The Bread of Life

Acknowledgments

We wish to express our deepest appreciation to Sally Russell, Vice President of Program for the Episcopal Church Women, who gently guided this manuscript to express the feminine voices of the church; to Carol Boker, our recipe editor, who used her knowledge of food preparation to make countless photocopied recipes into a timeless cookbook; to Mary Ann Drumel, who carefully chose the Scripture for its message about the power of the meal; to Julie Denham, who responded to the call; and to Debra Farrington, editorial director of Morehouse Publishing, who intuitively understood the importance of the eucharistic messages being the center of contemporary family, church, and community life and allowed this expression for the sake of all readers.

The Bread of Life

A Cookbook for Body and Soul

The Episcopal Church Women

Introduction by Phyllis Tickle
Meditations by the Reverend Beth Maynard

An Ellen Rolfes Book

MOREHOUSE PUBLISHING

Morehouse Publishing
P.O. Box 1321
Harrisburg, PA 17105

Morehouse Publishing is a division of The Morehouse Group.

The Scripture quotations contained herein are from the New Revised Standard Version Bible, copyright © 1989 by the Division of Christian Education of the National Council of the Churches of Christ in the U.S.A. Used by permission. All rights reserved.

The grace on page 240 is from the Third National UCC Women's Meeting Worship Book (June, 1996), copyright © Faith Johnson and The Coordinating Center in Church and Society, United Church of Christ. Used with permission.

Printed in the United States of America

Cover design by Corey Kent
Cover image © Visual Cuisines

Library of Congress Cataloging-in-Publication Data
The bread of life : a cookbook for body and soul / the Episcopal Church Women ; introduction by Phyllis Tickle ; meditations by the Reverend Beth Maynard.
     p. cm.
  Includes bibliographical references and index.
  ISBN 0-8192-1783-2
  1. Cookery, American. I. Episcopal Church Women.
TX715 .B834 2000
641.5973—dc21   99–053341

Contents

We are the Episcopal Church Women—unique, bold, and courageous in our work for Christ in His world. In the history of the Church, there has never been a more diverse group of women associated with cooking than the Episcopal Church Women. For well over 100 years, Episcopal women have prepared wedding receptions, potluck suppers, confirmation and funeral dinners, birthday celebrations, bake sales, and communion bread.

Our history as a church connects us strongly with boats arriving from England. We are an immigrant church as old as this new nation. Our present and future are a collaboration of women—both native to this land and those who continue to come to these shores from every hemisphere and continent.

Today our kitchen includes everything from soup pots to soul food, woks, tortillas, and bread machines. We delight in sharing the flavors that have changed the life of the Episcopal Church.

Welcome to our book!

Preface
When Two or More are Gathered

Ellen Robinson Rolfes

Sometimes, early in our lives, we begin to be shaped by the little things. I remember as a child in the Mississippi Delta being sent to my grandparents to stay for days at a time propped up on pillows to battle asthma. I was so weak that all I could do was activate my imagination by making up stories full of lively conversation between people. One day my grandfather came to my bedside bearing a gift. He handed me a small wicker basket filled with handmade toys—a cloth man and woman, a wooden table, two chairs, and a cooking pot. I was delighted and started "setting the table on the pillows." The man and woman began to cook together, to talk, and to "break bread." It was there in those childhood moments, I now realize, that my spiritual and professional life started a journey together at that tiny meal table. The Eucharist message was so clear even then: *when two or more are gathered* at mealtime, we are offered the chance to be in touch with the meaning and mystery of life. Thus, cookbooks are important for this very reason—they are manuals for food preparation, but on a deeper level, preparation for the sacred part of our lives together.

The compilation of *The Bread of Life: A Cookbook for Body and Soul* has been a beautiful path on my life's journey. The women collaborators have helped me reconnect to my Anglican taproot and granted me signs of acceptance and a means of experiencing spiritual strengthening through the ritual of the meal table. This nourishment, fulfillment, and wholeness, and most importantly, this sense of community is there waiting for all of us when we break bread with one another.

The scriptural stories now take on new meaning to me, as "meal memories"—the Jewish traveling wisdom teachers, seeking hospitality, finding a meal after the service in the homes of strangers; Mary at the Master's feet while Martha was dutifully in the kitchen; the loaves and the fishes, the wedding feast, on and on.

And finally, the messianic message appearing to us in the Upper Room is the ultimate meal memory. It was so simple; Mark 14:22 provides us with the best picture of what happened. Using his Jewish practice of hospitality, Christ invited his best friends to supper. Once they were seated, he called upon his teaching gifts to articulate his life's purpose of bringing the New Covenant, thus reshaping their lives (and ours) forever. As they were eating, he took bread, and blessed and broke it, and gave it to them and said:

"'Take, this is my body,' then he took a cup, and after giving thanks gave it to them, and all of them drank from it. He said to them, 'This is my blood of the covenant, which is poured out for many… Do this is in remembrance of me'" (Mark 14:22–14, Luke 22:19).

Each day, the young and old, the rich and poor, the strong and weak, the socially conscious and unconscious, gather still at the table to share a meal. The process of fulfilling a basic, human need is merely the catalyst for what happens when people sit together in a ritual designed to sustain life. Bringing a good thought to the table is as important as bringing good food to the table. While we eat in "community," we can speak about the events of the day, reminisce with childhood memories, proselytize our faith, review current events, teach social responsibility (and table manners), face our individual and collective fears, discover one another's truths, and speak our hearts about shared visions for tomorrow. *When two or more are gathered*, we participate in something far greater than ourselves. And if we are truly awake, we give thanks for the celebration of life through meal memories because these times afford us a holy connection with others.

All of this is only to say, recipe collections such as this compilation are powerful venues, offering us a chance to make more meal memories to become hosts at the Eucharist table. For the Christian, from the Last Supper forward, every meal becomes a sacrament. Even if it is just for peanut butter and jelly sandwiches or with cloth dolls at a table placed with pretend food on a pillow, we have the opportunity to take the sacred into the ordinary meal table of our homes and make a banquet of our lives.

Introduction

Phyllis Tickle

There is at large among us these days a new restiveness of the spirit. Like some kind of inarticulate homesickness, our discontent wanders *sotto voce* just below the hum of our mobile and unpredictable lives and whispers of the soul's yearning for some established place and rhythm of its own.

At times our unease presents as a sense of isolation from the lives of those around us. At other times, it is like an estrangement of sorts from any gentle or calming routine and from the security of the mundane and fixed. Sometimes, and they are the hard ones, it is the simple longing for quiet and familiar affection. Regardless of how we parse our contemporary disjuncture, however, it is just that—contemporary. Our forebears, had they even employed the word "disjuncture" in their daily conversations, would most certainly have puzzled over ours and eventually found it so alien as to be beyond their imagining. They would, in other words, have found life in isolation from community and physical rhythms to be inconceivable.

Historically, we Americans lived within community until our agricultural and industrial culture gave way in the mid-years of the twentieth century to a technological one. A community might be so small a thing as one family on one small homestead, or it might be the community of a tribe or clan moving together or settling together more or less in conclave. Community could be the nearest general store that offered even the most isolated folk news and the necessities. Community could be a village or a township or just a neighborhood within some emerging city.

Wherever one lived, in those not-so-distant times, and in whatever station, however, there was always connection with the larger fabric of humanity beyond the individual self. And dependency was the warp and weft that wove that fabric together. We needed each other for entertainment and information, for perspective and context, for encouragement and inspiration. We even needed each other for the larger chores of life and for physical survival. It was a neediness made tolerable—indeed, even sweet—by familiarity and human constancy.

But no more. For us Johnny-come-lately Americans, it is different. What once only a neighbor or kin could provide, now a dollar buys instead. We are entertained professionally and informed electronically. We attend fluid and dynamic small groups for context and meetings for perspective. We read books for inspiration and short features for encouragement. We hire experts to effect what we cannot accomplish alone, buy our luxuries as well as our necessities, and depend on the kindness of strangers when our distress exceeds our fiscal reach. And in that pivot from shared vulnerability and safe dependency to uniform packaging and increasing convenience, community as our great-grandparents experienced it was lost.

What was not lost—what apparently the soul cannot lose without losing itself—is our abiding, human need, if not for bartered goods and services, then still for connection to ourselves. And that is a connection that comes only when we give it to one another. As if joined by an intangible, invisible lace work of wisdom, souls in community are realized by each other. It is a holy process, as sacred as it is actual, and as beneficent.

Ironically, it is the smallest and most fundamental unit of community—the community of the shared table—that has managed to remain possible in a satisfying and credible way through all the cultural changes of the last few decades. It is at table that the routine and comfortingly ordinary needs of the body and the yearnings of the spirit to know and give itself are both satisfied, the delight of each being increased by the pleasure of the other.

The Eucharist's central place in the public exercise of our Christian faith rests, of course, upon the mystery of this very union, but we would be irresponsible as Christians if we relegated mystery strictly to our ecclesial lives. A gift of God freely given, the celebration in good food and good conversation of our human needs and human affections is to be enjoyed for the life-giving communion it is. It is also to be gratefully received for the antidote it provides to the aching of a restless heart.

This book is not a manual of prayer or a pastoral journal or even a treatise on theology. It is just exactly what it says it is, a cookbook compiled and published by some of the liveliest and most agreeable cooks currently wielding a spoon. But this book is as intentional as any religious manual or journal or treatise ever was or could be—intentional in its belief that food is the unbreakable bond that joins us, that food eaten together nourishes the soul as well as the body, and that grace attends wherever food is given and received. This book, in sum, is a celebration of the secular part of a great mystery, as well as a means to participate in it joyfully.

And Abraham hastened into the tent to Sarah, and said, "Make ready quickly three measures of choice flour, knead it, and make cakes."

Appetizers

Abraham ran to the herd, and took a calf, tender and good, and gave it to the servant, who hastened to prepare it. Then he took curds and milk and the calf that he had prepared, and set it before them; and he stood by them under the tree while they ate.

Genesis 18:6–8

1

A Potluck Kind of Name

S oon after graduating from college, I went to a party where all the guests were instructed to bring hors d'oeuvres. For some reason, an old family standby occurred to me, so I called my mother to find out how she made cheese straws. Despite the fact that I had never tried the recipe before, they came out well and received several compliments. In fact, from then on, every time I encountered a certain man whose acquaintance I had made for the first time that evening, he greeted me with, "Do you still make those marvelous cheese straws?"

Wherever that fellow is now, to this day, in his mind, I'm sure I'm still the Cheese Straw Lady. And why not? We automatically begin to locate people as we sample their food, to name them by what they bring to a supper or a party. This naming can even be literal: for example, when delegates from our region's parishes gathered last year for a potluck, my own parish, the Church of the Good Shepherd, thought it obvious that it was our duty to offer (what else?) shepherd's pie.

It should be no surprise, then, that at almost every church supper there are two unwritten rules. First, you have to try a little of everything, arranging small samples on your plate as you circle the buffet table. Then, you have to find out who made each dish and express appreciation—if not directly to the cook, at least to your tablemates. That's how we place each other and include each other. After years of experience, the history of shared meals can end up being written into the life of the community, as specific people become identified with specific food. "It's just not the same without Dick's Tomato Aspic... Muriel's Meat Pies... Joan's Butter Brickle."

In many places church suppers as such have faded away—much to the confusion of older people, who easily remember when they were held once a month and everyone wanted to attend. When the moment arrives to solicit suggestions for new programs, the idea of reviving church suppers inevitably comes up. Now, some would say those days are gone forever, and others would contend we'd better get busy bringing them back. But whatever the outcome of that particular debate, we need not fear that anything is going to stop us church people from bonding over food.

Even parish events that ostensibly have nothing to do with eating usually end up including it anyway. Choirs break for juice and cookies. House fellowships share a meal before the study begins. Search committees reserve a table for dinner at the nearest restaurant, and everyone will be watching for the answer to the important question of how the current candidate for rector says grace. The women's group brings desserts to its monthly meeting and debates whether the low-fat versions are adequately moist.

Whether or not we use the model of the church supper to encourage it, shared food will just go on forming community and helping us find our place there. For Episcopalians at least, the connection seems to be instinctive. But what do you expect, in a tradition that can't even imagine getting together without breaking out the bread and wine?

CHEESE STRAWS

1 pound sharp cheese,
  shredded
1/4 pound butter
1 3/4 cups all-purpose flour
1/2 teaspoon salt
1 teaspoon cayenne pepper

Cream the cheese and butter in a large bowl. Add flour, salt, and cayenne pepper; mix well. Place in a cookie press and press out in strips about 4 inches long. Bake on a cookie sheet at 350° until light golden brown.
Yields: 15 to 20 servings

Goodness Graces
St. Paul's Episcopal Church
Albany, Georgia

ZIPPY CHEESE DIP

4 ounces grated sharp
  cheddar cheese
1 (8-ounce) package
  cream cheese
1 teaspoon Worcestershire
  sauce
Dash of Tabasco sauce
6 slices bacon, cooked
  and crumbled
Parsley for decoration

Combine first 4 ingredients over low heat until smooth and bubbly. Blend in bacon; garnish with parsley and serve warm with crackers.
Yields: 4 to 6 servings

Trinity Episcopal Church Cookbook
Society of Mary and Friends
Gladstone, Michigan

WINE-CHEESE DIP

2 (3-ounce) packages
  cream cheese
1/3 pound bleu or Roquefort
  cheese, grated
1/4 cup white wine
1 tablespoon mayonnaise
1/4 teaspoon salt
1/4 teaspoon Worcestershire
  sauce
Dash of cayenne pepper
Dash of garlic salt

Combine cream cheese and bleu or Roquefort cheese in a bowl. Add remaining ingredients, mixing well. Chill for about 24 hours before serving.
Yields: 12 servings

All Angels Fare
All Angels by the Sea Episcopal Church
Longboat Key, Florida

CHEESE GOODIES

2 sticks butter, softened
2 cups grated sharp
  cheddar cheese
2 cups all-purpose flour
2 cups rice cereal
Dash of Worcestershire sauce
Dash of cayenne pepper

Cream butter and cheese in a large bowl. Add flour and rice cereal. Add Worcestershire sauce and cayenne pepper. Mix all ingredients thoroughly. Roll into tiny balls and place on a foil-covered pan. Flatten with a fork, and bake at 350° for 10 minutes or until slightly brown. (The cheese goodies will be about 1 1/2 inches in diameter when cooked.) Store in sealed plastic container; they will keep a while without any refrigeration.
Yields: 8 to 10 servings

St. Anne's Guild Cookbook
St. James the Less Church
Scarsdale, New York

BLEU CHEESE BITES

1 (10-count) package
  refrigerator biscuits
1/4 cup crumbled bleu cheese
1 stick butter or margarine

Cut raw biscuit dough into quarters. Put pieces in a greased baking pan in a single layer. Melt bleu cheese and butter in a small saucepan. Pour on dough. Bake at 400° for about 15 minutes. Serve warm.
Yields: 40 servings

Recipes from St. Paul's 1981
St. Paul's Episcopal Church
Naples, Florida

❖

THE LORD SAID TO MOSES AND AARON: THIS IS THE ORDINANCE FOR THE PASSOVER: NO FOREIGNER SHALL EAT OF IT, BUT ANY SLAVE WHO HAS BEEN PURCHASED MAY EAT OF IT AFTER HE HAS BEEN CIRCUMCISED; NO BOUND OR HIRED SERVANT MAY EAT OF IT. IT SHALL BE EATEN IN ONE HOUSE, YOU SHALL NOT TAKE ANY OF THE ANIMAL OUTSIDE THE HOUSE, AND YOU SHALL NOT BREAK ANY OF ITS BONES. THE WHOLE CONGREGATION OF ISRAEL SHALL CELEBRATE IT.

IF AN ALIEN WHO RESIDES WITH YOU WANTS TO CELEBRATE THE PASSOVER TO THE LORD, ALL HIS MALES SHALL BE CIRCUMCISED; THEN HE MAY DRAW NEAR TO CELEBRATE IT; HE SHALL BE REGARDED AS A NATIVE OF THE LAND. BUT NO UNCIRCUMCISED PERSON SHALL EAT OF IT; THERE SHALL BE ONE LAW FOR THE NATIVE AND FOR THE ALIEN WHO RESIDES AMONG YOU.

EXODUS 12:43–49
(PASSOVER INSTRUCTIONS)

BLEU CHEESE CAKE

2 tablespoons butter or
    margarine
1 cup crushed cheese crackers
2 (8-ounce) packages
    cream cheese, softened
1 (8-ounce) package bleu cheese
3 large eggs
1/4 cup all-purpose flour
1/4 teaspoon salt
1/4 cup medium picante sauce
1 cup sour cream
1/2 cup chopped green onions,
    tops included
1/2 cup chopped English
    walnuts
Fresh parsley, tomato roses, or
    green onions for garnish

Butter an 8-inch springform pan. Sprinkle cracker crumbs on bottom and sides. Blend cheeses, eggs, flour, salt, picante sauce, and sour cream in a large bowl. Fold in green onions. Pour into pan and sprinkle with walnuts. Bake at 325° for 1 hour. Cool and chill overnight. Garnish with parsley, tomato roses, or green onions, if desired. Serve at room temperature with crackers.
Yields: 20 servings

The Garden of Eatin' Cook Book
Diocese of Southwest Florida

STUFFED BAKED BRIE

3 green onions, sliced
1–2 cloves garlic, minced
1 tablespoon oil
1–2 tablespoons butter
1 tablespoon Dijon mustard
1/2 teaspoon each of basil,
    rosemary, and parsley
1/4–1/3 pound fresh
    mushrooms, sliced
1 large or 2 small rounds of
    Brie
Puff pastry sheet

Sauté green onions and garlic in oil and butter in a small skillet. Add mustard and herbs. Add mushrooms and continue to sauté. Place Brie in center of pastry. Place sautéed mixture over Brie. Pull up and squeeze pastry together. Bake on baking sheet at 400° for 20 minutes. Let sit for 10 minutes before serving.
Yields: 15 to 20 servings

St. Raphael's Cookbook Vol. II
St. Raphael's Episcopal Church
Brick, New Jersey

TORTILLA ROLL-UPS

5 large flour tortillas
2 (8-ounce) packages
  cream cheese
1 (8-ounce) carton sour cream
2 (4-ounce) cans chopped
  green chiles
1 (4-ounce) jar chopped
  pimientos
1/2 cup chopped nuts
Garlic salt to taste

Spread tortillas with cream cheese, sour cream, chopped green chiles, pimientos, and chopped nuts. Sprinkle with garlic salt and roll up. Slice rolls into 1/4-inch pieces to serve.
Yields: 20 to 24 servings

Breaking Bread with St. Nicholas
St. Nicholas Episcopal Church
Midland, Texas

GINGER DIP

1 cup mayonnaise
1 cup sour cream
1/4 cup minced onion
1 (8-ounce) can water chestnuts
1 tablespoon soy sauce
Dash of salt
2 tablespoons candied ginger
  (crystallized)
2 cloves garlic, minced
1/4 cup minced parsley

Combine all ingredients in a bowl; mix well. Refrigerate for about 3 days. Serve with crackers.
Yields: about 2 1/2 cups

St. David's Cookbook
St. David's Episcopal Church
Nashville, Tennessee

HUMMUS

1 (16-ounce) can chickpeas
1 clove garlic
Juice of 2 lemons
1/2 cup sesame seeds
1 teaspoon paprika
3 tablespoons parsley
2 tablespoons oil
2 tablespoons water

Combine first 6 ingredients in a blender. Slowly add oil and water alternately until smooth and pasty consistency. Serve with toasted wedges of pita bread.
Yields: 6 to 8 servings

Our Daily Bread and More
St. Christopher's Episcopal Church
Kingsport, Tennessee

ROASTED RED PEPPER DIP

1 (7-ounce) jar roasted red
  peppers, drained
1 tablespoon balsamic vinegar
1/4 cup plain low-fat yogurt
1/2 teaspoon minced garlic
1/4 teaspoon salt
1/4 teaspoon black pepper

Process peppers and vinegar in a blender until smooth. Scrape into a bowl and stir in remaining ingredients. Serve with pita bread wedges or crisp vegetables cut up for dipping.
Yields: 4 to 6 servings

Feeding Our Flock
St. Andrew's Episcopal Church
Longmeadow, Massachusetts

ARTICHOKE SPREAD

1 (16-ounce) can artichokes in
  water, drained
1 cup grated Parmesan cheese
1 cup mayonnaise
Dash of Worcestershire sauce
Paprika

Cut artichokes into tiny pieces. Add Parmesan cheese, mayonnaise, and Worcestershire sauce. Mix well. Place in small baking dish. Sprinkle paprika on top. Bake at 400° for 20 minutes. Serve hot with crackers.
Yields: 4 to 6 servings

Heavenly Hosts
St. John's Episcopal Church
Naples, Florida

CRUMB-COATED ZUCCHINI DIAGONALS

3 medium zucchini
1 large egg, slightly beaten
1/4 teaspoon salt
1/8 teaspoon black pepper
1/4 cup sour cream
20 round, butter-flavored
  crackers, crushed
2 tablespoons grated
  Parmesan cheese

Cut zucchini into 1/2-inch diagonal slices. Dip into a small bowl in which you've combined egg, salt, pepper, and sour cream; mix well. Then dip into another bowl with the combined cracker crumbs and cheese, turning zucchini to coat. Place in a shallow greased baking pan. Bake at 375° for 20 to 25 minutes or until zucchini is tender. Serve hot.
Yields: 12 to 15 servings

Potluck
Trinity Episcopal Church
Ware, Massachusetts

HOT STUFFED MUSHROOMS

1 pound hot sausage
1/4 cup butter, melted
2 tablespoons chives
1 teaspoon thyme
3 pounds large mushrooms
1 large egg, slightly beaten
1/2 teaspoon paprika

Cook sausage in a large skillet, stirring to crumble; drain well. Add melted butter to chives and thyme in a small bowl. Remove mushroom stems and brush caps with butter mixture. Chop stems finely and mix with cooked sausage; add egg and mix well. Fill caps with sausage mixture. Sprinkle with paprika. Place in a greased shallow baking pan. Bake at 400° for 10 to 15 minutes. Serve hot.
Yields: 10 to 12 servings

What's Cookin' at Epiphany?
Church of the Epiphany
Richmond, Virginia

MUSHROOM-NUT ROLLUPS

12 slices white bread
12 ounces fresh mushrooms, chopped
1 large onion, minced
1 tablespoon butter
Salt and black pepper to taste
2 (3-ounce) packages cream cheese
1/2 pound melted butter
1 cup pecans, finely chopped

Trim crusts off bread; roll bread thin with rolling pin. Sauté mushrooms and onion in 1 tablespoon butter until onion is transparent. Season with salt and pepper. Spread bread slices with cream cheese. Place 1 tablespoon or more of mushroom mixture on one end of the slice and roll up. Dip roll in melted butter and then in nuts; freeze. When ready to serve, slice rolls into thirds while still frozen. Bake at 450° for 20 minutes or until browned.
Yields: about 3 dozen

What's Cooking Along the King's Highway?
Diocese of El Camino Real
Monterey, California

DEVILISH DEVILED EGGS

6 hard-cooked eggs, peeled
1 tablespoon mayonnaise or
  salad dressing
1 teaspoon prepared mustard
1/2 teaspoon horseradish
Dash of soy sauce
Dash of Worcestershire sauce
1 teaspoon dried onion, soaked
Dash of celery salt
1/2 teaspoon powdered mustard
Paprika for garnish

Cut eggs in half lengthwise; scoop out yolks with a spoon. Mash yolks in a medium bowl with a fork to remove lumps. Stir in mayonnaise, mustard, horseradish, and next 5 ingredients; mix well. If mixture is too dry, add more mayonnaise until smooth and creamy. Fill each egg half with yolk mixture. Sprinkle with paprika.
Yields: 12 servings

Not by Bread Alone
Christ Church, the Episcopal Parish
Shrewsbury, New Jersey

PICKLED EGGS

1 (16-ounce) can red beets,
  drained
1/2 cup water
6 large hard-cooked eggs
1/2 cup sugar
1/2 cup vinegar

Put all ingredients in glass jar. Let stand in refrigerator for at least 24 hours.
Yields: 6 servings

Grace Cooks
Grace Episcopal Church
Chattanooga, Tennessee

CURRIED EGG SALAD

1 dozen large hard-cooked
  eggs, finely chopped
1 teaspoon chervil
1/4 teaspoon dry mustard
1/2 teaspoon salt
2/3 cup mayonnaise
1/8 teaspoon white pepper
1 tablespoon finely chopped
  parsley
1 teaspoon curry powder
  (optional)

Combine all ingredients in a bowl; mix well, then chill. Use for canapés or small tea sandwiches.
Yields: 8 to 10 servings

Blessed Are the Cooks
St. James Episcopal Church
Wichita, Kansas

SALMON CHEESE PÂTÉ

1 (7-ounce) can salmon
1 tablespoon lemon juice
1 tablespoon grated onion or
  1/2 teaspoon onion powder
1 tablespoon prepared
  horseradish
1/2 teaspoon salt
1/4 teaspoon black pepper
1/4 cup chopped pecans
  (or other nuts)
1 (8-ounce) package cream
  cheese, softened
1 (3-ounce) package cream
  cheese, softened
Snipped parsley and carrot
  slice

Drain salmon and flake fish in a bowl. Add lemon juice, onion, horseradish, salt, pepper, pecans, and cream cheese. Chill until firm, then shape into a fish on a plate. Sprinkle snipped parsley over fish to resemble scales. Make the eye with a carrot slice. Chill. Serve with crisp crackers.
Yields: 6 to 8 servings

What's Cooking?
St. John's Episcopal Church
Huntington, L.I., New York

CEVICHE

5 pounds firm-fleshed white
  fish, filleted
Salt
2 tablespoons olive oil
Juice of 12 lemons (about 3
  cups)
1 pound onions, minced
Hot peppers, minced

Skin raw fish and cut into small pieces (1/2-inch squares). Place in glass bowl. Salt to taste. Add olive oil and lemon juice to cover fish completely. Mix onion and peppers into fish. Refrigerate for about 12 hours. (The lemon juice "cooks" the fish.) Serve cold with crackers.
Yields: 20 servings

We Gather Together
Wives of Bishops, Episcopal Church

SHRIMP LOUIS

1 pound shrimp, cooked and
cut up
3/4 cup mayonnaise
1 (8-ounce) package cream
cheese, softened
1 medium onion, minced
1/2 cup celery, minced
3 tablespoons chili sauce
1 tablespoon lemon juice

Combine all ingredients in a bowl; mix well. Chill. Serve
with crackers.
Yields: 6 to 8 servings

The Book of Common Fare
Grace-St. Luke's Church
Memphis, Tennessee

COCONUT SHRIMP

1 large egg
3/4 cup milk
1/4 cup firmly packed brown
sugar
1 1/4 cups all-purpose flour
1 pound medium shrimp
2 (4-ounce) packages shredded
coconut
Vegetable oil for frying

Combine egg, milk, brown sugar, and flour in a small
bowl. Beat with rotary beater or whisk until smooth. Peel
and devein shrimp. If shrimp tails are larger than 2 inches,
cut in half lengthwise. Pour oil into deep skillet to a depth
of 1 inch. Heat to 375° on a deep-fat thermometer. Place a
small amount of coconut in a shallow dish. Dip each
shrimp in egg mixture, then coat thoroughly with coconut.
Fry in hot oil about 5 minutes or until golden brown.
Serve hot.
Yields: 20 servings

La Bonne Cuisine, Lagniappe
All Saints' Episcopal Church
River Ridge, Louisiana

PICKLED SHRIMP

1 1/2 cups vegetable oil
2 teaspoons salt
3/4 cup vinegar
3 teaspoons celery salt
2 1/2 tablespoons capers with sauce
Dash of Tabasco sauce
Onion, sliced in rings
8 bay leaves
2 1/2 pounds raw shrimp, peeled and deveined
3 quarts water, boiling
3 teaspoons salt
3/4 cup sliced celery
1/4 cup pickling spices or 2 bags crab boil

In a bowl combine the oil and next 7 ingredients; mix well and refrigerate. Add shrimp to the boiling water, along with the salt, celery, and pickling spices or crab boil; cook for 2 minutes after the water returns to a boil. Drain the shrimp and rinse them with cold water. In a glass container, combine the shrimp and sauce. Refrigerate the mixture for 24 to 30 hours. Remove the shrimp from the marinade to serve.
Yields: 10 to 12 servings

La Bonne Cuisine
All Saints' Episcopal Church
River Ridge, Louisiana

SHRIMP BUTTER

1/4 pound butter, softened
1 (8-ounce) package cream cheese, softened
1 (3-ounce) package cream cheese, softened
1 tablespoon chopped onion
2 (4-ounce) cans shrimp
1 teaspoon lemon juice

Combine butter and cream cheese in a bowl. Add remaining ingredients. Serve at room temperature on crackers or small rye bread.
Yields: 24 to 30 servings

Keep the Feast
Church of the Ascension
Middletown, Ohio

CRAB APPETIZERS

1/4 pound butter or margarine
1 (5-ounce) jar Old English
   cheese spread
1 1/2 tablespoons mayonnaise
1/2 teaspoon garlic salt
1/2 teaspoon seasoned salt
1 (7-ounce) can crabmeat,
   drained
6 English muffins, split

Blend first 6 ingredients and spread on muffins. Cut each muffin half into six pieces. Freeze on cookie sheet; place in a plastic bag for storage in freezer. To serve, broil until lightly browned and bubbly. Serve hot.
Yields: 6 dozen appetizers

Recipes—and Remembrances
Zion Episcopal Church
Avon, New York

CORNED BEEF CHEESE LOGS

1 (8-ounce) package cream
   cheese, softened
2 tablespoons milk
2 cloves garlic, crushed or
   minced
1 tablespoon Worcestershire
   sauce
1/8 teaspoon hot pepper sauce
1 (12-ounce) can corned beef,
   flaked and unchilled
3/4 cup minced parsley

Blend cheese with milk until smooth. Blend in garlic, Worcestershire sauce, and pepper sauce. Add corned beef; blend and chill for 1 to 2 hours. Divide mixture in half. Shape into 2 logs, 1 1/2 inches in diameter. Sprinkle parsley onto waxed paper. Roll logs in parsley to coat evenly. Wrap in plastic wrap and chill thoroughly. When ready to serve, remove plastic wrap, place on tray and surround with desired crackers.
Yields: 2 logs

Loaves and Fishes
St. Mark's Episcopal Church
Chenango Bridge, New York

HOT REUBEN DIP

1 (16-ounce) can sauerkraut,
   drained and squeezed dry
1 small onion, finely chopped
1/4 pound cooked corned beef
3 tablespoons prepared
   horseradish
1 cup shredded Swiss cheese
1 cup mayonnaise
1 cup sour cream

Place sauerkraut, onion, and corned beef in a food chopper or a mini chopper with cutting blade. Process until finely chopped. Combine the mixture with remaining ingredients in a 1-quart baking dish. Bake at 350° for 40 minutes. Serve with crackers.
Yields: 10 to 15 servings

125 Years of Cooking
St. Luke Episcopal Church
Niles, Ohio

HOT MACADAMIA DIP

1 (8-ounce) package cream
  cheese, softened
1 (3-ounce) package cream
  cheese, softened
2 tablespoons milk
1 (2 1/2-ounce) jar dried
  chipped beef
1/3 cup finely chopped onion
1/3 cup finely chopped green
  bell pepper
1 clove garlic, minced
1/2 teaspoon freshly ground
  black pepper
1/4 teaspoon ground ginger
3/4 cup sour cream
1/2 cup coarsely chopped
  macadamia nuts
1 tablespoon butter

Combine cream cheese and milk in a bowl, blending until completely smooth. Stir in chipped beef, onion, green pepper, garlic, pepper, and ginger. Fold in sour cream. Pour beef mixture into a glass pie plate or shallow baking dish. In small skillet, sauté nuts in butter until glazed. Sprinkle nuts over beef mixture. Bake at 350° for 20 to 25 minutes. Serve bubbling hot with crackers.
Yields: 12 to 15 servings

A Cook's Tour of the Bayou Country
Diocese of Louisiana Southwest Deanery

CHICKEN WINGS

1/2 stick melted butter
2–3 cloves garlic, chopped
1/2 cup firmly packed brown
  sugar
1/2 cup soy sauce
2–3 tablespoons lemon juice
1/4–1/2 cup water
White pepper to taste
Ginger to taste
Dab of molasses
1 tablespoon cornstarch
6 pounds chicken wings

Sauté butter and garlic in a skillet. Add sugar; stir until dissolved and a little thick. Add remaining ingredients, except cornstarch and chicken. Simmer. Clarify 1 tablespoon cornstarch in water; shake in a jar. Add to sauce. Continue cooking and stirring until sauce is thick and glossy. Bake chicken wings on a rack in a baking pan at 350° for about 45 minutes. Line roasting pan with foil. Add cooked wings and sauce. Cover with foil. Bake 30 minutes, stirring once. Remove foil last 10 minutes.
Yields: 12 to 15 servings

Potluck Favorites
St. Augustine's Episcopal Church
Kingston, Rhode Island

15

BOEREKS WITH MEAT FILLING

(Boereks are Greek appetizers that can be made with meat or cheese filling.)

2 tablespoons butter
1/2 pound ground beef
1 clove garlic
1 medium onion, grated
1 small tomato, diced
1 large egg
1 cup chopped parsley
Salt and black pepper
1/2 pound phyllo pastry sheets
1/4 pound butter, melted

Melt 2 tablespoons butter in skillet. Add meat, garlic, onion, and tomato and cook over medium heat for 15 minutes, stirring occasionally. Remove from heat. Add egg, parsley, salt, and pepper; mix well.

The pastry sheets will be piled on top of each other in a block, like sheets of paper of equal size. Put them on a flat surface and cut through all thicknesses crosswise, making two equal parts. Cut again lengthwise, making four equal parts. Place all parts on top of each other in an orderly pile and cover with a damp towel to prevent drying out. Phyllo sheets dry out very fast. Take one sheet from the pile and place it in front of you. Using a brush, butter the surface. Cut the rectangle lengthwise into three equal parts. Place 1 teaspoon of filling on each rectangle of pastry. Fold both sides over the filling. Fold end of pastry near filling over the filling and butter surface of the folded end. Roll like a cigarette, and butter end of pastry so that the end sticks together. Place on a buttered cookie sheet and butter the top. Bake for 25 to 30 minutes or until the boereks are golden brown. Do not overcook. These pastries freeze well.
Yields: 50 boereks

Canterbury Feasts
Canterbury School of Florida
St. Petersburg, Florida

❖

"When the Lord brings you into the land of the Canaanites, the Hittities, the Amorites, the Hivites, and the Jebusites, which he swore to your ancestors to give you, a land flowing with milk and honey, you shall keep this observance in this month. Seven days you shall eat unleavened bread, and on the seventh day there shall be a festival to the Lord. Unleavened bread shall be eaten for seven days; no leavened bread shall be seen in your possession, and no leaven shall be seen among you in all your territory. You shall tell your child on that day, 'It is because of what the Lord did for me when I came out of Egypt.'

It shall serve for you as a sign on your hand and as a reminder on your forehead, so that the teaching of the Lord may be on your lips; for with a strong hand the Lord brought you out of Egypt. You shall keep this ordinance at its proper time from year to year."

Exodus 13:5–10

LIVER PÂTÉ

1 pound chicken livers, cooked
1 cup cooked yams
1 clove garlic, mashed
1/2 cup butter
1/2 teaspoon powdered
  rosemary
1/2 cup vermouth
1 onion, chopped or sliced

Combine all ingredients in a blender. Puree until smooth and refrigerate. Serve as a spread with crackers or form into a loaf and slice.
Yields: 6 to 8 servings

St. Simons ECW Cookbook
St. Simons Episcopal Church
Miami, Florida

QUICHE LORRAINE

6 slices bacon
1 (9-inch) pie crust, baked 10
  minutes and cooled
1/2 pound Swiss or Gruyère
  cheese, grated
1 tablespoon all-purpose flour
4 large eggs
1/4 teaspoon salt
Dash of nutmeg
Dash of white pepper
Dash cayenne pepper
2 cups light cream
2 tablespoons butter or
  margarine

Lightly brown bacon; drain. Crumble bacon into pie crust with cheese that has been tossed with flour. Beat eggs, salt, nutmeg, pepper, and cayenne; then beat in cream. Slowly pour into pie crust over bacon and cheese. Dot with butter. Bake at 375° on middle rack for 25 minutes or until knife inserted comes out clean. Cut into wedges to serve. Cool 5 to 10 minutes before serving.
Yields: 6 to 8 appetizer servings

Angels in the Kitchen, II
Emmanuel Episcopal Church
Bristol, Virginia

CAVIAR PIE

1 (8-ounce) package cream
  cheese, softened
1/2 cup sour cream
1/2 medium onion,
  finely chopped
5 large hard-cooked eggs,
  chopped
3 tablespoons mayonnaise
1 (3 1/2-ounce) jar black caviar
Fresh parsley
Lemon slices

Mix cream cheese and sour cream until smooth. Place in center of large serving plate; shape into a circle. Top with onion. Mix eggs and mayonnaise; spread over onion, cover, and chill. About 3 hours before serving, spread caviar on top. Garnish with parsley and lemon slices.
Yields: 4 to 6 servings

Hometown Recipes of Palmetto
St. Mary's Episcopal Church
Palmetto, Florida

GLAZED NUTS

1 cup sugar
1/2 teaspoon nutmeg
1 teaspoon salt
2 teaspoons cinnamon
1/4 teaspoon cloves
1/2 cup water
2 cups pecan halves

Combine all ingredients except nuts in a heavy saucepan. Cook over medium heat, stirring constantly, until sugar is dissolved. Continue cooking to the soft ball (238°) stage. Remove from heat; add nuts. Stir gently until the mixture becomes creamy. Turn out onto waxed paper. Separate the nuts with a fork; let dry.
Yields: about 3/4 pound

The Loaves and Fishes, Act III
St. Stephen's Episcopal Church
Oak Ridge, Tennessee

When the layer of dew lifted, there on the surface of the wilderness was a fine flaky substance, as fine as frost on the ground.

Beverages

When the Israelites saw it, they said to one another, "What is it?" For they did not know what it was. Moses said to them, "It is the bread that the Lord has given you to eat. This is what the Lord has commanded: 'Gather as much of it as each of you needs, an omer to a person according to the number of persons, all providing for those in their own tents.'"

Exodus 16:14–16

Come and Dine

The first lesson I ever read in church, as a nervous high school student, was from the eighteenth chapter of Genesis. It told the story of three men visiting Abraham and Sarah by the oaks of Mamre, and the first sentence of the reading clarified who the three men were: The LORD. I wasn't sure how to understand that (perhaps I'm still not), but it was definitely what the book said.

The story pleased me very much. It went like this: Abraham was sitting outside his tent one afternoon, reading a magazine or something, and noticed some travelers approaching. Immediately he ran to meet them, bowed, and asked if they would care to sit a spell. While Abraham was getting his guests a cool drink, Sarah started a loaf of fresh bread, and one of the servants put meat on the grill; they even provided a milky yogurt dip on the side.

The visitors sat down under the shade of a tree, and everyone dug into the meal. While they were eating, the LORD, or the men, or whoever, told Abraham that they had come with news: within a year, Sarah was going to bear a male child. The boy was the first step in the fulfillment of a divine promise that this couple would have a lineage as vast as the stars (and so it has come to pass, because even you and I are part of it.)

The reading has remained a favorite of mine, and an icon depicting the scene now hangs in my kitchen. Painted (or to use the traditional term, "written") by the fifteenth-century Russian Andrew Rublev, the icon incorporates later Christian reflection on the story by calling itself "The Holy Trinity."

When you gaze at the image, you first notice three angels seated in a circle around a simple table, their golden wings and halos shining against the deep and varied colors of their robes. Their sensitive faces, nearly identical, are serenely viewing the meal in front of them, which the angel who depicts the Son is blessing with an outstretched hand. In the background you glimpse a home and a tree, presumably one of those oaks of Mamre.

Sarah and Abraham are nowhere to be seen, but I think there is a good reason for that. As you focus on the composition of the picture, it occurs to you that while the angels are indeed seated in a circle, they fill out only three of its four points. The Father sits at nine o'clock, the Son at twelve, and the Spirit at three; the six o'clock space has been left open for someone else to take.

And of course, that someone else is you. You are the one who now fulfills the role of the absent Abraham and Sarah. By even standing in front of the icon, you are already automatically put into that six o'clock space. And if you remain there, giving the image time to unfold its meaning, the icon draws you in, invites you.

George Herbert wrote a whole poem about that feeling: "You must sit down, says Love, and taste my meat." The icon invites you to become ready to sit down and dine with the three men, or three angels, or the LORD, or Love. Ready to receive back from them the hospitality that they were once offered by Abraham. Ready to hear what promises may become your own as you break bread with God.

This kind of fellowship did not just happen once in Genesis 18. It happens every time we enter into community with the God whose very nature is a community. It happens when we ourselves dare to be God's guest and sit down at that empty chair, and just as much when we consciously hold a place at our table open for some visitor, who, after all, might just (just?) be a man, or an angel, or the LORD, or Love.

MINT ICED TEA

3 cups boiling water
4 tea bags
12 mint sprigs
1 cup orange juice
1/4 cup lemon juice
6 cups cold water

Combine the boiling water, tea bags, and mint in a large bowl. Allow to steep for about 10 to 15 minutes; remove tea bags. Combine orange juice, lemon juice, and cold water; stir into tea.
Yields: about 2 1/2 quarts

Savoring Grace
St. Alban's Episcopal Church
Hixson, Tennessee

OLD-FASHIONED LEMONADE

2 large lemons
1 medium orange
1/2 cup sugar
1 quart cold water
Fresh mint leaves

Squeeze juice from lemons and orange into a pitcher. Add sugar, water, and mint. Stir well and serve over ice cubes.
Yields: 4 servings

Angel Food
St. Timothy's Episcopal Church
Signal Mountain, Tennessee

HONEY LIMEADE

5 cups water
1 cup lime juice (4 to 5 limes)
2/3 cup sugar
2 tablespoons honey

In a 2-quart pitcher, combine water, lime juice, sugar, and honey. Stir to dissolve sugar. Serve over ice cubes.
Yields: 6 servings

Recipes from "the Hill"
Boys' Home Inc.
Covington, Virginia

PINK LASSIE

1 cup cranberry juice
1 cup vanilla ice cream,
  softened
1/4 cup orange juice

Put all ingredients into blender. Cover and process until smooth. Serve in cocktail glasses.
Yields: about 2 1/2 cups

Taste & See
St. Peter's Episcopal Church
Louisville, Kentucky

VIRGIN BLOODY MARYS

1 (46-ounce) can tomato juice
3/4 cup water
1/3 cup vinegar
1/3 cup steak sauce
1/3 cup chili sauce
6 tablespoons confectioners'
  sugar
2 tablespoons Worcestershire
  sauce
1 tablespoon prepared mustard
1 tablespoon salt
Garlic powder to taste

Combine all ingredients in a large pitcher; mix well and chill. Serve over ice in tall glasses. You may add a celery stalk or shrimp on a skewer for decoration.
Note: Add a shot of vodka to each glass for Bloody Marys.
Yields: 6 to 8 servings

Holy Chow
Church of Ascension and Holy Trinity
Wyoming, Ohio

COFFEE PUNCH

1 pint milk
2 teaspoons vanilla
2 quarts strong coffee, cooled
1/2 cup sugar
1 quart vanilla, chocolate, or
  coffee ice cream
1 cup heavy cream, whipped
Nutmeg

Combine milk, vanilla, coffee, and sugar in a large pitcher; mix well and chill. Just before serving, place chunks of ice cream in a punch bowl. Cover with coffee mixture. Cover top with whipped cream and nutmeg.
Yields: 12 to 15 servings

Our Daily Bread
Church of the Incarnation
Mineral, Virginia

FROSTY GOLDEN PUNCH

2 (20-ounce) cans crushed
   pineapple with juice
2 (6-ounce) cans frozen
   lemonade concentrate
1/4 cup sugar
1 (28-ounce) bottle club soda
1 tray ice cubes

Combine pineapple and its juice, one can at a time, in a blender for 15 to 20 seconds or until thickened. Combine pineapple, lemonade concentrate, and sugar in a punch bowl. Stir in soda and ice. Serve immediately.
Note: You can add one 4/5 quart bottle of champagne for variation.
Yields: about 20 servings

All Saints' Cooks
All Saints' Episcopal Church
Kappaa, Kauai, Hawaii

"ORDINATION" PUNCH

1 (14-ounce) can pineapple
   juice, chilled
1 (6-ounce) can frozen pink
   lemonade concentrate, thawed
3/4 cup sugar
2 1/4 cups water
1 quart strawberry ice cream,
   softened
2 quarts chilled ginger ale

Combine pineapple juice, lemonade concentrate, sugar, and water in a punch bowl; mix well. Add ice cream and stir until blended. Stir in ginger ale and serve immediately.
Yields: 25 servings

Angels' Food
St. Mary's Episcopal Church
Napa, California

❖

THESE ARE THE APPOINTED FESTIVALS OF THE LORD, THE HOLY CONVOCATIONS, WHICH YOU SHALL CELEBRATE AT THE TIME APPOINTED FOR THEM. IN THE FIRST MONTH, ON THE FOURTEENTH DAY OF THE SAME MONTH, AT TWILIGHT, THERE SHALL BE A PASSOVER OFFERING TO THE LORD, AND ON THE FIFTEENTH DAY OF THE SAME MONTH IS THE FESTIVAL OF UNLEAVENED BREAD TO THE LORD; SEVEN DAYS YOU SHALL EAT UNLEAVENED BREAD.

LEVITICUS 23:4–6
(PASSOVER AND FESTIVAL OF UNLEAVENED BREAD)

SPRING PUNCH

1 (12-ounce) can frozen orange
   juice
1 (28-ounce) can pineapple
   juice
1 (32-ounce) bottle white grape
   juice
1/4 cup lemon juice
1 quart lime sherbet
1 2-liter bottle ginger ale

Mix first 4 ingredients together in punch bowl. Add sherbet in scoops. Add ginger ale and stir briefly.
Yields: 25 to 30 servings

Parish Collection
Trinity Episcopal Church
Richlands, Virginia

BANANA PUNCH

1 (12-ounce) can frozen orange
   juice, thawed
1 (46-ounce) can pineapple-
   grapefruit drink
2 cups sugar
4 ripe bananas, mashed
6 cups water
1 (2-liter) bottle ginger ale

Mix together the first 5 ingredients in a large bowl; place into freezer container and freeze. To serve, let stand 2 to 3 hours at room temperature (should be slushy). Pour the ginger ale over mixture. (Add more ginger ale as needed.)
Yields: 40 servings

Favorite Recipes of St. Stephen's
St. Stephen's Episcopal Church
Spokane, Washington

ST. FRANCIS PUNCH

64 ounces cranberry juice
64 ounces apple juice
64 ounces club soda
12 ounces frozen lemonade
   concentrate
64 ounces water

Chill all the ingredients. Pour into a punch bowl and combine; serve over ice.
Yields: 30 to 35 servings

Cooking with St. Francis by the Sea II
St. Francis by the Sea Episcopal Church
Blue Hill, Maine

CRANBERRY SPARKLE

1/4 cup lemon juice
1 1/2 quarts cranberry juice
  cocktail
1 1/2 cups orange juice
1 quart ginger ale

Blend all ingredients well in large bowl. Serve over ice.
Note: For a festive touch, garnish with citrus slices or
lemon sherbet. An "ice ring" with citrus slices and oranges
makes a pretty bowl.
Yields: 25 (4-ounce) servings

Shared Treasures
St. James Episcopal Church
Wichita, Kansas

SPICED CRANBERRY PUNCH

4 (6-ounce) cans frozen
  lemonade
4 pints cranberry juice
1/2 teaspoon salt, optional
1/2 teaspoon cinnamon
1/2 teaspoon allspice
4 cups water

Combine all ingredients in a large saucepan. Simmer for
10 to 15 minutes. Serve warm.
Yields: 1 gallon

Second Helpings
Holy Trinity Episcopal Church
Ukiah, California

HOT ORCHARD PEACH CUP

1 (46-ounce) can peach juice
1/4 cup firmly packed brown
  sugar
2 cinnamon sticks
2 tablespoons butter or
  margarine
1/2 cup peach schnapps
  (optional)

Combine juice, brown sugar, cinnamon, and butter in 4-
quart saucepan. Heat to boil, then remove from heat. Add
schnapps and pour into cups.
Yields: 6 servings

St. Raphael's Cookbook Vol. II
St. Raphael's Episcopal Church
Brick, New Jersey

SUNBURN

2 cups pineapple juice
1 cup fresh orange juice
1/4 cup dark rum
1/4 cup light rum
2 tablespoons amaretto
2 tablespoons bourbon
12–16 ice cubes
Grenadine syrup

Combine first 6 ingredients in a large pitcher and stir well. Divide ice cubes into 4 glasses. Pour juice mixture over ice. Add dash of grenadine to each. Stir to blend and serve.
Yields: 4 servings

Home Cookin'
St. Matthias Episcopal Church
Monument, Colorado

MILK PUNCH

1 fifth bourbon, chilled
1/2 gallon milk
1/2 gallon vanilla ice cream,
    softened
Nutmeg (optional)

Blend first 3 ingredients well in a large bowl. Sprinkle with nutmeg, if desired.
Yields: 24 (4-ounce) servings

A Cook's Tour of the Bayou Country
Diocese of Louisiana Southwest Deanery

❖

"WE REMEMBER THE FISH WE USED TO EAT IN EGYPT FOR NOTHING, THE CUCUM-BERS, THE MELONS, THE LEEKS, THE ONIONS, AND THE GARLIC; BUT NOW OUR STRENGTH IS DRIED UP, AND THERE IS NOTHING AT ALL BUT THIS MANNA TO LOOK AT." NOW THE MANNA WAS LIKE CORIANDER SEED, AND ITS COLOR WAS LIKE THE COLOR OF GUM RESIN. THE PEOPLE WENT AROUND AND GATHERED IT, GROUND IT IN MILLS OR BEAT IT IN MORTARS, THEN BOILED IT IN POTS AND MADE CAKES OF IT, AND THE TASTE OF IT WAS LIKE THE TASTE OF CAKES BAKED WITH OIL.
NUMBERS 11:5–9
(GOD SENDS MEAT TO COMPLAINING PEOPLE)

CLASSIC VIRGINIA EGGNOG

12 large eggs, separated
1 cup sugar
2 cups bourbon
1 cup rum
1 quart milk
1 quart whipping cream,
  whipped
1 teaspoon ground nutmeg

Beat egg whites until stiff but not dry; set aside. Beat egg yolks and sugar in a large bowl until fluffy and lemon in color. Add bourbon slowly while beating; then add rum and milk. Fold in egg whites and the whipped cream. Sprinkle with nutmeg.
Yields: 24 servings

What's Cookin' at Epiphany?
Church of the Epiphany
Richmond, Virginia

FRENCH CHOCOLATE

1 1/2 squares unsweetened
  chocolate
3/4 cup boiling water
2 1/2 tablespoons sugar
Dash of salt
1 cup milk, scalded
2 cups half-and-half or canned
  evaporated milk, scalded
Marshmallows

Melt the chocolate in a small pot over hot water; add boiling water very slowly, stirring constantly. Add sugar and salt; when well blended, bring to a boil for 3 minutes, stirring constantly. Place pan over hot water again and gradually add the scalded milk and cream, stirring constantly until well mixed. Keep warm. Beat with rotary beater until frothy just before serving. Top with marshmallows.
Yields: 4 servings

The Galveston Island Cookbook
Trinity Episcopal Church
Galveston, Texas

BISHOP'S PUNCH

6 (10-ounce) cans beef
  consommé
6 (10-ounce) cans tomato juice
2 (10-ounce) cans vegetable
  cocktail
Juice of 3 lemons
4 tablespoons Worcestershire
  sauce
1/2 teaspoon Tabasco sauce
2 pinches Bouquet Garni

Heat consommé in large pot; add remaining ingredients and bring almost to a boil. Serve hot.
Yields: 50 cups

Gracing Your Table
Christ Episcopal Church
Hudson, Ohio

FOR THE LORD YOUR GOD IS BRINGING

YOU INTO A GOOD LAND, A LAND WITH

FLOWING STREAMS, WITH SPRINGS AND

UNDERGROUND WATERS WELLING UP IN

VALLEYS AND HILLS, A LAND OF WHEAT AND

BARLEY, OF VINES AND FIG TREES AND

Breads

POMEGRANATES, A LAND OF OLIVE TREES

AND HONEY, A LAND WHERE YOU MAY EAT

BREAD WITHOUT SCARCITY, WHERE YOU

WILL LACK NOTHING, A LAND WHOSE

STONES ARE IRON AND FROM WHOSE HILLS

YOU MAY MINE COPPER. YOU SHALL EAT

YOUR FILL AND BLESS THE LORD YOUR

GOD FOR THE GOOD LAND THAT HE HAS

GIVEN YOU.

DEUTERONOMY 8:7–10
(PROMISED LAND)

Homemade Ritual

American Christians tend to go light on religious rituals at home. Even though, at least for Episcopalians, the resources are out there (Advent wreaths, various Lenten traditions, daily devotions from the Prayer Book), our household observances tend to be more cultural than religious. We put up a tree at Christmas, but so does everyone else, and we're not all that likely to say a prayer around it. We may dye eggs at Easter, but we probably don't bless them or read a Bible passage about resurrection first.

The same thing is true of table traditions. Fewer people observe meatless Fridays now, and what food customs there are have often been gifts from a particular ethnic heritage. Ask around for a true-blue American Christian table tradition, and after someone hesitantly replies, "Well, turkey at Thanksgiving…" the room will likely fall silent.

In this area, we could learn much from our sisters and brothers in faith who worship God in the Jewish tradition. For these believers, rituals and meals at home are often as important a part of religious holidays as public worship.

There are customs about what to serve at various occasions: round challah bread for Rosh Hashanah, fried foods at Hanukkah, Hamentaschen at Purim. And of course, the Passover Seder features foods symbolic of slavery and of the Exodus from Egypt. The whole family can easily be involved in traditional meals like these, making memories and building identities that will last a lifetime.

In grade school, I remember preparing for an experiment in a science class that required bread to be brought in. A student from a Jewish home immediately volunteered, and he arrived the next day with matzo, proudly explaining that this was the special kind of bread his family ate during Passover. I was not a Christian then; but even had I been, I suspect I would still have been flooded with the same disappointing realization. "We don't have anything like that," I thought to myself.

Christian educator John Westerhoff speaks of the way children pass through a period of what he calls "affiliative faith," when believing means belonging. In this stage the stories, customs, and behavior of a faith tradition play a crucial role in building a sense of communal identification. (Who are we? We are the ones who do things this way.) Reclaiming those traditions of shared meals and special traditions can make it easier for our children to connect with their spiritual heritage. Deeds, as much as words—perhaps more than words—convey values.

Someone has said that through the ages, more than the Jewish people having kept the Sabbath with its weekly family meal, it has been the Sabbath that has kept the Jewish people. The more we, like they, learn to incorporate into our family life the practice of memorized actions, classic rituals, and special foods, the more our heritage will keep us, too.

NO-KNEAD ROLLS

1 package dry yeast
1 cup warm water
1/3 cup shortening
1 cup milk, scalded
1/3 cup sugar
1 teaspoon salt
6 cups all-purpose flour
1 large egg

Dissolve the yeast in warm water. Melt shortening in scalded milk and add sugar and salt. Mix some flour in yeast mixture. Add milk mixture after cooled slightly and stir in more flour. Stir in egg and remaining flour. Let rise until doubled in bulk. Punch down and let rise 3/4 as much again. Shape into rolls. Let rise and bake at 425° for 10 minutes.

Note: This recipe makes delicious cinnamon or pecan rolls. Pour a mixture of 2 cups brown sugar, 1/2 cup softened butter, and 5 tablespoons light corn syrup in the bottom of the pan before placing rolls on top. Bake as directed

Yields: about 3 dozen

St. Luke's Episcopal Church
Parish Collection
Delta, Colorado

ICE BOX ROLLS

1 quart milk
1 cup shortening
1 cup mashed potatoes
1 teaspoon baking powder
1 cup sugar
1 tablespoon salt
1 teaspoon baking soda
2 yeast cakes or 2 packages
  dry yeast
9 cups all-purpose flour,
  divided

Bring milk to a boil in a saucepan and pour over the shortening, mashed potatoes, baking powder, sugar, salt, and soda in a large bowl. Let mixture stand until luke-warm; add yeast and stir until dissolved. Add 6 cups flour or enough to make a batter. Let rise in warm place for 1 to 1 1/2 hours. Add about 3 cups flour or enough to make a soft dough, beating with a spoon. Place dough in a well-greased bowl, cover with plastic wrap, and refrigerate. Should stay in refrigerator for at least 2 hours. Can be kept in refrigerator for as long as 3 days. Roll out and cut on lightly floured surface, or put balls of dough in greased muffin tins, 2 to each, or 3 for cloverleaf rolls, rolling the balls of dough in melted butter. Let rise 2 hours. Bake at 400° for 10 to 20 minutes, or until brown.

Yields: 4 to 5 dozen

Burnt Offerings
Grace Episcopal Church
Vernon, Texas

ALABAMA BISCUITS

1 package dry yeast
1/4 cup warm water
2 1/2 cups all-purpose flour
1 teaspoon salt
2 teaspoons baking powder
1 tablespoon sugar
3 tablespoons shortening
3/4 cup milk
Melted shortening

Dissolve yeast in warm water. Sift flour and add salt, baking powder, and sugar and sift again. Cut 3 tablespoons shortening into flour as you would biscuits. Add milk and yeast to flour. Roll thin and cut out. Dip in melted shortening. Place 2 together. Let stand 2 hours. Bake at 450° for 10 to 15 minutes.
Yields: 2 to 3 dozen

Our Daily Bread and More
St. Christopher's Episcopal Church
Kingsport, Tennessee

ANGEL BISCUITS

1 package dry yeast
1 cup lukewarm water
7 cups all-purpose flour
1/4 cup sugar
4 teaspoons baking powder
1/4 teaspoon baking soda
1/2 teaspoon salt
2 cups buttermilk
3/4 teaspoon vegetable oil

Dissolve yeast in lukewarm water. Sift together dry ingredients; add remaining ingredients. Beat well; turn out on floured board and knead until elastic and smooth. Place in greased bowl and refrigerate. For rolls, cut with biscuit cutter (fairly thick) and bake at 400° for 15 to 20 minutes. Dough may be frozen for later use.
Yields: 3 to 4 dozen

More Manna… and a Little Quail
St. Luke's on the Lake
Austin, Texas

MAYONNAISE BISCUITS

1 cup self-rising flour
1/2 cup milk
2 tablespoons mayonnaise

Combine all ingredients in a small bowl; mix well. Pour into greased muffin pans. Bake at 375° until brown.
Yields: 6 biscuits

Give Us This Day
Grace Memorial Episcopal Church
Lynchburg, Virginia

SPOON BREAD

1 cup cornmeal
2 cups milk
4 large eggs, separated
1 tablespoon sugar
1 teaspoon salt
2 tablespoons butter

Cook cornmeal and milk in a double boiler, stirring until it thickens like a hot cereal. Add 4 egg yolks, sugar, salt, and butter. Beat egg whites and fold into mixture. Bake in greased casserole in slow oven, 325° for about 45 minutes, until brown.
Yields: 8 servings

Parish Collection
St. Peter's Episcopal Church
Altavista, Virginia

WHOLE-KERNEL CORN BREAD

1 1/2 cups self-rising cornmeal
2 large eggs
3/4 cup vegetable oil
1 (8-ounce) container sour
  cream
1 cup cream-style corn
1 small onion, chopped
1 teaspoon salt

Combine all ingredients in a large bowl; mix well. Pour into a greased and warmed pie pan. Bake at 400° for about 30 minutes or until golden brown.
Note: Add chopped green or jalapeño peppers for variety.
Yields: 6 to 8 servings

The Book of Common Fare
Grace-St. Luke's Church
Memphis, Tennessee

❖

BUT MOSES SAID, "THE PEOPLE I AM WITH NUMBER SIX HUNDRED THOUSAND ON FOOT; AND YOU SAY, 'I WILL GIVE THEM MEAT, THAT THEY MAY EAT FOR THE WHOLE MONTH'! ARE THERE ENOUGH FLOCKS AND HERDS TO SLAUGHTER FOR THEM? ARE THERE ENOUGH FISH IN THE SEA TO CATCH FOR THEM?" THE LORD SAID TO MOSES, "IS THE LORD'S POWER LIMITED? NOW YOU SHALL SEE WHETHER MY WORD WILL COME TRUE FOR YOU OR NOT."

THEN A WIND WENT OUT FROM THE LORD, AND IT BROUGHT QUAILS FROM THE SEA AND LET THEM FALL BESIDE THE CAMP, ABOUT A DAY'S JOURNEY ON THIS SIDE AND A DAY'S JOURNEY ON THE OTHER SIDE, ALL AROUND THE CAMP, ABOUT TWO CUBITS DEEP ON THE GROUND. SO THE PEOPLE WORKED ALL THAT DAY AND NIGHT AND ALL THE NEXT DAY, GATHERING THE QUAILS; THE LEAST ANYONE GATHERED WAS TEN HOMERS; AND THEY SPREAD THEM OUT FOR THEMSELVES ALL AROUND THE CAMP.

NUMBERS 11:21–23, 31–32
(GOD PROVIDES)

JOHNNY CAKE

(Often called a hoe cake, Johnny cakes were usually made on a griddle like pancakes.)

1 cup all-purpose flour
1 cup cornmeal
2 teaspoons baking powder
2 tablespoons sugar
1/2 teaspoon salt
1 large egg, beaten with 1 cup milk
4 tablespoons shortening

Stir all ingredients together; mix lightly but do not beat. Bake in an 8-inch square pan at 375° for 25 to 30 minutes.
Yields: 6 to 8 servings

Heavenly Delights
St. Paul's Episcopal Church
Waterloo, New York

INDIAN FRY BREAD

3 cups flour
2 tablespoons baking powder
1 tablespoon sugar
1 teaspoon salt
1 teaspoon shortening
About 2 cups water
Shortening for deep frying

Combine flour, baking powder, sugar, and salt in a large bowl; mix well. Cut in shortening with a pastry knife or mix well with hands. Add enough water to make a dough. Knead well. Break off a handful of dough. Roll flat on a floured surface using a rolling pin. Make a small hole in center of dough. Fry in shortening in a large skillet on both sides.

Navajo Indian Recipe
Good Shepherd Church
Fort Defiance, Arizona

BAKERS BROWN BREAD

1 cup bran or bran buds
1 cup sour milk
1 large egg, beaten
1 tablespoon molasses
2 tablespoons shortening
1/4 teaspoon salt
1 cup all-purpose flour
1 teaspoon baking soda
1/2 cup sugar
l/2–3/4 cup raisins

Soak bran in milk in a large bowl. Add egg, molasses, and shortening. Sift dry ingredients and add with raisins. Pour batter into a greased loaf pan. Bake at 350° for 35 minutes. Freezes well.
Yields: 1 loaf

Loaves and Fishes
St. Mark's Episcopal Church
Chenango Bridge, New York

WHOLE WHEAT ENGLISH MUFFIN BREAD

3/4 cup wheat germ
1 1/4 cups whole wheat flour
4 cups white bread flour,
  divided
2 packages dry yeast
1 tablespoon brown sugar
1/4 teaspoon baking soda
2 cups milk
1/2 cup water

Combine wheat germ, whole wheat flour, 1 cup white flour, yeast, sugar, and soda in a large bowl. Heat milk and water to 120° to 130°. Pour into dry ingredients; beat well. Stir in remaining flour to make a stiff batter. Spoon into two 8 1/2 × 4 1/2-inch pans that have been greased and floured with cornmeal. Sprinkle tops of dough with additional cornmeal. Cover and let rise in warm place for 45 minutes. Bake at 400° for 25 minutes. Remove from pans immediately and cool.
Yields: 2 loaves

St. Philip's Cooks
St. Philip's Episcopal Church
Brevard, North Carolina

MUFFULETTA BREAD

1 cup warm water
1 teaspoon sugar
1 package dry yeast
3 cups all-purpose flour
1 1/2 teaspoons salt
2 teaspoons shortening
Sesame seeds

In a 2-cup glass measuring cup, combine water and sugar. Stir in yeast. Let stand 5 minutes until foamy. In a food processor, fitted with a steel blade, combine flour, salt, and shortening. Add yeast mixture. Process until dough forms a ball, about 5 seconds. It should be smooth and satiny. If dough is too dry, add more water, 1 teaspoon at a time, and process just until blended. If too sticky, add a little flour. Process 20 seconds to knead. Lightly oil a large bowl. Place dough in bowl and turn to grease all sides. Cover bowl with plastic wrap, let rise until double in size, about 1 to 1 1/2 hours. Lightly grease a baking sheet. When dough has doubled, punch down and turn out on a lightly floured surface. Form dough into a 10-inch round and place on the baking sheet. Sprinkle top with sesame seeds and press. Cover loosely and let rise until doubled in size, about 1 hour. Place on rack in center of oven. Bake bread at 425° for 10 minutes. Reduce heat to 375° and bake 25 minutes. Remove from oven when bread sounds hollow when thumped. Cool completely on rack.
Yields: 1 loaf

A Book of Favorite Recipes
Church of the Redeemer
Ruston, Louisiana

CARDAMOM BREAD

2 cups milk
1/2 cup butter or margarine
2 packages dry yeast
1/2 cup warm water
1 1/4 cups sugar
4 large eggs, beaten
1 1/4 teaspoons ground cardamom
1 teaspoon salt
9 1/2–10 1/2 cups unsifted all-purpose flour
2 tablespoons butter, softened
2 tablespoons all-purpose flour
2 tablespoons sugar
1/4 cup water
1 large egg yolk
2 tablespoons sugar

Heat milk in medium saucepan; stir in 1/2 cup butter. Set aside to melt butter. Cool until lukewarm. In a large bowl, sprinkle yeast over 1/2 cup warm water. Let stand 5 minutes. Beat 1 1/4 cups sugar, 4 eggs, cardamom, and salt into milk mixture, stir into yeast mixture. Gradually add 5 cups of flour, beating after each addition until smooth. Let stand 10 minutes. Beat in another 4 1/2 cups flour until soft dough forms. Turn dough out onto floured board and knead until smooth. (Hand kneading will require more flour than kneading with a mixer.) Place dough in oiled bowl. Cover and let rise for 60 to 70 minutes. Grease 3 baking sheets. Punch down dough. Shape into 9 equal-size balls. Roll each ball into a rope. Braid 3 ropes together to form a loaf. Place on greased sheet. Repeat to make 2 more loaves. Cover and let rise in warm place until double size, about 30 to 45 minutes. Heat oven to 325°. Combine 2 tablespoons butter, 2 tablespoons flour, and 2 tablespoons sugar. Sprinkle down center of braids. Bake loaves 25 minutes or until golden brown. Combine 1/4 cup water, 1 egg yolk, and 2 tablespoons sugar in a small bowl. Brush over loaves. Bake 5 minutes longer. Brush again and bake until loaves sound hollow when tapped on top.

Yields: 3 loaves

Episcopal Churchwomen Cookbook
Church of the Transfiguration
Ironwood, Michigan

YORKSHIRE PUDDING

2 large eggs
1 cup milk
1 cup sifted all-purpose flour
1/2 teaspoon salt

Preheat oven to 450°. Slide pans into oven to heat. (Use muffin pans or a loaf pan if you do not have Yorkshire pudding pans.) Beat eggs and milk in a bowl until eggs are fluffy and light. Add sifted flour and salt all at once. Beat until batter is smooth. Grease hot pans with oil and fill half full of batter. Bake 30 minutes. Reduce temperature to 350°. Bake 15 minutes. Serve with roast beef.
Yields: 6 to 8 servings

Canterbury Fare
St. George's-by-the-River
Rumson, New Jersey

HOMEMADE PIZZA DOUGH

1 package dry yeast
1 cup warm water
1/4–1/2 tablespoon salt
3–4 cups flour (may be all
  white flour or 1 cup whole
  wheat in with white)
1 tablespoon sugar
2 tablespoons vegetable oil

Dissolve yeast in warm water. Let mixture stand for 10 minutes, then stir. Blend in other ingredients. Knead about 10 minutes until smooth and elastic. Place in greased bowl; turn dough to grease all sides. Cover with towel. Let rise 1 1/2 hours. Punch down and divide in half. Spread on 2 pizza pans. Top with favorite ingredients. Bake at 350° until dough is done.
Yields: enough for 2 pizzas

St. Martin's Spoon-Lickers
St. Martin's Episcopal Church
Chattanooga, Tennessee

SWEET HUSH PUPPIES

1 cup all-purpose flour
1/2 cup sugar
1/2 cup yellow cornmeal
1/8 cup baking powder
1/4 teaspoon salt
1/8 teaspoon cayenne pepper
1 cup onion, finely chopped
1/2 cup green bell pepper,
  finely chopped
1/2 cup green onions
  (tops only), finely chopped
2 large eggs, beaten
Vegetable oil for deep frying

Combine first 6 ingredients in a large bowl. Add other ingredients and blend thoroughly. Allow to set for 1 1/2 to 2 hours to moisten. Cook batter in fryer oil, 1 tablespoon at a time, and fry until golden.
Yields: 20 servings

Home Cookin'
St. Matthias Episcopal Church
Monument, Colorado

LEMON BREAD

1 cup sugar
1/2 cup shortening
2 large eggs
1 1/2 cups all-purpose flour
1 teaspoon baking powder
1/2 teaspoon salt
1/2 cup milk
1 lemon, rind and juice
1/4 cup sugar

Combine the sugar and shortening in a large bowl. Add the eggs, and beat well. Combine the flour, baking powder, and salt in a bowl. Stir into the egg mixture alternately with the milk. Stir in the lemon rind. Pour into a greased and floured loaf pan. Bake at 350° for 50 minutes. Combine lemon juice and 1/4 cup sugar in a cup; stir well. Pour over warm bread. Let cool before removing from pan.
Yields: 1 loaf

Saint Peter's Recipes
St. Peter's Episcopal Church
Rockland, Maine

CRANBERRY LOAF

2 cups sifted all-purpose flour
1 teaspoon baking soda
1 teaspoon salt
3/4 cup sugar
1 large egg, slightly beaten
2/3 cup milk
1/4 cup melted margarine
1 cup chopped walnuts
1 cup canned whole cranberry
   sauce

Sift dry ingredients together in a large bowl. Add egg, milk, and margarine, mixing until blended. Fold in nuts and cranberry sauce. Pour into a greased loaf pan and bake at 350° for 1 hour.
Yields: 1 loaf

St. Anne's Guild Cookbook
St. James the Less Church
Scarsdale, New York

ORANGE BLOSSOM PRUNE BREAD

1 cup pitted prunes
2 cups all-purpose flour
1 cup sugar
2 1/2 teaspoons baking powder
3/4 teaspoon salt
2 large eggs, beaten
3 tablespoons vegetable oil
1 tablespoon grated orange
   peel
3/4 cup chopped nuts
3/4 cup orange juice

Place prunes in sauce pan; add water to 1/2 inch above prunes. Bring to boil, reduce heat, and simmer about 5 minutes; drain, saving 3/4 cup liquid. Combine flour, sugar, baking powder, and salt in a bowl; mix well. Combine reserved liquid, eggs, oil, and orange peel in a bowl; add to dry ingredients. Add prunes and nuts; mix well and pour into greased pan. Bake at 350° for 1 hour or until done. Let stand 10 minutes. Remove from pan and cool.
Yields: 10 to 12 servings

One Hundred Years of Heavenly Cooking
St. Paul's Episcopal Church
Lynchburg, Virginia

PANCAKES

1 large egg
2 cups buttermilk
2 cups all-purpose flour
1 teaspoon baking soda
1 teaspoon salt
1 tablespoon melted shortening

Beat egg in a large bowl; add buttermilk, mixing well. Sift flour, baking soda, and salt. Add to egg mixture. Stir in melted shortening. Cook spoonfuls of batter on hot griddle or skillet.
Yields: 6 to 8 pancakes

Shared Treasures
St. James Episcopal Church
Wichita, Kansas

WELSH TEA LOAF

2 3/4 cups water
1 (15-ounce) package raisins
4 teaspoons baking soda
3 sticks butter or margarine,
  softened
1 1/2 cups sugar
3 large eggs
2 tablespoons molasses
1 tablespoon vanilla
1/8 teaspoon salt
4 cups all-purpose flour

Combine water and raisins in medium saucepan. Bring to boil over high heat. Reduce heat to low and simmer 2 minutes. Stir in baking soda; let cool. Cream butter with sugar in large bowl of electric mixer. Add eggs, one at a time, beating well after each addition. Add molasses, vanilla, and salt; continue beating until well blended, 2 or 3 minutes. Beat in flour. Add raisin mixture and beat on low speed until well blended, about 2 minutes. Spoon batter into prepared 9 × 5-inch loaf pans. Bake at 350° for 50 to 60 minutes, or until tester inserted in center comes out clean. Cool in pans on rack. Serve at room temperature.
Yields: 2 (9 × 5-inch) loaves

Parish Collection
St. Luke the Evangelist
Roselle, New Jersey

BLUEBERRY MUFFINS

1 large egg
Milk
1 3/4 cups all-purpose flour
1 teaspoon baking soda
2 teaspoons cream of tartar
1/4 cup sugar
1 teaspoon salt
1/3 cup melted shortening
1 cup fresh blueberries

Break egg into 1-cup measure; add milk to make a full cup. Whisk together. Sift together flour, soda, cream of tartar, sugar, and salt in a large bowl. Add egg mixture and shortening; mix lightly. Fold in blueberries. Bake at 400° in a greased muffin pan for 20 to 30 minutes.
Yields: 1 dozen

Angels in the Kitchen
Holy Trinity Episcopal Church
Gainesville, Florida

❖

WHILE THE ISRAELITES WERE CAMPED IN GILGAL THEY KEPT THE PASSOVER IN THE EVENING ON THE FOURTEENTH DAY OF THE MONTH IN THE PLAINS OF JERICHO. ON THE DAY AFTER THE PASSOVER, ON THAT VERY DAY, THEY ATE THE PRODUCE OF THE LAND, UNLEAVENED CAKES AND PARCHED GRAIN. THE MANNA CEASED ON THE DAY THEY ATE THE PRODUCE OF THE LAND, AND THE ISRAELITES NO LONGER HAD MANNA; THEY ATE THE CROPS OF THE LAND OF CANAAN THAT YEAR.
JOSHUA 5:10–12

APPLE MUFFINS

1 large egg
1/2 cup milk
1/4 cup vegetable oil
1 1/2 cups all-purpose flour
1/2 cup sugar
1 teaspoon cinnamon
2 teaspoons baking powder
1/2 teaspoon salt
3 apples, peeled and diced

Beat egg, milk, and oil in a large bowl. Stir in dry ingredients; mix well. Stir in apples. Bake in muffin tins at 400° for 20 to 30 minutes.
Yields: 1 dozen

Potluck
Trinity Episcopal Church
Ware, Massachusetts

HOT CROSS BUNS

1 package dry yeast
1/4 cup warm water
3/4 cup milk
1/2 cup butter, softened
2 tablespoons sugar
1 teaspoon salt
1/2 teaspoon cinnamon
1/2 teaspoon nutmeg
3 large eggs
2/3 cup raisins
4–5 cups all-purpose flour
1/4 cup light corn syrup
Frosting

Dissolve yeast in warm water in a large bowl. Heat milk and butter in a saucepan until lukewarm (butter doesn't need to melt). Stir into yeast mixture. Add sugar, salt, and spices. Whisk in eggs until blended. Stir in raisins. Stir in about 4 cups of flour (enough to make an easily managed dough). On a smooth, floured surface, knead until smooth and elastic, about 5 minutes, using additional flour if needed. Place in a greased bowl; turn to grease top of dough; cover. Let rise in a warm, draft-free place until double in bulk (about 1 hour). Punch dough down. Let rest 10 minutes. Divide into 24 equal balls. Place in a greased, floured 9 × 13-inch baking pan. Put in a warm place, and let rise until double in bulk (about 45 minutes). Bake at 375° for 15 minutes. Brush with corn syrup. Return to oven for 5 minutes. Remove rolls from oven; let cool for 10 minutes. Pipe a frosting "cross" on each bun.
Yields: 2 dozen

FROSTING
1 tablespoon light corn syrup
1 tablespoon hot water
1 1/2 cups confectioners' sugar

Combine syrup and water in a medium bowl; gradually stir in confectioners' sugar. Turn into a pastry bag for piping.

St. Martin's Spoon-Lickers
St. Martin's Episcopal Church
Chattanooga, Tennessee

SOUR CREAM BUNS

1 cup sour cream
2 tablespoons shortening
3 tablespoons sugar
1/8 teaspoon baking soda
1 teaspoon salt
1 large egg
1 package dry yeast
3 cups all-purpose flour
2 tablespoons soft butter
1/3 cup firmly packed brown
   sugar
1 teaspoon cinnamon

Heat the sour cream to lukewarm in a large saucepan; stir in shortening, sugar, soda, and salt until well blended. Add the egg and yeast. Stir until yeast is dissolved. Mix in the flour. Turn out onto lightly floured board. Knead lightly a few seconds to form a smooth ball. Cover with damp cloth and let rise 5 minutes. Roll dough 1/4 inch thick into rectangle, 6 × 24 inches.

    Spread dough with the butter; sprinkle brown sugar and cinnamon over top. Roll up, beginning at wide side. Cut into slices about 1 1/2 inches thick. Place in greased muffin cups. Cover with damp cloth and let rise about 1 hour. Bake 12 to 15 minutes at 375°. While still warm, frost with a confectioners' sugar icing.
Yields: 16 servings

Trinity Episcopal Church Cookbook
Society of Mary and Friends
Gladstone, Michigan

JAMAICAN EASTER SPICED BUNS

1 yeast cake
1/2 pint milk
1 cup water
1/2 pound butter
1 cup firmly packed brown
   sugar
1 teaspoon salt
1 whole nutmeg, grated
1 teaspoon cinnamon
Pinch of mixed spice
1 large egg, beaten
4 cups all-purpose flour,
   divided
1/4 pound crystallized cherries,
   chopped
1/4 pound currants, chopped
1/4 pound raisins, chopped

Dissolve yeast in a small amount of lukewarm water. Scald the milk and boil the cup of water; combine liquids. Place butter, sugar, salt, and spices in a large bowl; add liquids. Stir in egg. Sift half the flour into the liquid; stir well. Add yeast and fruit. Add sufficient amount of remaining flour to make a stiff dough. Cover and let rise until double in bulk. Knead dough, then sprinkle in remaining flour and knead well. Shape into loaves and let rise again until double in bulk. Bake at 350° in greased loaf pans until buns leave side of tins and are springy to the touch.
Yields: 2 loaves

Diocese Collection
Iglesia Episcopal Costarricense
Costa Rica

RAISIN SCONES

2 cups all-purpose flour
2 teaspoons baking powder
1/2 teaspoon baking soda
1/2 teaspoon nutmeg
1/2 teaspoon salt
8 tablespoons cold unsalted
   butter
1 cup raisins
2 tablespoon sugar
1 large egg yolk
3/4 cup buttermilk or plain
   yogurt
1 large egg white
Sugar

Combine flour, baking powder, baking soda, nutmeg, and salt in a large bowl; mix well. Cut in butter. Add raisins and sugar, tossing to distribute evenly. Add egg yolk to buttermilk in a measuring cup and whisk together. Pour over the flour mixture and stir until a soft dough forms. Turn out dough and knead 10 to 12 times. Cut dough in half. Knead each half briefly into a ball, turn smooth side up and pat into a 6-inch circle. Cut in 6 wedges. Do not separate wedges. Brush with egg white and sprinkle with sugar. Carefully transfer each circle to an ungreased cookie sheet, keeping edges of each wedge touching. Bake at 375° for 18 to 22 minutes. Cool on a wire rack; after 5 minutes, pull wedges apart and cover loosely with a dish towel.
Yields: 12 servings

Loaves & Fishes and Other Dishes
St. Andrew's Episcopal Church
Turners Falls, Massachusetts

CINNAMON ROLLS

1/2 cup warm water
2 packages dry yeast
1 1/2 cups lukewarm milk
1/2 cup sugar
2 teaspoons salt
2 large eggs
1/2 cup soft shortening
7 cups all-purpose flour,
   or more as needed, divided
8 tablespoons melted butter,
   divided
Cinnamon sugar
Raisins, optional
1/2 cup firmly packed
   brown sugar
Nuts, optional

Dissolve yeast in warm water in a large bowl. Stir in milk, sugar, salt, eggs, shortening, and enough flour so dough remains slightly sticky. Turn out onto a lightly floured surface and knead for about 5 minutes. Place in a greased bowl; cover with a damp cloth. Let rise in warm place until doubled in bulk, about 30 minutes. Divide dough in half. Roll each into a 9 × 15-inch oblong. Spread each with 2 tablespoons butter. Sprinkle with cinnamon sugar. Add raisins, if desired. Roll up tightly, beginning at wide side. Stretch slightly to even. Spread the remaining 4 tablespoons of butter in 2 baking pans. Add brown sugar and spread evenly. Sprinkle with nuts, if desired. Cut rolls and place on top of brown sugar mixture. Let rise until doubled in bulk. Bake at 350° for 25 to 30 minutes. Invert immediately onto serving platter.
Yields: 1 1/2 to 2 dozen

Savoring Grace
St. Alban's Episcopal Church
Hixson, Tennessee

BEIGNETS

1/2 cup boiling water
2 tablespoons shortening
1/4 cup sugar
1/2 teaspoon salt
1/2 cup evaporated milk
1/2 package dry yeast
1/4 cup warm water
1 large egg, beaten
3 3/4 cups sifted all-purpose
  flour
Confectioners' sugar

In a large mixing bowl pour the boiling water over the shortening, sugar, and salt. Add the milk and let stand until warm. In a small bowl dissolve the yeast in the warm water and add to the milk mixture along with the egg. Stir in 2 cups flour and beat. Add enough flour to make a soft dough. Place the dough in a greased bowl turning to grease the top. Cover with wax paper and a cloth, and chill until ready to use. On a lightly floured surface, roll the dough to 1/8 inch thickness. Do not let dough rise before frying. Cut into 2-inch squares and fry, a few at a time, in deep hot fat (360°). Brown on 1 side; turn and brown on the other side. Drain on paper towels. Sprinkle with the confectioners' sugar and serve hot.
Yields: 30 doughnuts

La Bonne Cuisine
All Saints' Episcopal Church
River Ridge, Louisiana

FRENCH BAKED DOUGHNUTS

5 tablespoons margarine
1/2 cup sugar
1 large egg
1 1/2 cups all-purpose flour
2 1/4 teaspoons baking powder
1/4 teaspoon salt
1/4 teaspoon nutmeg
1/2 cup milk
Melted butter
Cinnamon and sugar

Mix margarine, sugar, and egg together in a large bowl. Add flour and next 3 dry ingredients, mixing alternately with milk. Fill muffin tins half full (use muffin papers). Bake at 350° for 25 minutes. While hot, dip each baked doughnut into melted butter, then into cinnamon and sugar mixture.
Yields: about 2 dozen

Cooking with Grace
St. Luke's Episcopal Church
Lanesboro, Massachusetts

GERMAN COFFEE CAKE
(A German recipe from the early 1900s)

1 large egg
2/3 cup sugar
1/4 teaspoon salt
1/2 teaspoon cinnamon
1 cup sour cream
1 teaspoon soda
2 cups all-purpose flour
Butter, cinnamon, and sugar
  for topping

Combine egg and next 6 ingredients in a large bowl; mix well. Pour into a greased 9 × 13-inch baking pan. Dot with butter, cinnamon, and sugar. Bake at 350° for about 30 minutes.
Yields: 8 to 10 servings

St. Stephen's Parish Cookbook
St. Stephen's Episcopal Church
Schuylerville, New York

PUMPKIN COFFEE CAKE

1 (2-layer) package yellow
  cake mix
3 large eggs
1/2 cup softened butter
3/4 cup raisins
2/3 cup canned pumpkin
2/3 cup water
1 teaspoon cinnamon
1/4 teaspoon ground cloves
1/8 teaspoon ginger
Heavy dash nutmeg
Topping

Mix all ingredients except topping together in a large bowl; stir well for 2 minutes. Pour into a greased and floured 13 × 9-inch pan. Sprinkle with Topping. Bake at 350° for 30 to 35 minutes.
Yields: 10 to 12 servings

TOPPING
1/2 cup butter
1/3 cup firmly packed light
  brown sugar
2/3 cup chopped pecans
1/3 cup butterscotch chips

Cut butter and sugar together into large crumbs. Mix in pecans and butterscotch chips.

Parish Collection
Trinity Episcopal Church
Richlands, Virginia

COTTAGE CHEESE HOTCAKES

1 cup creamed cottage cheese
4 large eggs, well beaten
6 tablespoons all-purpose flour
6 tablespoons melted butter
Pinch of salt

Press cottage cheese through a sieve into a mixing bowl using the back of a large spoon. Stir in eggs. Add flour, butter, and salt; mix well. Drop by spoonfuls onto hot buttered griddle. Cook until brown, turning once. Serve for breakfast or as a dessert with confectioners' sugar and strawberry preserves.
Yields: 10 to 15 hotcakes

Kitchen Confessions II
St. Edward's Episcopal Church
Lawrenceville, Georgia

DATE AND NUT BREAD

3/4 cup chopped walnuts
1 cup chopped pitted dates
1 1/2 teaspoons baking soda
1/2 teaspoon salt
3 tablespoons shortening
3/4 cup boiling water
2 large eggs
1 teaspoon vanilla
1 cup sugar
1 1/2 cups sifted all-purpose
   flour

Mix first 4 ingredients in a large bowl with a fork. Add shortening and water. Let stand 20 minutes. Beat eggs with fork in a separate bowl. Add vanilla, sugar, and flour, beating with fork. Stir in date mixture, mixing to just blend. Pour into greased 9 × 5 × 3-inch loaf pan. Bake at 350° for 1 hour and 5 minutes, or until done.
Yields: 1 loaf

Treasure of Personal Recipes
Church of Our Fathers
Hulls Cove, Maine

GRANDMA'S BANANA BREAD

3 ripe bananas, mashed
1 cup sugar
1/2 cup shortening
2 large eggs
2 cups all-purpose flour
1 teaspoon salt
1 teaspoon baking powder
1 teaspoon baking soda
1 tablespoon water
1/4 cup chopped nuts

Mix bananas and sugar in a large bowl; let stand 15 minutes. Add shortening and eggs; mix well. Mix together dry ingredients except baking soda. Add dry ingredients to banana mixture, then add baking soda dissolved in water. Stir in nuts. Divide batter into two greased and lightly floured loaf pans. Bake 1 hour at 350°. Check with toothpick for doneness.
Yields: 2 loaves

Recipes—and Remembrances
Zion Episcopal Church
Avon, New York

MONASTERY BREAD

4 cups whole wheat flour
4 teaspoons baking powder
2 teaspoons salt
1/2 cup honey
1/2 cup vegetable oil
3/4 cup milk
3/4 cup hot water

Sift together dry ingredients in a large bowl. Combine wet ingredients and pour into flour mixture, using enough to make smooth, soft dough that's not too sticky to handle. Knead gently on floured surface. Roll out to 3/16 inch thick. Cut either 6 or 8 inches in diameter. Place on lightly greased baking sheet. Cut cross on top. Bake at 400° for 10 to 15 minutes.
Yields: several small round loaves

Kitchen Confessions
St. Edward's Episcopal Church
Lawrenceville, Georgia

AT MEALTIME BOAZ SAID TO HER, "COME
HERE, AND EAT SOME OF THIS BREAD, AND
DIP YOUR MORSEL IN THE SOUR WINE." SO

SHE SAT BESIDE THE REAPERS, AND HE
HEAPED UP FOR HER SOME PARCHED
GRAIN. SHE ATE UNTIL SHE WAS SATISFIED,
AND SHE HAD SOME LEFT OVER.

RUTH 2:14

Balancing
a Feast

Our mothers told us, and we've passed it on down: always eat a balanced meal. If you need help planning one, the U.S. Food and Drug Administration is ready to help you out with its 1995 Food Guide Pyramid. This visual aid gives advice on how to balance servings from several different food groups. The primary concern in the pyramid's system is ensuring that the human body gets the right amount and variety of nutrients. Not too many fats, oils, and sweets ("use sparingly"), but plenty of grain products like rice and pasta ("6 to 11 servings" a day.) Mom would be proud.

But there is another instinct apart from just sheer nutrition that tells us something about balancing meals. There may be times in our own lives when we just grab some yogurt for lunch, or enjoy a quick piece of fruit. When we invite others to dine with us, however, the meal never works out that way. Something tells us, as we gather in community, that diversity is required. As soon as the invitations go out, we start planning for how we can offer our guests many different kinds of enjoyment at a shared table.

Let's start with those stuffed cherry tomatoes… or maybe a cheese plate. Then the chilled cucumber soup, the recipe I got from Margaret. Shall we just marinate the chicken, throw it on the grill and do peppers along with it, or would Mom's chicken casserole be a better idea? We'll need vegetables, too, and then dessert: Jack doesn't eat chocolate, of course, so what about angel food cake with… what, raspberries? Or a glaze?

On the big day—whatever it is—the Greeks savor *meze* and the Spanish pass *tapas*. In America, our Thanksgiving tables can end up requiring every serving dish in the house. Our bodies seem instinctively to know that that feasting involves not mere quantity, but the feeling of options, the experience of differences. And our souls, if we listen to them for a while, tell us the same thing.

Diversity and variety surround us when we gather at church. We don't just sing five hymns in a row and head home. Nor do we politely listen to an extended lecture. We stand and sit and stand and sit and kneel and stand in a ritual often humorously called "Episcopal aerobics."

Sometimes we chant; sometimes we confess; sometimes we clasp hands—and we always eat and drink together the bread and wine that show forth and bring about our union with our Host.

The Food and Drug Administration's Food Guide Pyramid, in some mysterious way, seems to have a spiritual analogue. If you want abundance, wholeness, and feasting, you have to offer yourself and others variety. Humanity cannot thrive on bread, or private prayer, alone.

When we meet with each other and with God, it enriches us to let that meeting touch many different parts of who we are. We know, even without a reminder from the FDA, how good it is to move with each other through the process of a meal—or a Meal—in which there is something for everyone to savor.

WATERCRESS SALAD

2 (4-ounce) bunches
  watercress, cleaned
1 (3-ounce) package slivered
  almonds
1 tablespoon butter
1 pound fresh mushrooms,
  sliced
3–5 stalks of heart of palm,
  sliced
1 cup vegetable oil
1/3 cup cider vinegar
2 teaspoons sugar
1 tablespoon salt
1 tablespoon capers
2 tablespoons grated onion
1/2 tablespoon dried parsley
1 large hard-cooked egg, grated
Dash of red pepper

Place watercress in large bowl. Sauté almonds in butter; add to watercress. Add mushrooms and heart of palm. Toss well. Combine oil and remaining ingredients in a bowl; mix well. Toss with vegetables just before serving.
Yields: 8 to 10 servings

Saints Preserve Us Cookbook
St. Edward's Episcopal Church
Lawrenceville, Georgia

GARLICKY TOSSED SALAD

3 tablespoons olive oil
1 tablespoon seasoned gourmet
  rice vinegar
4 large cloves garlic, pressed
5–6 cups mixed salad greens,
  torn
1 medium red onion,
  thinly sliced
Croutons, optional

Combine oil, vinegar, and garlic (may use same proportions—3 to 1 of oil to vinegar—if more dressing is desired). Pour over mixture of greens and onion in a large bowl. Add croutons, if desired. Serve immediately.
Yields: 4 to 6 servings

Entertaining Grace-fully
Grace Episcopal Church
Hutchinson, Kansas

SPINACH SALAD

1/2 pound bacon, cooked and
  crumbled
2 large hard-cooked eggs
1 pound spinach, washed and
  destemmed
Croutons
2/3 cup vegetable oil
1/3 cup sugar
1 teaspoon celery seed
1/3 cup wine vinegar
1 tablespoon prepared mustard
1 1/2 teaspoons brown mustard
1 onion, finely chopped

Combine the bacon, eggs, spinach, and croutons in a large
bowl; mix well. Combine oil and remaining ingredients in
a bowl; mix well. Pour over spinach mixture.
Yields: 4 servings

Savoring Grace
St. Alban's Episcopal Church
Hixson, Tennessee

SPINACH-STRAWBERRY SALAD

1 package prewashed spinach
  leaves
1 pint strawberries, destemmed
  and sliced
Dressing

DRESSING
1/2 cup sugar
2 tablespoons sesame seeds
1 tablespoon poppy seeds
1 1/2 teaspoons minced onion
1/4 teaspoon Worcestershire
  sauce
1/4 teaspoon paprika
1/2 cup olive or vegetable oil
1/4 cup cider vinegar

Toss spinach leaves and strawberries. Top with Dressing;
toss lightly.
Yields: 4 to 6 servings

Blend all ingredients well in a small bowl.

Parish Collection
Holy Trinity Episcopal Church
Iron Mountain, Michigan

SEVEN-LAYER SALAD

1 medium head lettuce,
  shredded
1 cup chopped celery
1/2 cup chopped green bell
  pepper
1 cup chopped Spanish onion
1 (10-ounce) package frozen
  peas, separated
1 1/2 cups mayonnaise
2 tablespoons sugar
2 1/2 cups shredded mild
  Cheddar cheese
8 strips bacon, cooked, drained,
  and crumbled

Arrange lettuce in bottom of deep glass bowl or a 9 × 13-inch dish. Layer other vegetables; do not toss. Spread mayonnaise evenly over layer of peas. Sprinkle with sugar and cheese. Cover and refrigerate for at least 4 hours. Sprinkle bacon over salad before serving.

Yields: 10 to 12 servings

All Angels Fare
All Angels by the Sea Episcopal Church
Longboat Key, Florida

CHINESE SALAD

1 medium head Napa (Chinese
  cabbage), shredded
1 bunch green onions, chopped
1/2 bottle sesame seeds
1/4 cup slivered almonds
2 (3-ounce) packages ramen
  noodles
3–4 tablespoons butter or
  margarine
1/4 cup vinegar
1/2 cup sugar
3/4 cup vegetable oil
2 tablespoons soy sauce

Mix together Napa and green onions in a large bowl. Toast sesame seeds, almonds, and noodles with flavor packet in skillet with butter until very brown. Combine vinegar, sugar, oil, and soy sauce in a saucepan; boil for 1 minute, then cool. Toss all three mixtures right before serving.

Note: Mixtures can be made and refrigerated 1 or 2 days ahead of time.

Yields: 4 servings

Recipes & Remembrances
St. Timothy's Episcopal Church
Cincinnati, Ohio

ORANGE-AVOCADO SALAD

3 tablespoons balsamic vinegar
1/2 cup vegetable oil
2 tablespoons orange juice
2 teaspoons orange zest
1/4 teaspoon salt
1/4 teaspoon black pepper
2 large oranges, peeled and
thinly sliced
1 large avocado, peeled and
sliced
1 medium onion, peeled and
sliced
1 head romaine lettuce, torn
into bite-size pieces

Combine vinegar and next 5 ingredients in a small bowl;
mix well. Combine oranges, avocados, onion, and lettuce
in a large bowl. Toss with vinegar dressing.
Yields: 4 to 6 servings

Angels' Food
St. Mary's Episcopal Church
Napa, California

BEAN SALAD

2 (14 1/2-ounce) cans French-
style green beans
1 (14 1/2-ounce) cans green
peas
4 stalks celery, chopped
1 small onion, chopped
1 green bell pepper, chopped
1/3 cup pimientos, chopped
Dressing

Drain beans and peas. Combine with the celery, onion,
green pepper, and pimientos in a large bowl. Pour
Dressing over top. Refrigerate for 24 hours; drain before
serving.
Yields: 6 to 8 servings

DRESSING
1/4 cup vegetable oil
1/2 teaspoon salt
1 cup sugar
1/2 cup cider vinegar
1 tablespoon water
1 teaspoon paprika

Mix all ingredients together; blend well.

Angels in the Kitchen, II
Emmanuel Episcopal Church
Bristol, Virginia

GREEK GREEN BEAN AND FETA SALAD

1 1/2 pounds fresh green beans, washed and cut
3/4 cup olive oil
1/2 cup packed fresh mint leaves, finely chopped
1/4 cup white wine vinegar
1 tablespoon lemon juice
3/4 teaspoon salt
1 teaspoon sugar
1/4 teaspoon ground black pepper
1/2 teaspoon minced garlic
1 cup chopped onion
1 cup crumbled feta cheese
1 cup chopped walnuts

Place beans in a saucepan of salted water. Bring to a boil for a few minutes; drain. Place in a bowl in the refrigerator to cool. Combine oil, mint, vinegar, lemon juice, salt, sugar, pepper, and garlic in blender; blend well, then refrigerate. When ready to assemble, arrange beans on platter; sprinkle with onions, then feta cheese, then walnuts. Pour salad dressing over and serve.
Yields: 4 servings

Diocese of Central Pennsylvania
Diocese Board Collection

CAULIFLOWER SALAD

1 medium head cauliflower, broken into florets
1 medium tomato, chopped
1 medium cucumber, peeled and chopped
3 green onions with tops, chopped
1 stalk celery, chopped
2 tablespoons sweet pickle relish
1/2 cup mayonnaise
1/2 teaspoon salt
1/2 teaspoon black pepper
1 tablespoon lemon juice
4 slices bacon, cooked and crumbled

Cook cauliflower, covered, in a large saucepan in a small amount of boiling water for 10 minutes; drain well. Add next 9 ingredients; toss gently. Cover and refrigerate several hours. Place in serving containers; sprinkle with bacon.
Yields: 8 servings

Lunches & Brunches
St. Mark's Episcopal Church
Plainview, Texas

BEAN SPROUT SALAD

2 cups grated carrots
2 cups grated cabbage
2 cups fresh bean sprouts
1 onion, diced
1 stalk celery, diced
1/2 cup raisins
Salt to taste
1/2 cup mayonnaise

Combine carrots and next 6 ingredients in a large bowl; mix well. Fold in mayonnaise. Serve cold.
Yields: 6 to 8 servings

St. Mary's Favorite Recipes
St. Mary's Episcopal Church
Fleeton, Virginia

BROCCOLI AND CAULIFLOWER SALAD

1 bunch broccoli, cut in bite-size pieces (about 2 cups)
1 bunch cauliflower, cut in bite-size pieces (about 2 cups)
1 pound bacon, cooked and crumbled
1 small onion, diced
1 cup light mayonnaise
1/3 cup sugar
2/3 tablespoon vinegar

Toss broccoli and cauliflower with bacon and onion in a large bowl. Make dressing with remaining ingredients and mix thoroughly. Toss with vegetables and bacon. Keep refrigerated.
Yields: 4 to 6 servings

Give Us This Day
Grace Memorial Episcopal Church
Lynchburg, Virginia

MARINATED TOMATOES

6–8 large tomatoes
1/4 teaspoon coarse ground black pepper
1/4 cup parsley
2/3 cup vegetable oil
1/4 cup tarragon vinegar
1 teaspoon salt
1/2 teaspoon thyme
1/4 cup chopped chives or green onion tops

Slice tomatoes and place in one or two layers in a 13 × 9-inch dish. Combine other ingredients and pour over tomatoes. Refrigerate for several hours or overnight.
Yields: 8 to 10 servings

Angels in the Kitchen
Holy Trinity Episcopal Church
Gainesville, Florida

TREES 'N' SEEDS

1 bunch fresh broccoli, broken
   into florets
1/2 cup red onion, chopped
1 cup celery, chopped
1 pound bacon, cooked and
   crumbled
1/2 cup hulled sunflower or
   sesame seeds
1/2 cup white raisins
Dressing

DRESSING
3/4 cup mayonnaise
1/4 cup sugar
2 tablespoons vinegar

In a large mixing bowl, combine all ingredients. Pour Dressing over salad and stir to blend. Refrigerate until chilled. Serve chilled.
Yields: 12 servings

Combine all ingredients and blend thoroughly.

Served with Love
Diocese of West Missouri

TABBOULEH

1 1/2 cups very fine-grain
   bulgur (cracked) wheat
Juice of 3 lemons
Vegetable oil
1 1/2 teaspoons salt
1 teaspoon freshly ground
   black pepper
1 teaspoon allspice
3/4 cup fresh or canned peeled,
   chopped tomatoes
2 large onions, finely chopped
3 bunches parsley, finely
   chopped
1 handful mint, finely chopped
3 pounds romaine or leaf
   lettuce, chopped
Fresh cabbage leaves or pita
   bread wedges

Put bulgur in a large pan. Pour very hot tap water on it. Drain through a fine mesh strainer, pushing out excess water with your hands. Place wheat in a glass bowl. Add lemon juice. Add salad oil to cover wheat. Then add salt, pepper, and allspice. Layer tomato, onion, parsley, mint, and lettuce on top. Refrigerate until ready to serve. Toss well before serving and adjust seasonings. Serve with cabbage leaves or pita bread wedges to scoop up salad.
Yields: 6 to 8 servings

Love, Loaves, and Fishes
St. John's Episcopal Church
Lafayette, Indiana

COPPER PENNY SALAD

6 cups sliced carrots
2 onions, sliced into rings
2 green bell peppers, sliced into
  rings
1 (10-ounce) can tomato soup
3/4 cup vinegar
2/3 cup sugar
1/2 cup vegetable oil
1 teaspoon mustard
1 teaspoon Worcestershire
  sauce

Combine carrots, onions, and peppers in a large bowl. Combine the soup, vinegar, sugar, oil, mustard, and Worcestershire sauce in a saucepan. Bring to a boil; cool and pour over vegetables. Refrigerate. Let marinate overnight. Keeps well for a long time in the refrigerator.
Yields: 10 cups

Parish Collection
Epiphany Episcopal Church
Cape Coral, Florida

MARINATED VEGGIE SALAD

1 (16-ounce) can petit point
  peas, drained
1 (11-ounce) can white shoe
  peg corn, drained
1 (16-ounce) can French-style
  green beans, drained
1 (2-ounce) jar chopped
  pimiento, drained
1 green bell pepper, chopped
1 cup chopped celery
1/2 cup finely chopped onion
1 (4-ounce) can chopped olives,
  drained
1 cup crisp-cooked carrots
1/2 cup sugar
1/2 cup vegetable oil
1/2 cup vinegar
1 teaspoon salt
1/2 teaspoon black pepper

Combine peas and next 8 ingredients in a large bowl; mix well. Combine sugar, oil, vinegar, salt, and pepper in a small saucepan. Bring to a boil; pour over vegetables and mix well. Refrigerate for at least 12 hours. Drain before serving.
Yields: 8 to 10 servings

St. John the Baptist Centennial Cookbook
St. John the Baptist Episcopal Church
Seattle, Washington

VEGETARIAN SALAD

1 1/2 cups chicken substitute,*
   cut in chunks
2 navel oranges, peeled and
   sectioned
2 celery stalks, diced
2 green onions, sliced
1/3 cup light mayonnaise
Salt and black pepper
   as needed

Combine all ingredients in a bowl, toss gently. Serve on lettuce or spinach leaves.

Note: Vegetarian substitutes for chicken can be found in many health stores and are frequently found in general food stores.

Yields: 4 servings

Parish Collection
St. Hilary's Church
Fort Myers, Florida

CHRISTMAS SALAD

1 pound marshmallows
1 (8-ounce) package cream
   cheese
1–2 (20-ounce) cans crushed
   pineapple
1–2 (8-ounce) jars maraschino
   cherries
1 (3-ounce) package lemon
   gelatin
1 pint whipping cream
Nuts (optional)
1 (6-ounce) package cherry
   gelatin

Place marshmallows and cream cheese in double boiler. While this is melting, drain the pineapple and save the juice. Cut the cherries to desired size. Add enough water to pineapple juice to make 2 cups. Heat in the microwave for 40 seconds. Dissolve the lemon gelatin in the juice. Beat whipping cream very stiff, and stir in the cherries and pineapple. When the marshmallows and cream cheese are fully melted, remove from heat and cool. When it gets ropey, add the pineapple juice/lemon gelatin mixture and stir well. Then add the whipping cream/cherries/pineapple mixture and stir. Place in one large dish, or several smaller dishes or molds. Place nuts on top in a design, if desired, or sprinkle liberally over the top. Place in the refrigerator to set. Then add the cherry gelatin to the top. If desired, sprinkle additional marshmallows or nuts over the top for a decorative look. Allow several hours for salad to set. Unmold before serving, if desired.

Yields: 8 to 10 servings

Parish Collection
Stras Memorial Episcopal Church
Tazewell, Virginia

ST. CHRISTOPHER'S CRANBERRY SALAD

2 cups ground cranberries
(1 pound)
2 cups sugar
2 cups crushed pineapple,
drained
2 (3-ounce) packages lemon
gelatin, dissolved in 1 1/2
cups hot water
2 cups pineapple juice
2 cups celery, cut fine
1 cup chopped pecans

Combine cranberries and sugar and set aside. Combine pineapple, dissolved gelatin, pineapple juice, and celery in a large bowl; stir in cranberries. Refrigerate until mixture is syrupy. Stir in pecans. Refrigerate until set.
Yields: 20 to 25 servings

St. Christopher's Cookbook
St. Christopher's Episcopal Church
El Paso, Texas

CRANBERRY-ORANGE SALAD

3 cups cranberries
1 orange, seeded but unpeeled
2 cups sugar
1 (6-ounce) package lemon
gelatin
2 cups boiling water

Grind cranberries and orange in blender; cover with sugar. Let stand 1 hour. Combine gelatin and boiling water; add fruit and pour into a large ring mold. Chill until set.
Yields: 8 to 10 servings

Heavenly Hosts
St. John's Episcopal Church
Naples, Florida

DAVID CAME TO NOB TO THE PRIEST AHIMELECH. AHIMELECH CAME TREMBLING TO MEET DAVID, AND SAID TO HIM, "WHY ARE YOU ALONE, AND NO ONE WITH YOU?" DAVID SAID TO THE PRIEST AHIMELECH, "THE KING HAS CHARGED ME WITH A MATTER, AND SAID TO ME, 'NO ONE MUST KNOW ANYTHING OF THE MATTER ABOUT WHICH I SEND YOU, AND WITH WHICH I HAVE CHARGED YOU.' I HAVE MADE AN APPOINTMENT WITH THE YOUNG MEN FOR SUCH AND SUCH A PLACE. NOW THEN, WHAT HAVE YOU AT HAND? GIVE ME FIVE LOAVES OF BREAD, OR WHATEVER IS HERE." THE PRIEST ANSWERED DAVID, "I HAVE NO ORDINARY BREAD AT HAND, ONLY HOLY BREAD—PROVIDED THAT THE YOUNG MEN HAVE KEPT THEMSELVES FROM WOMEN." DAVID ANSWERED THE PRIEST, "INDEED WOMEN HAVE BEEN KEPT FROM US AS ALWAYS WHEN I GO ON AN EXPEDITION; THE VESSELS OF THE YOUNG MEN ARE HOLY EVEN WHEN IT IS A COMMON JOURNEY; HOW MUCH MORE TODAY WILL THEIR VESSELS BE HOLY?" SO THE PRIEST GAVE HIM THE HOLY BREAD; FOR THERE WAS NO BREAD THERE EXCEPT THE BREAD OF THE PRESENCE, WHICH IS REMOVED FROM BEFORE THE LORD, TO BE REPLACED BY HOT BREAD ON THE DAY IT IS TAKEN AWAY.
1 SAMUEL 21:1–6
(DAVID ASKS A PRIEST FOR BREAD)

FROZEN FRUIT SALAD

2 cups sour cream
3/4 cup sugar
1/8 teaspoon salt
2 tablespoons lemon juice
1/2 cup chopped nuts
4 tablespoons maraschino
  cherries, chopped
3 bananas, diced
1 (8-ounce) can crushed
  pineapple

Mix sour cream, sugar, and salt in a bowl; beat well. Add lemon juice, nuts, cherries, bananas, and crushed pineapple (use about half of liquid with pineapple). Put mixture in cupcake liners. Freeze.
Yields: 12 to 14 servings

One Hundred Years of Heavenly Cooking
St. Paul's Episcopal Church
Lynchburg, Virginia

ORANGE BUTTERMILK SALAD

1 (6-ounce) package orange
  gelatin
1 cup boiling water
1 cup miniature marshmallows
1 (16-ounce) can crushed
  pineapple, chilled
1 cup buttermilk
1 (8-ounce) container frozen
  whipped topping

Mix gelatin and water. Add marshmallows, pineapple, and buttermilk. Mix in metal bowl; add whipped topping when it starts to congeal.
Yields: 6 to 8 servings

Parish Collection
St. Peter's Episcopal Church
Altavista, Virginia

VEGETABLE ASPIC SALAD

3 tablespoons plain gelatin
1/2 cup cold water
2 cups boiling water
1 tablespoon salt
1 1/2 cups sugar
Juice of 1 lemon
1/2 cup vinegar
1 cup chopped celery
1 cup fresh tomatoes, cut fine
1 small onion, chopped
1 green bell pepper, chopped

Dissolve gelatin in cold water. Combine boiling water, salt, and sugar; add to gelatin. Stir in lemon juice and vinegar. Cool until almost set; then fold in vegetables. Allow to set completely before serving.
Yields: 12 servings

Parish Collection
St. Luke's Episcopal Church
Delta, Colorado

CONGEALED VEGETABLE SALAD

1 1/2 cups sugar
1/2 cup vinegar
3 cups water, divided
4 envelopes plain gelatin
4 tablespoons lemon juice
2 teaspoons salt
2 tablespoons onion flakes
2 (5-ounce) cans water
  chestnuts, drained and sliced
2 cups chopped celery
2 (4-ounce) jars sliced
  pimiento, drained
2 (8-ounce) cans cut asparagus,
  drained

Heat sugar, vinegar, and 2 cups water in a saucepan; cook until sugar dissolves. Dissolve gelatin in 1 cup cold water. Add lemon juice, salt, and onion flakes. Add remaining ingredients; pour into mold. Chill until set.
Yields: 8 to 10 servings

Christ Episcopal Church Cookbook
Christ Episcopal Church
Pearisburg, Virginia

TEXAS COLESLAW

1 medium head cabbage,
  shredded
1 medium green bell pepper,
  finely chopped
1 large onion, finely chopped
1 carrot, grated
Dressing

Combine vegetables in a large mixing bowl; toss lightly. Pour Dressing over vegetables; toss lightly. Cover and refrigerate overnight. Keeps well.
Yields: 4 to 6 servings

DRESSING
1 12 cups vegetable oil
1/2 cup vinegar
1 cup sugar
1 1/4 teaspoons black pepper
1 teaspoons salt
1/2 teaspoon dry mustard
2 tablespoons chopped parsley

Combine all ingredients. Beat until smooth and well blended.

Recipes—and Remembrances
Zion Episcopal Church
Avon, New York

FROZEN COLE SLAW

l teaspoon salt
1 medium head cabbage,
   shredded
1 carrot, grated
1 green bell pepper, chopped
1 cup vinegar
1 teaspoon mustard seed
1 teaspoon celery seed
2 cups sugar
l/4 cup water

Mix salt and cabbage in a large bowl; let stand 1 hour. Squeeze out excess moisture. Add remaining vegetables. Combine the remaining ingredients in a saucepan and boil 1 minute. Cool to lukewarm and pour over the slaw. Put into freezer containers and freeze. This thaws quickly for serving and can be refrozen.
Yields: 6 to 8 servings

Trinity Episcopal Church Cookbook
Trinity Episcopal Church
Gladstone, Michigan

GREEK SLAW

1 large egg, slightly beaten
3/4 cup water
1/4 cup vinegar
3/4 cup sugar
1 teaspoon prepared mustard
1 teaspoon salt
1/4 teaspoon black pepper
1 medium head cabbage,
   shredded
1/2 cup mayonnaise
1 teaspoon celery seed

Combine egg, water, vinegar, sugar, mustard, salt, and pepper in a saucepan. Cook, stirring constantly, over low heat until mixture thickens, about 10 minutes. Combine cabbage and mayonnaise in large bowl. Stir in celery seed. Pour hot mixture slowly over cabbage and stir well. Cover and refrigerate for 24 hours before serving. Will keep for 2 or 3 days.
Yields: 6 to 8 servings

The Way to a Man's Heart
All Saints' Episcopal Church
Norton, Virginia

CREAMY POTATO SALAD

5–7 new potatoes
1/2 onion, finely minced
3 stalks celery, finely chopped
Salt and black pepper to taste
1 tablespoon sugar
4–5 large hard-boiled eggs
Salsa rosa or French dressing
Mayonnaise

Cut potatoes in half; leave skin on. Put in cold water to cover in a large saucepan. Boil for 25 or 30 minutes or until soft when pierced with a fork; drain and cool. Peel and dice potatoes into a large bowl. Add onion, celery, salt, pepper, sugar, and eggs; mix thoroughly. Taste and adjust seasoning. Mix in salsa or French dressing for color and special taste. Let stand in refrigerator overnight to absorb flavors. Add mayonnaise a few hours before serving.
Yields: 6 to 8 servings

Diocese Collection
Iglesia Episcopal Costarricense
Costa Rica

GOURMET POTATO SALAD

3/4 cup sour cream
1/4 cup prepared mustard
3/4 cup diced celery
2 tablespoons chopped chives
1/4 cup minced onion
1 teaspoon salt
1/4 teaspoon black pepper
1/4–1/2 pound crisp fried
   bacon, diced
6 cups cubed, cooked potatoes,
   chilled

Combine sour cream and next 7 ingredients in a large bowl, blend gently. Fold in chilled potatoes. Serve chilled.
Yields: 4 to 6 servings

Cooking with Grace
St. Luke's Episcopal Church
Lanesboro, Massachusetts

SWEET POTATO SALAD

2 pounds sweet potatoes,
   peeled and cubed
2 tablespoons lemon juice
1 cup mayonnaise
2 tablespoons orange juice
1 tablespoon honey
1 teaspoon grated orange peel
1/2 teaspoon ground ginger
1/4 teaspoon salt
1/8 teaspoon nutmeg
1 cup sliced celery
1/3 cup chopped dates
1/2 cup chopped pecans
Lettuce leaves
1 (11-ounce) can mandarin
   oranges, drained

Cook sweet potatoes in boiling salted water in a saucepan just until tender; drain. Toss with lemon juice. Combine mayonnaise and next 6 ingredients in a large bowl. Add the warm potatoes, celery, and dates. Toss lightly to coat well; cover and chill. Gently stir in pecans before serving. Spoon salad onto a lettuce-lined platter. Arrange orange slices around salad.
Yields: 6 to 8 servings

The Garden of Eatin' Cook Book
Diocese of Southwest Florida

WALNUT MACARONI SALAD

1 1/2 cups uncooked macaroni
2 cups sliced celery
1/2 cup sweet pickle relish or
   sweet pickles, diced
1/4–1/2 cup chopped onion
Salt and black pepper
3/4 cup coarsely chopped
   walnuts
1/2 cup mayonnaise
1 teaspoon prepared mustard
2 tablespoons lemon juice
1 large hard-cooked egg, sliced,
   chopped, or cut into wedges
Walnut halves (optional)

Cook macaroni in salted water in a saucepan until tender; drain and rinse in cold water. Place in a large bowl. Add celery, relish, onion, salt, and pepper. Stir in chopped nuts. Combine mayonnaise, mustard, and lemon juice in a small bowl. Stir into macaroni mixture. Chill. Serve in a lettuce-lined bowl. Garnish with hard-cooked egg and walnut halves, if desired.
Yields: 4 to 6 servings

The Vicar's Guild Cookbook
Episcopal Church of the Resurrection
Loudon, Tennessee

PASTA SALAD WITH PESTO MAYONNAISE

1 pound rotini or rotelle pasta,
   cooked
2 bunches green onions,
   chopped
1 medium red bell pepper,
   finely chopped
1 1/2 cups thinly sliced celery
2–3 tablespoons white wine
   vinegar or rice wine vinegar
Juice of 1 lemon
2/3 cup Pesto Sauce
1 cup mayonnaise
2/3 cup olive oil
Salt and freshly ground black
   pepper

Combine the pasta, green onions, red pepper, and celery in a large bowl. Combine the vinegar, lemon juice, 2/3 cup Pesto Sauce, mayonnaise, and olive oil in a medium bowl; mix well. Fold into pasta mixture until well combined. Add salt and pepper. Refrigerate several hours before serving.
Yields: 4 to 6 servings

PESTO SAUCE
4 cups fresh basil
2/3 cup olive oil
4–5 cloves garlic, crushed
8 sprigs parsley
Salt and black pepper to taste
1/3 cup pine nuts

Place the basil in a food processor or blender. Add the oil, a little at a time, along with the garlic, parsley, salt, and pepper. Blend until finely chopped. Add the nuts; blend well.

Not by Bread Alone
Christ Church, the Episcopal Parish
Shrewsbury, New Jersey

CHICKEN SALAD

4 cups chopped cooked chicken
2 tablespoons chopped onion
1 cup chopped celery
1 1/2 cups green bell pepper
1 (6.5-ounce) can mandarin
  oranges, drained
1 (15-ounce) can pineapple
  chunks, drained
1 cup mayonnaise
1 tablespoon mustard
1 cup Chinese noodles

Combine chicken and next 5 ingredients; mix well. Combine mayonnaise and mustard and stir into chicken mixture; blend well. Stir in Chinese noodles right before serving.
Yields: 6 to 8 servings

Diocese Board Collection
ECW Diocese of New Jersey

CHUTNEY CHICKEN SALAD

2 cups chopped cooked chicken
1 (13-ounce) can pineapple
  tidbits, drained
1 cup diagonally sliced celery
1 green onion, sliced
1/4 cup peanuts or cashews
2/3 cup mayonnaise
2 tablespoons chopped chutney
1/2 teaspoon grated lime rind
2 tablespoons lime juice
1/2 teaspoon curry powder

Toss together first 5 ingredients in a bowl. Combine remaining ingredients and stir into chicken mixture. Chill, then serve on lettuce.
Yields: 4 servings

Keep the Feast
Church of the Ascension
Middletown, Ohio

❖

IN THE OPEN COUNTRY THEY FOUND AN EGYPTIAN, AND BROUGHT HIM TO DAVID. THEY GAVE HIM BREAD AND HE ATE, THEY GAVE HIM WATER TO DRINK; THEY ALSO GAVE HIM A PIECE OF FIG CAKE AND TWO CLUSTERS OF RAISINS. WHEN HE HAD EATEN, HIS SPIRIT REVIVED; FOR HE HAD NOT EATEN BREAD OR DRUNK WATER FOR THREE DAYS AND THREE NIGHTS.

1 SAMUEL 30:11–12
(DAVID HELPS AN EGYPTIAN)

TURKEY SALAD

4 cups cooked turkey breast
2/3 cup uncooked rice, steamed
  or boiled
1 (8-ounce) can chopped water
  chestnuts
2 tablespoons finely chopped
  onion
1/2 teaspoon black pepper
1 teaspoon salt
1 (8-ounce) can pineapple
  tidbits
1/2 cup flaked coconut
1/2 cup mayonnaise
1 tablespoon lemon juice
1/2 teaspoon curry powder
Dash of soy sauce
Paprika
Lettuce leaves
Cranberry sauce, sliced
1 large hard-cooked egg, sliced

Combine turkey and next 7 ingredients in a large bowl. Combine mayonnaise, lemon juice, curry powder, and soy sauce; stir into turkey mixture. Refrigerate overnight. Sprinkle with paprika and serve on lettuce leaves. Garnish with a slice of cranberry sauce and a slice of hard-cooked egg.
Yields: 6 to 8 servings

St. John the Baptist Centennial Cookbook
St. John the Baptist Episcopal Church
Seattle, Washington

THAI HOT BEEF SALAD

1 clove garlic, minced
1/3 cup vegetable oil
3 tablespoons lime juice
2 tablespoons soy sauce
2 tablespoons light molasses
2 tablespoons minced
  ginger root
1–2 small hot peppers, minced
1 pound lean ground beef
6 cups loosely packed salad
  greens
1 large tomato, cut into thin
  wedges
2 sliced green onions

Combine garlic, oil, lime juice, soy sauce, molasses, ginger, and hot peppers in a small bowl; set aside. Cook ground beef in a skillet, stirring frequently, until all pan juices evaporate; drain well. Add dressing; stir to loosen browned bits from pan. Arrange greens and tomato wedges on large platter. Pour beef mixture over greens; sprinkle with green onions.
Yields: 4 servings

Second Helpings
Holy Trinity Episcopal Church
Ukiah, California

SHRIMP SALAD

2 cups frozen, cooked shrimp
1/2 cup mayonnaise
1 1/2 cups cooked rice
Juice of 1/2 lemon
1 cup raw cauliflower, sliced
1/4 teaspoon paprika
1/2 green bell pepper, chopped
Dash of Tabasco sauce
2 tablespoons diced green
   onion
12 stuffed olives, sliced
Salt and black pepper to taste

Thaw shrimp; place in a large bowl. Add remaining ingredients and toss well. Chill and serve.
Yields: 4 servings

Another Touch of Basil
St. Basil's Episcopal Church
Tahlequah, Oklahoma

FRESH HERB DRESSING

1/4 cup salad oil
3 tablespoons dry white wine
2 tablespoons lemon juice
1 tablespoon sugar
1 tablespoon snipped fresh
   basil, crushed
1 teaspoon salt
Several dashes of bottled hot
   pepper sauce
1/4 teaspoon black pepper

Combine salad oil, wine, lemon juice, sugar, basil, salt, hot pepper sauce, and pepper in a screw-top jar. Cover and shake thoroughly. Use for tossed salad.
Yields: 1/2 cup

All Saints' Cookbook
All Saints' Episcopal Church
Morristown, Tennessee

CREAMY GARLIC DRESSING

1 large head garlic
1/2 cup mayonnaise
1/4 cup grated Parmesan
   cheese
1 tablespoon lemon juice
1/4 cup chopped chives
1/2–1 cup buttermilk
Salt and fresh ground black
   pepper to taste

Roast garlic in baking dish at 350° for 30 minutes to 1 hour, depending on size of garlic. Stick knife into garlic to check for tenderness. Cool garlic, then squeeze into glass bowl. Add mayonnaise, cheese, lemon juice, and chives. Stir in buttermilk to thin to appropriate consistency and season to taste with salt and pepper. Serve on mixed greens with garlic croutons.
Yields: 6 servings

What's Cookin' at Epiphany?
Church of the Epiphany
Richmond, Virginia

FRENCH DRESSING

1 1/2 cups sugar
1 teaspoon salt
1 teaspoon dry sweet peppers
1/8 teaspoon celery seed
2 tablespoons ketchup
1 tablespoon lemon juice
2/3 cup salad oil
1/2 teaspoon dry mustard
1 teaspoon paprika
1 1/2 cups vinegar

Beat all ingredients in a bowl with electric beater until thickened; store in sealed container. Keeps well in the refrigerator.
Yields: about 2 cups

Recipes—and Remembrances
Zion Episcopal Church
Avon, New York

SWEET-AND-SOUR SALAD DRESSING

1 cup sugar
1 cup tomato ketchup
1 cup salad oil
1/2 cup finely chopped onion
1 teaspoon lemon juice
1 teaspoon black pepper
1/2 teaspoon Worcestershire
  sauce
1/2 teaspoon salt
1 cup vinegar

Combine sugar and next 7 ingredients in a bowl; mix well. Add vinegar; stir well.
Yields: about 3 1/2 cups

Seasoned with Love
St. Andrew's Episcopal Church
Taft, California

BLEU CHEESE SALAD DRESSING

1 pound bleu cheese
4 tablespoons vinegar
4 tablespoons lemon juice
1 teaspoon Worcestershire
  sauce
1 teaspoon salt
1 teaspoon black pepper
1 quart mayonnaise
1 (16-ounce) container sour
  cream

Crumble bleu cheese in a large bowl. Add vinegar, lemon juice, Worcestershire sauce, salt, and pepper. Stir well to make sure cheese is well crumbled. Add mayonnaise and sour cream; stir well. Refrigerate and serve cold.
Yields: about 8 cups

Angels in the Kitchen
Holy Trinity Episcopal Church
Gainesville, Florida

MUSTARD DRESSING

2 tablespoons grated onion
1/2 teaspoon salt
1/2 teaspoon black pepper
2 tablespoons Dijon mustard
2 tablespoons wine vinegar
6–8 tablespoons olive oil
1/2 teaspoon lemon juice

Combine onion, salt, pepper, and mustard in a bowl; beat with a wire whisk. Add vinegar. Beat in oil, one tablespoon at a time, until smooth. Stir in lemon juice. Serve with a salad of spinach, bacon, and hard-cooked egg.
Yields: 4 to 6 servings

Canterbury Fare
St. George's-by-the-River
Rumson, New Jersey

CELERY SEED DRESSING

1 1/2 cups sugar
2 teaspoons salt
1 tablespoon onion juice
2 teaspoons prepared mustard
2/3 cup vinegar, divided
2 cups salad oil
2 tablespoons celery seed

Mix sugar, salt, onion juice, mustard, and half the vinegar in a small bowl. Alternately add remaining vinegar with oil until mixed. Add celery seed last. Great over assorted fresh fruit.
Yields: about 3 cups

Feed My Sheep
St. Peter's Episcopal Church
Lebanon, Indiana

CUCUMBER SAUCE

1 medium cucumber, unpeeled
1/4 cup mayonnaise
1/2 cup sour cream
1 tablespoon grated onion
1 teaspoon vinegar
Salt and black pepper to taste

Cut cucumber in half and scoop out seeds. Grate the cucumber; drain. Combine all ingredients in a bowl and blend well. Chill and serve over tomato aspic, tossed salad greens, or congealed vegetable salads.
Yields: 1 1/2 cups

What's Cooking Along the King's Highway?
Diocese of El Camino Real
Monterey, California

HONEY DRESSING

2/3 cup sugar
1 tablespoon lemon juice
1 teaspoon mustard
1 tablespoon grated onion
1 teaspoon paprika
1/3 cup honey
1/2 teaspoon salt
5 tablespoons vinegar
1 cup vegetable oil

Combine all ingredients except oil in blender; gradually add oil. Beat until thick. Keep refrigerated.
Yields: about 2 1/2 cups

St. Andrew's 75th Celebration
St. Andrew's Episcopal Church
Maryville, Tennessee

MAPLE RAISIN DRESSING

1/2 cup plain yogurt
1 teaspoon honey
2 tablespoons maple syrup
1/2 teaspoon dried orange rind
1/4 cup raisins
1/4 cup chopped walnuts

Combine yogurt, honey, and maple syrup in a bowl; mix well. Fold in orange rind, raisins, and nuts. Cover and chill until ready to use on fresh fruit salad.
Yields: 1 cup

Miracles in the Kitchen
St. Luke's Episcopal Church
Farmington, Maine

WHEN DAVID CAME TO MAHANAIM, SHOBI

SON OF NAHASH FROM RABBAH OF THE

AMMONITES, AND MACHIR SON OF AMMIEL

FROM LO-DEBAR, AND BARZILLAI THE

GILEADITE FROM ROGELIM, BROUGHT BEDS,

BASINS, AND EARTHEN VESSELS, WHEAT,

Soups & Stews

BARLEY, MEAL, PARCHED GRAIN, BEANS AND

LENTILS, HONEY AND CURDS, SHEEP, AND

CHEESE FROM THE HERD, FOR DAVID AND

THE PEOPLE WITH HIM TO EAT; FOR THEY

SAID, "THE TROOPS ARE HUNGRY AND

WEARY AND THIRSTY IN THE WILDERNESS."

2 SAMUEL 17:27–29
(DAVID FLEES FROM SAUL)

More than a Sum of Its Parts

There is something especially homey about soup. When you head into the kitchen to start a recipe from scratch, you know that the steaming pot on the stove will be your companion for the rest of the day. The scent of the broth will permeate your house, and as family or friends begin to arrive, they will comment on it. "What are you making? It smells wonderful!" But it won't be ready for three more hours, and everybody just has to wait. That's all there is to it.

This afternoon, I'm making thirty-two bean soup. The beans, bought in bulk at a whole foods store, are sitting on my counter; and yes, there really are 32 different varieties. I know that because after filling my bag in the bulk-foods aisle, I picked up the little card by the barrel that lists them. Pinto, adzuki, garbanzo, snow cap, appaloosa, scarlet runner, black turtle. Some of the names are familiar, others exotic.

As I begin measuring out sixteen cups of water for the pot, it occurs to me that I don't quite know what the result will taste like, although I expect it will be good this evening and better tomorrow. In fact, the result may keep changing as it occurs to me to throw in a few extra things.

Using the recommended ingredients is enough to make an acceptable pot of soup, but it is as you begin to add little pieces of personal kitchen history that the soup really becomes your own. Things that were intended for one purpose get recycled and used for another one. Wasn't there some wine left in the bottle from last night? Or how about that leftover lettuce, which I know perfectly well will just disappear into the broth? Maybe a bunch of the herbs from outside, too, since they won't survive the frost that has to be coming any night now. Whatever I think to drop in—totally different from what someone else might add—makes the soup more complex and deep.

You can put anything into a soup pot, almost. But when you do, it will affect the outcome. In this way, soup is like a parish community; a parish can absorb almost anyone, but at the end it may not be quite the same parish anymore. And usually, that's a good thing.

This is why learning stories about a church's past will always help you appreciate its present. Communities are like soup: much more has gone into creating them than is evident. Contributions, specialties, leftovers, and the dreams and hopes of specific people have all made your parish, and every other parish, what it is.

As you sit down to share a bowl of soup with family and friends, they will only see the end result of your afternoon of work. No one will ask whether this green stuff is just your old salad fixings. No one (unless you are entertaining other cooks) will request the whole story of what went into the pot; they'll all simply enjoy what has come out. But you are especially blessed, because you will remember and appreciate the particularities. You will know what has been contributed, whose offerings are whose, and which individual flavors have now become a part of the whole.

AVOCADO SOUP

1 large ripe avocado
2 cups beef broth
1 cup sour cream
Salt to taste
Chili powder to taste
White or cayenne pepper
1/2 small onion, grated
Dill for garnish

Peel avocado. Blend in blender until smooth. Add broth, sour cream, and next 4 ingredients; blend well. Chill thoroughly. Serve garnished with dill.
Yields: 4 servings

Recipes From St. Paul's 1981
St. Paul's Episcopal Church
Naples, Florida

SPANISH GAZPACHO SOUP

3 ounces olive oil
1 tablespoon lime juice
Salt and black pepper to taste
1 (32-ounce) can vegetable
  juice cocktail
1 cucumber, thinly sliced
1 (6-ounce) can pimiento
3 large ripe tomatoes, chopped
3 cloves garlic
2 large onions, chopped

Combine oil, lime juice, salt, and pepper in the container of an electric blender. Add the remaining ingredients until coarsely ground. Place soup in refrigerator for at least 2 hours. Serve cold. Enjoy on a warm day.
Yields: 8 servings

Heavenly Tastes, Earthly Recipes
St. Andrew's Episcopal Church
Lake Worth, Florida

GREEK SOUP

6 cups chicken broth
1/3 cup barley, raw
1/2 cup mint leaves
3 cups plain yogurt

Cook broth with barley in a large saucepan; cool this mixture. In blender combine mint leaves and plain yogurt. Blend with barley and broth. Serve cold as first course for luncheon or dinner, usually in warm weather.
Yields: 6 to 8 servings

Parish Collection
Christ Episcopal Church
Bradenton, Florida

TURKISH CUCUMBER SOUP (CACIK)

3 cucumbers
3 cups plain yogurt
2 cloves garlic, crushed
1/2 teaspoon salt
2 tablespoons chopped walnuts
2 large hard-cooked egg yolks,
  crumbled
Freshly ground pepper
1 tablespoon melted butter
1 tablespoon wine vinegar
2 tablespoons chopped parsley
2 tablespoons chopped fresh
  dill or 1 tablespoon dried
  dillweed

Mix all ingredients in blender and chill in refrigerator for at least 1 hour. Serve cold with crusty brown bread.
Yields: 6 servings

Food and Gladness
St. Francis Episcopal Church
Norris, Tennessee

ORANGE-TOMATO SOUP

5 cups tomato juice
2 tablespoons brown sugar
1 small onion, chopped
1/2 cup concentrated
  orange juice
2 tablespoons lemon juice
1 tablespoon lemon peel
Salt and black pepper to taste

Combine tomato juice, sugar, and onion in a large saucepan; add orange and lemon juices. Bring to a boil. Reduce heat and simmer for 5 minutes. Garnish with grated lemon peel and season to taste.
Note: Use 1/2 teaspoon nutmeg and cinnamon, if desired. May also be served chilled.
Yields: 4 servings

Cooking with Grace
Grace Church
Bath, Maine

❖

THEY BROUGHT IN THE ARK OF THE LORD, AND SET IT IN ITS PLACE, INSIDE THE TENT THAT DAVID HAD PITCHED FOR IT; AND DAVID OFFERED BURNT OFFERINGS AND OFFERINGS OF WELL-BEING BEFORE THE LORD. WHEN DAVID HAD FINISHED OFFERING THE BURNT OFFERINGS AND OFFERINGS OF WELL-BEING, HE BLESSED THE PEOPLE IN THE NAME OF THE LORD OF HOSTS, AND DISTRIBUTED FOOD AMONG ALL THE PEOPLE, THE WHOLE MULTITUDE OF ISRAEL, BOTH MEN AND WOMEN, TO EACH A CAKE OF BREAD, A PORTION OF MEAT, AND A CAKE OF RAISINS. THEN ALL THE PEOPLE WENT BACK TO THEIR HOMES.

2 SAMUEL 6:17–19
(DAVID BRINGS THE ARK TO JERUSALEM)

ONION SOUP GRATINEE

3 tablespoons unsalted butter, divided
1 1/2 pounds yellow onions, thinly sliced
6 tablespoons dry red wine
3 tablespoons dry sherry
5 cups beef stock or canned broth
1 teaspoon Worcestershire sauce
1 teaspoon dried thyme, crumbled
1/2 teaspoon dried oregano, crumbled
1/2 teaspoon white pepper
1 bay leaf
2 shallots, thinly sliced
2 green onions, thinly sliced
1 large garlic clove, minced
8 toasted French bread baguette slices
8 slices Gruyere cheese

Melt 2 tablespoons butter in heavy large pot over medium-high heat. Add yellow onions and cook until very soft and caramelized, about 40 minutes, stirring frequently. Add wine and sherry and bring to boil, scraping up any browned bits. Add stock, Worcestershire sauce, thyme, oregano, pepper, and bay leaf. Reduce heat and simmer soup for 30 minutes, stirring occasionally.

Melt remaining 1 tablespoon butter in heavy medium skillet over medium heat. Add shallots, green onions, and garlic; cook until golden, stirring frequently, for about 10 minutes. Add to soup and stir to combine. (You can prepare soup 1 day ahead. Cover and refrigerate. Bring to simmer before continuing.) Preheat broiler. Ladle soup into 4 broiler-proof soup crocks. Top each with 2 toasted bread slices and 2 cheese slices. Broil until cheese bubbles.
Yields: 4 servings

Home Cookin'
St. Matthias Episcopal Church
Monument, Colorado

BROCCOLI SOUP

1 (14-ounce) can chicken broth
1 (10-ounce) package frozen chopped broccoli
1 medium chopped onion
1/4 cup flour
1/4 cup margarine
1 (12-ounce) can evaporated milk

Mix chicken broth, broccoli, and onion together in a saucepan; bring to boil to cook broccoli. Mix flour and margarine in a bowl to make a paste; add to broccoli mixture. Add milk and cook until thickened. Add salt and pepper to taste. Add more milk before serving if soup is too thick.
Yields: 4 servings

Butter 'n Love Recipes
St. Matthew's Episcopal Church
Unadilla, New York

THE VICAR'S BLACK BEAN SOUP

2 cups dried black beans,
  rinsed
3 cups water
1/2 cup olive oil
2 teaspoons salt (or up to 2
  tablespoons)
2 tablespoons olive oil
1 medium onion, diced
2–3 garlic cloves, crushed
1 carrot, diced
1/2 green bell pepper, diced
1 teaspoon ground coriander
1/2 teaspoon ground cumin
1/2 cup red wine
Black pepper to taste
Pinch (or more) cayenne
  pepper

Soak the beans overnight in water to cover in a medium saucepan. In the morning, drain the liquid and add 3 cups of water, 1/2 cup olive oil, and salt. Bring to a boil; reduce heat and simmer, covered, over very low heat for at least 1 to 2 hours. In a medium skillet, heat the 2 tablespoons olive oil and sauté the onion, garlic, carrot, green pepper, coriander, and cumin. When the vegetables are softened, add to the beans and continue to simmer for another 1 to 2 hours. Add the remaining ingredients and simmer for at least 30 minutes before serving. Serve with slices of oranges and avocados, tortilla chips, chopped onions, a dollop of sour cream, and Dos Equis beer.
Yields: 4 to 6 servings

Cooking with St. Francis by the Sea II
St. Francis by the Sea Episcopal Church
Blue Hill, Maine

HUNGARIAN MUSHROOM SOUP

4 tablespoons butter
2 pounds mushrooms,
  sliced thin
8 tablespoons fresh dill,
  chopped
2 tablespoons soy sauce
2 tablespoons hot or regular
  imported Hungarian paprika
8 tablespoons butter
5 tablespoons all-purpose flour
2 cups milk
4 cups chicken stock
Salt and black pepper to taste
Sour cream
Fresh dill and parsley for
  garnish

In a large heavy saucepan or soup pot, melt 4 tablespoons butter and sauté the mushrooms. Once the mushrooms start to ooze their juices, add chopped dill, soy sauce, and paprika. Continue to cook 1 minute. Place contents of pan into a large bowl and set aside. Using the same pan, melt the 8 tablespoons butter; add flour to make a roux, cook a little, and whisk in the milk. Continue to cook on low-medium heat, and stir as mixture thickens and flour cooks. Add chicken stock and continue cooking for a few minutes, checking the consistency. Add the mushroom and dill mixture, cover, and simmer for 15 minutes. Taste for salt and pepper. Serve with a dollop of sour cream on top of each serving and sprinkle on mixed dill and parsley.
Yields: 10 to 12 servings

Suppers in Season
All Saints' Episcopal Church
Wolfeboro, New Hampshire

SPLIT PEA SOUP

1 (16-ounce) package dried
  split green peas
3 quarts water
1 small ham shank or pork
  tenderloin
1 large onion, chopped
2 chicken bouillon cubes
1/2 teaspoon garlic powder
1/2 teaspoon pepper
1 bay leaf
1/2 teaspoon oregano leaves
1 1/2 cups thinly sliced carrots
1 cup chopped celery

Soak peas in water overnight in a large pot. Drain and combine with new water, ham, onion, chicken bouillon, and seasonings. Simmer, uncovered, for 1 1/2 hours. Stir in carrots and celery. Simmer, uncovered, 1 hour or until soup reaches desired thickness; stir often. Remove meat; cut up and return to soup.

Yields: 6 servings

Blest Be These Feasts
St. Francis of Assisi
Levittown, New York

HOT AND SOUR SOUP

3 ounces lean boneless pork,
  thinly shredded
1 ounce dried Chinese
  mushrooms, soaked in
  warm water
1 tofu cake
2 large eggs
1 teaspoon sesame oil
1 quart chicken broth
2 teaspoons sugar
3 tablespoons cider vinegar
1/2 teaspoon white pepper
2 tablespoons dark soy sauce
1 tablespoon cornstarch mixed
  with 1 tablespoon cold water
2 tablespoons chopped green
  onions
1 teaspoon hot chili oil
  (optional)

Blanch pork in hot water for 2 minutes. Drain meat, and set aside. Soak mushrooms for 20 minutes; drain and squeeze. Discard stems and chop the caps. Drain tofu, and cut into small pieces. Beat eggs and sesame oil together in a small bowl. Bring broth to a simmer; add pork, mushrooms, tofu, sugar, vinegar, white pepper, and soy sauce. Simmer for 3 minutes, then thicken with cornstarch mixture. Simmer with heat as low as possible. When very hot, pour egg mixture in soup in a steady stream and pull egg into strands with a fork. Stir in green onions and chili oil, if desired.

Yields: 4 to 6 servings

Not by Bread Alone
Trinity Episcopal Church
Oak Ridge, Virginia

POTATO CHEESE SOUP

10–15 red or new potatoes
1 medium yellow onion, diced
1/2 stick butter
1 cup cream, divided
3–4 tablespoons all-purpose
  flour
3/4–1 cup shredded Cheddar
  cheese
Salt and black pepper to taste
7–8 strips cooked bacon,
  crumbled, for garnish
Chopped green onions for
  garnish

Scrub and cut potatoes into chunks (do not peel). Cook the potatoes and onion in enough water to cover in a large saucepan until tender. Add butter and let boil until the butter is melted. Add 3/4 cup cream and reduce heat. Use remaining 1/4 cup cream to mix with flour and make a paste. Slowly stir into boiling potatoes until mixture thickens. Stir in shredded cheese. Season to taste. Serve garnished with crumbled bacon and chopped green onions.

Yields: 4 to 6 servings

Celebrating Our Roots
St. Thomas' Episcopal Church
Knoxville, Tennessee

POTATO SOUP WITH CLAMS

3 potatoes, cut into cubes
3 onions, sliced
Pat of butter
1 pint half-and-half or milk
Salt and black pepper
Celery salt
1 (6-ounce) can minced clams
  with liquid

Cook potatoes and onions in enough water to cover in a saucepan until soft; add butter and mash lightly with potato masher. Add half-and-half, salt and pepper, celery salt, and clams with liquid. Serve hot.

Yields: 4 to 6 servings

Parish Collection
St. Mary's Episcopal Church
Mitchell, South Dakota

CABBAGE AND BEEF SOUP

1 pound ground beef
1 (28-ounce) can stewed
  tomatoes, undrained
1 tomato can of water
1/4 teaspoon black pepper
2 stalks celery, chopped
4 beef bouillon cubes
1 (16-ounce) can kidney beans,
  not drained
1/2 medium head cabbage,
  chopped
Garlic powder, if desired
Salt and chili powder to taste

Brown beef in skillet. Place beef and next 8 ingredients in a stockpot. Bring to a boil. Reduce heat and simmer, covered, for 2 hours. Add salt and chili powder to taste.

Yields: 4 servings

Recipes from "the Hill"
Boys' Home Inc.
Covington, Virginia

ITALIAN SAUSAGE AND BEAN SOUP

1 pound mild Italian sausage
1 clove garlic, minced
1 large onion, chopped
1/2 cup chopped parsley, divided
2 carrots, thinly sliced
1 cup thinly sliced mushrooms
1 (16-ounce) can garbanzo beans
3 cups water
2 beef bouillon cubes
1/2 teaspoon rubbed sage
Salt and black pepper

Remove casings from sausage and slice or crumble into bite-size pieces. Cook sausage in a 3-quart saucepan over medium-high heat, stirring often until meat is browned. Add garlic, onion, 1/4 cup parsley, carrots, and mushrooms. Cook, stirring frequently, until onion is limp. Add beans (including liquid), water, bouillon cubes, and sage. Bring to a boil, then lower heat and simmer, covered, until beans are hot and carrots are tender, about 10 minutes. Add salt and pepper. Skim off and discard any excess fat. Garnish with remaining parsley.
Yields: 3 or 4 servings

125 Years of Cooking
St. Luke Episcopal Church
Niles, Ohio

FRENCH MARKET SOUP

1 package "16-bean soup"
  beans
3 quarts water
1 ham hock
1 tablespoon salt
1 teaspoon bouquet garni
1 (28-ounce) can tomatoes
2 medium onions, chopped
2 cloves garlic, minced
6 stalks celery, chopped
Salt and black pepper to taste
1 pound Polish sausage, sliced
2 chicken breasts, cut up
1/2 cup sherry (optional)
Hot cooked rice

Wash beans. Simmer, covered, in large saucepan in 3 quarts water with the ham hock, 1 tablespoon salt, and bouquet garni for 2 1/2 to 3 hours. Add tomatoes, onions, garlic, celery, and salt and pepper. Simmer 1 1/2 hours or until creamy. Add sausage and chicken. Simmer for 30 to 45 minutes. Add sherry, if desired, and serve with a scoop of rice in center.
Yields: 12 to 16 servings

Holy Chow
Church of Ascension and Holy Trinity
Wyoming, Ohio

TURKEY SOUP

1 turkey carcass
3 cups turkey broth
3 cups turkey meat
1 1/2 cups thinly sliced carrots
1/2 cup chopped celery
1/2 cup chopped onion
2 cloves garlic, minced
1/3 cup butter
1 1/2 cups chopped apple
3 tablespoons all-purpose flour
1 1/2 teaspoons salt
3/4 teaspoon curry
3/8 teaspoon nutmeg
Dash of black pepper
3 chicken bouillon cubes
1 (8-ounce) can tomatoes
1 1/2 cups milk

Cover carcass with water; boil 1 hour. Save broth and meat to make 3 cups each. Sauté carrots, celery, onion, and garlic in butter in a large stockpot. Add apple and cook until tender. Stir in flour and seasonings; stir well. Stir in broth gradually. Add bouillon cubes, tomatoes, and turkey meat; simmer for 1 hour. Add milk and heat well just before serving.

Yields: 6 servings

Second Helpings
Holy Trinity Episcopal Church
Ukiah, California

STEAK SOUP

1 pound ground chuck
1 cup chopped onions
1/2 cup chopped carrots
1/2 cup chopped celery
1/2 tablespoon minced garlic
1 1/2 (10-ounce) cans chicken broth
1 cup canned tomatoes
1 tablespoon Worcestershire sauce
1/2 teaspoon hot pepper sauce
1/4 teaspoon black pepper

Brown ground meat in a skillet; drain and set aside. Brown onions. Add to meat. Sauté carrots, celery, and garlic. Add to meat. Add chicken broth, tomatoes, Worcestershire sauce, hot pepper sauce, and black pepper. Bring to a boil. Simmer 30 minutes.

Yields: 4 servings

Recipes & Remembrances
St. Timothy's Episcopal Church
Cincinnati, Ohio

CHUPE

2 pounds beef (with bones)
1 green onion, with stem
2 cloves garlic
6 plum tomatoes
Chopped chile or sweet pepper
    to taste
2 tablespoons salt, or to taste
2 laurel leaves
1 sprig thyme
2 tablespoons cooking oil
2 carrots, sliced
1 *pataste*, cubed
1/2 cup baby corn
1/2 cup carob beans
1/2 pound small shrimp, cleaned
1 quart milk, heated
1 tablespoon ground oregano
2 tablespoons chopped parsley
Black pepper to taste
1/4 ounce cheese, cubed
4 ounces butter
10 large eggs

Place the meat in cold water in a large stock pot; add with the onion, garlic, tomatoes, chile pepper, salt, laurel, and thyme. Cook until meat is tender. Strain the broth and set aside; debone meat and use in another recipe.

Place cooking oil in a large skillet. Stir-fry carrots and next 3 ingredients until tender. Add the shrimp. Place strained vegetables from broth in blender; liquefy and add to skillet. Add the reserved broth and cook mixture for 10 to 15 minutes.

Add the hot milk, oregano, parsley, and black pepper; boil for 5 minutes longer. Add the cheese and butter. Serve by placing 1 raw egg in each individual soup bowl; pour hot soup over top (broth will cook egg).

Yields: 10 servings

Sabor a Mas
Guatemala, Guatemala

CALDO GALLEGO

(This recipe, from northern Spain, was a soup of the peasants or farmers because it was cheap but nourishing.)

3/4 cup dried white beans
1/4 pound smoked ham
1/4 pound lean smoked bacon
    or salt pork
7 cups cold water
1/2 medium onion, sliced
1/2 small head white cabbage,
    coarsely chopped
3 turnips and a few turnip
    greens, coarsely chopped
1 chorizo (Spanish sausage) or
    1 stick pepperoni
Salt and black pepper to taste

Pour water over beans, ham, and bacon in a large pot (earthenware is best). Cover and simmer for 2 1/2 hours. Add sliced onion, cabbage, turnips, turnip tops and chorizo or pepperoni. Mix together carefully so beans are not mashed. Add salt and pepper to taste, and simmer 1 1/2 hours longer. Remove meat and chop into bite-size servings. Return to soup. Serve in large soup bowls.

Yields: 4 servings

Canterbury Feasts
Canterbury School of Florida
St. Petersburg, Florida

MULLIGATAWNY SOUP

4 tablespoons butter
1 onion, diced
1 carrot, diced
1 stalk celery, diced with leaves on
1 green, red, or yellow bell pepper, diced
1 apple, peeled and diced
1 pound uncooked chicken, cut up
1/3 cup all-purpose flour
1/4 teaspoon grated nutmeg
2 cloves, crushed
5 cups chicken stock
Few sprigs parsley
1 cup tomatoes, peeled and seeded
2 teaspoons curry powder (or more to taste)
Salt and black pepper to taste

Melt the butter in a large stockpot with a good, solid bottom. Sauté the onion until tender and then add the carrot and next 3 ingredients, cooking slowly for 15 minutes or so, so that the onions are translucent but not browned. Add the chicken, and cook on low heat for 10 minutes or so. Stir in the flour, nutmeg, and cloves, and cook for about 10 minutes longer. Add the stock, parsley, and tomatoes. Simmer for about 1 hour on very low heat. Add the curry powder to taste, as well as salt and pepper, and cook for a few more minutes until the flavors blend and you are satisfied with the taste. (Additional curry powder will make a sharper taste.)
Yields: about 8 (1-cup) servings

Parish Collection
St. Luke the Evangelist
Roselle, New Jersey

❖

THE WORD OF THE LORD CAME TO HIM, SAYING, "GO NOW TO ZAREPHATH, WHICH BELONGS TO SIDON, AND LIVE THERE; FOR I HAVE COMMANDED A WIDOW THERE TO FEED YOU." SO HE SET OUT AND WENT TO ZAREPHATH. WHEN HE CAME TO THE GATE OF THE TOWN, A WIDOW WAS THERE GATHERING STICKS; HE CALLED TO HER AND SAID, "BRING ME A LITTLE WATER IN A VESSEL, SO THAT I MAY DRINK."

AS SHE WAS GOING TO BRING IT, HE CALLED TO HER AND SAID, "BRING ME A MORSEL OF BREAD IN YOUR HAND." BUT SHE SAID, "AS THE LORD YOUR GOD LIVES, I HAVE NOTHING BAKED, ONLY A HANDFUL OF MEAL IN A JAR, AND A LITTLE OIL IN A JUG; I AM NOW GATHERING A COUPLE OF STICKS, SO THAT I MAY GO HOME AND PREPARE IT FOR MYSELF AND MY SON, THAT WE MAY EAT IT, AND DIE." ELIJAH SAID TO HER, "DO NOT BE AFRAID; GO AND DO AS YOU HAVE SAID; BUT FIRST MAKE ME A LITTLE CAKE OF IT AND BRING IT TO ME, AND AFTERWARDS MAKE SOMETHING FOR YOURSELF AND YOUR SON. FOR THUS SAYS THE LORD THE GOD OF ISRAEL: THE JAR OF MEAL WILL NOT BE EMPTIED AND THE JUG OF OIL WILL NOT FAIL UNTIL THE DAY THAT THE LORD SENDS RAIN ON THE EARTH." SHE WENT AND DID AS ELIJAH SAID, SO THAT SHE AS WELL AS HE AND HER HOUSEHOLD ATE FOR MANY DAYS. THE JAR OF MEAL WAS NOT EMPTIED, NEITHER DID THE JUG OF OIL FAIL, ACCORDING TO THE WORD OF THE LORD THAT HE SPOKE TO ELIJAH.

1 KINGS 17:8–16
(ELIJAH MIRACULOUSLY SUPPLIES FOOD)

OYSTER BISQUE

1 pint fresh oysters
1 1/2 tablespoons butter or
  margarine
1 1/2 tablespoons all-purpose
  flour
2 1/2 cups milk
1 teaspoon salt
1/2 cup cream
1/2 teaspoon paprika
2 large egg yolks mixed with 2
  tablespoons water (optional)

Heat oysters in liquid until edges curl. Drain and save liquid. Chop oysters or grind in meat grinder. Melt butter in a large skillet; add flour and cook but don't brown, for 5 minutes. Add oyster liquid, milk, and salt; heat but do not boil. Simmer 15 minutes and add cream. Add ground oysters and paprika. If desired, add egg yolk mixture, and simmer 10 more minutes.
Yields: 3 to 4 servings

Hometown Recipes of Palmetto
St. Mary's Episcopal Church
Palmetto, Florida

OYSTER CHOWDER

1 quart fresh oysters
Water
4 slices bacon
1 large onion, chopped
3 medium potatoes, peeled
  and cubed (3 cups)
1 teaspoon salt
1/4 teaspoon ground white
  pepper
4 cups milk
2 cups half-and-half
Paprika

Drain oysters, reserving liquid. Add water to liquid to measure 2 cups. In 5-quart Dutch oven, cook bacon over medium heat until crisp, stirring occasionally. Using a slotted spoon, transfer bacon to paper towels to drain. Crumble. Add onion to bacon fat. Cook 1 minute. Add potatoes, salt, pepper, and reserved oyster liquid. Heat to boiling over high heat. Reduce heat to low. Cover and simmer until potatoes are very tender, about 20 minutes. Add milk and half-and-half. Heat just until bubbles appear around side of pan. Stir in drained oysters. Cook until edges of oysters curl. Do not boil soup. Ladle into soup tureen. Sprinkle with bacon and paprika.
Yields: about 14 servings

Keeping the Feast
St. Thomas Episcopal Church
Abingdon, Virginia

CORN CHOWDER

4 slices bacon
1 medium onion, chopped
4 tablespoons all-purpose flour
2 cups milk
2 tablespoons chopped green
  bell pepper
2 medium potatoes, cubed
1 (8-ounce) can whole kernel
  corn
1 (8-ounce) can creamed corn
1/4 teaspoon sugar
1 teaspoon salt
1/2 teaspoon black pepper

Sauté bacon in a large saucepan; remove from drippings and chop. Sauté onion in bacon drippings. Add flour and stir in milk. Add green pepper and potatoes. Simmer slowly until potatoes are almost soft. Add corn and seasonings and simmer until heated through. Stir in crumbled bacon.
Yields: 6 to 8 servings

The Book of Common Fare
Grace-St. Luke's Church
Memphis, Tennessee

CATFISH GUMBO

3 ounces olive oil
3 ounces all-purpose flour
1/2 cup okra
1/2 cup diced onions
1/2 cup diced celery
1/2 cup diced green bell peppers
1 1/2 cups whole tomatoes
1 clove garlic, crushed
Salt, paprika, black pepper, and
  cayenne pepper to taste
Thyme, basil, and marjoram to
  taste
6 cups water
1 pound catfish (about 4
  fillets), diced
Gumbo filé
Vegetable oil

Make a roux of olive oil and flour in a large stockpot, stirring constantly. Add all vegetables, herbs, and spices; sauté until tender. Add water and catfish. Simmer for 45 minutes. Cook gumbo filé in vegetable oil and then add to gumbo. Simmer for 5 minutes.
Yields: 4 to 6 servings

Goodness Graces
St. Paul's Episcopal Church
Albany, Georgia

CHICKEN GUMBO

1 small round onion, chopped
4 cloves garlic, chopped
3 stalks celery, sliced
10 medium okra
3 chicken breasts, sliced
1 (14-ounce) can stewed
  tomatoes
1 can water
1 bay leaf
1 teaspoon basil
2 tablespoons soy sauce
2 tablespoons Worcestershire
  sauce
1 tablespoon gumbo filé
  powder

Sauté the onion, garlic, celery, and okra in a large skillet until translucent; add chicken. Pour in the stewed tomatoes and water. Add bay leaf, basil, soy sauce, and Worcestershire sauce. Bring to a boil and simmer for 1 to 2 hours. Add gumbo filé powder for thickening, just before serving.
Yields: 6 servings

…and Sew We Eat!
Diocese of Hawaii/Diocesan Altar Guild
Honolulu, Hawaii

CHICKEN ANDOUILLE GUMBO

2 pounds boned chicken meat
  (without skin), cut into
  bite-size pieces
Cayenne pepper
1 cup oil
1 1/2 pounds andouille
  sausage, cut into bite-size
  pieces
1 cup all-purpose flour
4 cups chopped onion
2 cups chopped celery
2 cups chopped green bell
  pepper
1 tablespoon chopped garlic
8 cups chicken stock
Salt, cayenne pepper, and filé
  powder to taste
1 cup chopped green onions
1 cup chopped parsley
Cooked rice

Sprinkle chicken with cayenne pepper; brown in oil over medium heat in a Dutch oven. Add sausage and sauté with chicken. Remove both from the pot. Remove from heat and strain fat. To make roux, over low heat, add flour to hot fat gradually, stirring constantly with a whisk. Over low heat, brown the roux, stirring constantly, until it turns a nutty brown color. Add onion, celery, bell pepper, and garlic. Continue cooking over low heat until vegetables are tender, stirring constantly. Gradually add the stock; mix well. Add the chicken and sausage and bring to a boil. Reduce to simmer and cook for 1 hour or more. Season to taste. Approximately 10 minutes before serving, add green onions and parsley. Gumbo may or may not be served over rice.
Note: Two to three drops of sherry or 1/4 to 1/2 teaspoon filé may be added to each serving as a flavor option at the table. Filé is a fine green powder of young, dried, ground sassafras leaves used in gumbo for flavor and thickening.
Yields: 10 to 15 servings

Cooking New Orleans Style!
All Saints' Episcopal Church
River Ridge, Louisiana

GUMBO Z'HERBES

1 bunch each, in any combination, but use at least five:
spinach, collard, mustard or
turnip greens, watercress,
chicory, beet tops, carrot tops,
pepper grass, radish tops
1 bunch parsley, chopped
1/2 bunch green onions, chopped
1 small head green cabbage,
chopped
1 gallon water
4 tablespoons all-purpose flour
4 tablespoons shortening
1 large onion, diced
1 pound boiled ham, diced
1/2 pound Creole or Polish
smoked sausage, cubed
2 bay leaves
2 sprigs thyme
1/4 teaspoon allspice
Salt and black pepper to taste
Cayenne pepper to taste
2 cups rice, cooked

Wash the greens, parsley, green onions, and cabbage thoroughly and remove the stems and hard centers. Boil in a large stockpot in the 1 gallon water for 2 hours. Drain the greens and reserve the water. Chop the greens finely. In a soup kettle make a brown roux of the flour and shortening. Add the onion, ham, and sausage and sauté for 5 minutes or until soft. Add the greens and simmer for 15 minutes. Add the reserved cooking water, herbs, spices, and seasonings. Simmer for 1 hour. Serve over rice.
Yields: 8 servings

La Bonne Cuisine
All Saints' Episcopal Church
River Ridge, Louisiana

JAMBALAYA

6–8 chicken breasts
1 pound link sausage
1/4 cup vegetable oil
1 cup chopped onion
1 cup chopped celery
1 cup chopped bell pepper
1 tablespoon minced garlic
2 cups raw rice
2 1/2 cups water
Dash cayenne
1/2 cup chopped parsley
1 cup chopped green onions

Cut chicken and sausage in bite-size pieces. Brown in oil, then remove. Sauté onion, celery, green pepper, and garlic. Return meat and mix with vegetables. Add rice, water, and cayenne. Bring to a boil; reduce heat and simmer, covered, 35 to 40 minutes. Stir in parsley and green onions before serving.
Yields: 6 to 8 servings

A Book of Favorite Recipes
Church of the Redeemer
Ruston, Louisiana

CHUNKY VEGETABLE CHILI

2 medium onions, chopped
2 medium green bell peppers,
  chopped
2 ribs celery, sliced
3 carrots, thinly sliced
1 clove garlic, minced
1 tablespoon vegetable oil
1 (16-ounce) can crushed
  tomatoes
1 (15-ounce) can red kidney
  beans, drained
1 (8-ounce) can tomato sauce
2 tablespoons red wine vinegar
1 tablespoon firmly packed
  brown sugar
1 tablespoon chili powder
1 teaspoon dried oregano
1 teaspoon ground cumin
1 tablespoon salt

Sauté onions, peppers, celery, carrots, and garlic in oil in a large saucepan until soft. Stir in remaining ingredients. Bring to a boil; reduce heat, cover, and simmer for 35 minutes.
Yields: 6 servings

Blest Be These Feasts
St. Francis of Assisi
Levittown, New York

CABBAGE AND WHITE BEAN STEW

1 large onion, diced
1 tablespoon olive oil
1 tablespoon butter
2 carrots, sliced
1 large stalk celery, chopped
2 cups chopped cabbage
2 cups water
1 tablespoon brown sugar
1 (16-ounce) can tomatoes in
  juice, chopped
1 (15-ounce) can white beans,
  drained
1 tablespoon vinegar

Sauté onion in oil and butter in large saucepan for 3 minutes. Add carrots and celery and sauté for 3 more minutes. Stir in cabbage, water, and brown sugar; simmer covered for 5 minutes. Stir in tomatoes with juice. Simmer for 20 minutes. Add beans and vinegar; simmer until hot.
Yields: 4 to 6 servings

Potluck Sunday
St. Mary's Episcopal Church
Madisonville, Kentucky

PORTUGUESE FISH STEW

3 leeks, white part only
2 medium onions
1/2 bunch parsley
6 cloves garlic, minced
4 tablespoons olive oil
1/2 teaspoon ground cumin
1/2 teaspoon ground coriander
1/2 teaspoon ground thyme
1/4 teaspoon ground saffron
2 bay leaves, finely cut
2 (28-ounce) cans chopped,
  peeled tomatoes with puree
1 1/2 cups dry white
  Portuguese or Italian wine
2 cups clam juice
1 cup fish stock or water
4 pounds fresh fish (variety)

Clean the leeks. Chop the leeks and onions finely; stem the parsley and chop it fine. In a large stockpot, sauté leeks, onions, and garlic in olive oil until the onion softens. Stir in the parsley, cumin, and next 4 ingredients and sauté another minute or two. Add the tomatoes, wine, clam juice, and stock. Bring to a boil and simmer, covered, for 10 minutes.

Cut fish into 2-inch chunks, or use whole in the case of shrimp and small scallops. (Good seafood choices are cusk, scrod, sword, halibut, haddock, or any firm white fish, plus shrimp and scallops.) Add fish to the stew in the order of time it takes each variety to cook. Continue to simmer in the covered stockpot as each seafood is added. Ladle into heated bowls, garnish with chopped parsley, and serve with a crusty loaf of sourdough or French bread.
Yields: 8 servings

Suppers in Season
All Saints' Episcopal Church
Wolfeboro, New Hampshire

BRUNSWICK STEW

1 (4-pound) stewing chicken
1 cup chopped onion
3 1/2 cups stewed tomatoes
2 cups whole kernel corn
2 cups lima beans
1 1/2 teaspoons salt
1/4 teaspoon black pepper
1 teaspoon Worcestershire
  sauce
1 teaspoon marjoram flakes
Cayenne pepper to taste

Bring chicken to a boil in salted water to cover in a large stockpot. Reduce heat and cook until tender. Pull meat from bones and remove skin. Leave meat in large chunks. Return meat to the broth and add remaining ingredients. Simmer stew for about 2 hours.
Yields: 8 servings

The Way to a Man's Heart
All Saints' Episcopal Church
Norton, Virginia

WINTER WINE STEW

2 pounds round steak, cut into
  chunks
3 tablespoons vegetable oil
1/2 cup dry sherry
2 large onions, sliced
1 cup beef stock
2 bay leaves
1/4 cup vinegar
3 tablespoons ketchup
1/2 cup raisins
3–4 potatoes, cut into chunks

Wipe meat dry and brown meat in oil in a baking dish or Dutch oven. Remove from pan. Pour sherry over meat and toss lightly. Add onions to the meat drippings in the pan and sauté briefly. Return meat and sherry to pan and stir in remaining ingredients, except potatoes. Bake, covered, at 325° for 3 to 4 hours, or until meat is tender. Add potatoes to pan during the last 2 hours of cooking. Add extra liquid (bouillon), if necessary. Thicken gravy, if desired. Serve with assortment of sliced and diced cheeses and a loaf of warm bread or rolls.

Yields: 6 to 8 servings

Memories from the Kitchen
St. Paul's Episcopal Church
Mount Lebanon, Pennsylvania

GOURMET VENISON STEW

3 pounds tender venison,
  cubed
2 tablespoons teriyaki sauce
1 clove garlic, mashed
5 medium white onions,
  chopped
1 1/2 pounds small carrots
5 pounds potatoes, peeled and
  cubed
2 cups beef stock
1 cup all-purpose flour
Salt and freshly ground black
  pepper
4 tablespoons canola oil
1 cup dry white wine
2 cups water
2–3 bay leaves
Juice of 1/2 lemon
1 teaspoon Tabasco sauce

Marinate meat in teriyaki sauce and garlic for about 30 minutes. Place vegetables in large stockpot. Simmer, covered, in beef stock about 15 minutes. Coat meat in flour, salt, and pepper. Brown in oil in a large skillet. Add wine and 2 cups water. Spoon meat and liquid into vegetables. Add bay leaves, lemon juice, and Tabasco sauce. Simmer on low for about 20 minutes or until meat is tender. Remove from heat and let stand, covered, for about 1 1/2 hours or longer; remove bay leaves before serving.

Yields: 6 to 8 servings

Goodness Graces
St. Paul's Episcopal Church
Albany, Georgia

KENTUCKY BURGOO

1 (2-pound) pork shank
1 (2-pound) veal shank
1 (2-pound) beef shank
1 (2-pound) breast of lamb
1 (4-pound) hen
8 quarts cold water
1 1/2 pounds potatoes
1 1/2 pounds onions
1 bunch carrots, sliced
2 green bell peppers, chopped
2 cups chopped cabbage
2 cups whole corn, fresh or
   canned
2 pods red pepper
2 cups diced okra
1 cup lima beans
1 cup diced celery
1 quart tomato puree
Steak sauce and Worcestershire
   sauce to taste
Salt and cayenne pepper to
   taste
Tabasco sauce
Chopped parsley

Put all the meat into cold water in a stockpot and slowly bring to a boil. Simmer until meat is tender enough to fall from the bones. Lift meat out of stock. Cool and chop up meat, removing bones. Pare potatoes and onions; dice. Return meat to stock. Add potatoes, onions, and next 9 ingredients. Allow to simmer until thick, stirring frequently. Burgoo should be very thick but not soupy. Season when burgoo is almost done. Add chopped parsley just before serving.
Yields: 16 to 20 servings

Gifts from the Kitchen
Church of the Advent
Cynthiana, Kentucky

THEN DAVID SAID TO THE WHOLE ASSEMBLY, "BLESS THE LORD YOUR GOD." AND ALL THE ASSEMBLY BLESSED THE LORD, THE GOD OF THEIR ANCESTORS, AND BOWED THEIR HEADS AND PROSTRATED THEM-

Meats

SELVES BEFORE THE LORD AND THE KING. ON THE NEXT DAY THEY OFFERED SACRIFICES AND BURNT OFFERINGS TO THE LORD, A THOUSAND BULLS, A THOUSAND RAMS, AND A THOUSAND LAMBS, WITH THEIR LIBATIONS AND SACRIFICES IN ABUNDANCE FOR ALL ISRAEL; AND THEY ATE AND DRANK BEFORE THE LORD ON THAT DAY WITH GREAT JOY.

1 CHRONICLES 29:20–22
(DAVID OFFERS SACRIFICES)

Upside-down Hospitality

If you could assemble a dinner party and invite anyone you could choose from history, who would grace your table? Would you prefer to enjoy classical observations from Socrates and Sappho? Twentieth-century wisdom from John F. Kennedy and Eleanor Roosevelt? Ask around, and you will discover a huge variety of nominations: Marie Antoinette, John Lennon, William Shakespeare, Emily Dickinson, Wolfgang Amadeus Mozart. No two lists are the same.

You can discover something about people by how they respond to this question: are they more interested in historical importance, in the guests' reputed wit, in fame? Or would they look forward to designing an event where the debate between characters was likely to be, let's say, somewhat spirited?

When we put dinners together, whether we do it for real or in our imaginations, we tend to select guests with whom we'd enjoy dining: people we would "get something out of" spending time with. And that's only natural. Unless we are doggedly repaying some perceived social obligation, it's obvious, isn't it, that we will invite people we like?

As is so often true, however, Jesus invites us to move beyond the natural. "When you give a luncheon or a dinner," he suggests in the Gospel of Luke, "do not invite your friends or your brothers or your relatives or rich neighbors, in case they may invite you in return, and you would be repaid… Invite the poor, the crippled, the lame, and the blind. And you will be blessed, because they cannot repay you, for you will be repaid at the resurrection of the righteous."

In Jesus' vision, we will offer hospitality not to people whose presence would nourish us, but to people who would benefit from the nourishment we have to offer. Our table is, like everything else, a gift from God, meant to be shared. We have a duty to be proactive and to make room for more than just those individuals whom we naturally enjoy.

It is not uncommon for families to issue this kind of invitation for one special holiday meal, welcoming an international student or a widower who has nowhere else to go. But such offers tend to come thick and fast the last six weeks of the year; why not open your home in February or June, when no one else is likely to think of it? In the same way, why not deliberately wait to volunteer or to donate to your local soup kitchen until the holidays are well past?

Or for those of us who live in an urban environment, there is another regular challenge to hospitality. When a panhandler asks for spare change, have you ever invited the person to join you for a meal instead? She may shake her head and wave you off, of course, but on the other hand, she just may say yes. Start a conversation over a casserole (or whatever she'd like; you aren't going to force her to order the cheapest thing on the menu, are you?), and you are on the way to Jesus' kind of dinner.

When we build community at our tables, we lose something if the hospitality is limited to our friends alone. And we lose even more if the motivation is limited to what we ourselves will get out of the event. Take the risk; set a place, somehow, for the outcast and the unlikely. This is the way of Jesus: not to give and welcome because of what we get out of it, but because giving and welcoming is built into the very life of God.

IRISH BAKED HAM

(Serve on St. Patrick's Day with Cocannon, Irish soda bread, spinach salad, and Irish coffee.)

1 (10- to 12-pound) ham
1 (12-ounce) bottle Guinness
  stout beer
1/2 cup chopped onion
1/4 cup sugar
4 sprigs parsley
1 teaspoon thyme
1 bay leaf, crumbled
1/4 cup firmly packed brown
  sugar

Put ham, fat side up, in roasting pan. Pour stout into pan. Combine onion, granulated sugar, parsley, thyme, and bay leaf. Sprinkle over ham. Cover pan tightly with foil. Bake at 325° for 3 hours, basting every 30 minutes with stout. Remove ham from oven. Increase oven temperature to 400°. Strain liquid and put back into pan. Pat brown sugar on top of ham. Bake, uncovered, for 30 minutes, basting every 10 minutes. Let stand for 20 minutes before carving.
Yields: 18 to 20 servings

Canterbury Feasts
Canterbury School of Florida
St. Petersburg, Florida

HAM LOAF

1 pound ground ham
1/2 pound ground pork
1/2 pound ground beef
1/4 teaspoon salt, optional
2 cups crushed corn flakes
1 tablespoon chopped onion
1 tablespoon chopped green
  bell pepper
2 large eggs, beaten
1 cup milk
Horseradish Sauce

Combine all ingredients except Horseradish Sauce; mix well. Pack into a greased loaf pan. Bake at 350° for 1 hour. Serve with Horseradish Sauce.
Yields: 6 to 8 servings

HORSERADISH SAUCE
5 tablespoons mayonnaise
4 teaspoons horseradish
1 1/2 teaspoons prepared
  mustard
Paprika

Blend the first 3 ingredients in a small bowl; sprinkle with paprika.

Christ Church Classics
Christ Church
Lexington, Kentucky

PORK LOIN WITH ORANGE LIQUEUR

1 (6-ounce) can frozen orange juice concentrate, thawed
1/2 cup honey
1/3 cup vinegar
1 teaspoon prepared mustard
1 teaspoon soy sauce
5–6 drops Tabasco sauce
1 (4- to 5-pound) boneless pork loin (center cut)
4 teaspoons cornstarch
1/4 cup orange liqueur
1/2 cup sour cream
1/3 cup water

Combine orange juice concentrate and next 5 ingredients in a saucepan. Bring to a boil; reduce heat and simmer for 5 minutes, then cool. Place pork loin in a large plastic bag. Add sauce. Close bag tightly and refrigerate overnight.

Remove pork from bag; place in roasting pan. Bake at 325° for 2 1/2 to 3 hours. Baste with marinade during last 30 minutes. Combine remaining marinade in saucepan. Stir in cornstarch, then liqueur. Heat gently, stirring constantly. Blend in sour cream and serve with pork.
Yields: 8 to 10 servings

All Angels Fare
All Angels by the Sea Episcopal Church
Longboat Key, Florida

SWEET AND SOUR PORK ROAST

1 (3 1/2- to 4-pound) pork roast
Salt and black pepper to taste
1 (8-ounce) can tomato sauce
2 tablespoons lemon or lime juice
1 teaspoon grated lemon on lime rind
1/2 cup water
1/2 teaspoon salt
2 tablespoons brown sugar
1/2 teaspoon allspice or nutmeg
1 (16-ounce) can pineapple chunks with juice
1/2 cup seedless raisins

Sprinkle pork with salt and pepper. Roast in a baking pan at 325° for 1 hour; drain fat from pan. Combine tomato sauce, lemon or lime juice and rind, water, 1/2 teaspoon salt, brown sugar, allspice, and pineapple juice in saucepan. Simmer for 10 minutes. Add pineapple chunks and raisins to sauce. Pour over pork. Roast, basting occasionally, for 2 hours. Add hot water to sauce if it thickens too rapidly.
Yields: 6 servings

Food for the Flock
St. Catherine's Episcopal Church
Jacksonville, Florida

PORK AND PRUNES

24 pitted prunes
1 cup dry white wine
6 (3/4-inch-thick) boneless
  pork chops
Salt and black pepper to taste
All-purpose flour
3 tablespoons butter
1/2 cup chicken broth
1/2 cup heavy cream
1 teaspoon currant jelly

Soak prunes in wine for 12 hours. Simmer in same liquid for 10 minutes. Drain and reserve liquid. Sprinkle pork with salt, pepper, and flour. Sauté in butter in skillet until brown on both sides; remove to side dish. Add prune-flavored wine to skillet and boil until reduced to half. Add pork and chicken broth; cover and simmer until pork is tender, about 30 minutes. Remove meat. Add cream and jelly to pan. Bring to a boil and add prunes. Arrange pork on a platter and spoon sauce and prunes around and over the pork.
Yields: 4 to 6 servings

Parish Collection
Christ Episcopal Church
Bradenton, Florida

PORK CHOPS, FAMILY STYLE

6 pork chops
6 onion slices
6 lemon slices
2/3 cup firmly packed brown
  sugar
1/8 teaspoon salt (optional)
1/8 teaspoon black pepper, or
  to taste
3 teaspoons lemon juice
2/3 cup chili sauce

Brown pork chops in large skillet. Drain excess grease. Arrange in large baking dish lined with aluminum foil. Cover each chop with onion and lemon slice. Blend remaining ingredients. Pour over chops. Bake, covered, for 30 minutes in preheated oven at 325°. Uncover and bake 30 minutes or longer if needed.
Yields: 6 servings

Keeping the Feast
St. Thomas Episcopal Church
Abingdon, Virginia

❖

SHE RISES WHILE IT IS STILL NIGHT AND PROVIDES FOOD FOR HER HOUSEHOLD AND TASKS FOR HER SERVANT-GIRLS. SHE CONSIDERS A FIELD AND BUYS IT; WITH THE FRUIT OF HER HANDS SHE PLANTS A VINEYARD.

PROVERBS 31:15–16
(VIRTUOUS WOMAN)

STICKY BONES

2–3 pounds country-style
  pork ribs
2–3 medium onions
1/2 cup ketchup
1/3 cup firmly packed brown
  sugar
3 tablespoons vinegar
1/2 teaspoon Worcestershire
  sauce
2 tablespoons molasses
1 teaspoon dry mustard
1/2 cup water

Place the ribs in a baking dish sized to the quantity of ribs so they fill the dish. Slice the onions over the ribs. Combine the remaining ingredients in a saucepan and simmer 10 to 15 minutes. Pour over the onions and ribs. Cover and bake at 350° for 2 1/2 hours; uncover during the last 1/2 hour.

Yields: 4 servings

Heavenly Delights
St. Paul's Episcopal Church
Waterloo, New York

OKTOBERFEST SAUSAGE SKILLET

3 tablespoons bacon drippings
1 small onion, thinly sliced
1 pound smoked sausage,
  quartered
1 (16-ounce) can sauerkraut
  with caraway seeds, rinsed
  and drained
1 medium apple, peeled, cored,
  and thinly sliced
1/4 teaspoon salt
1/2 teaspoon celery seed
1 tablespoon sugar
1/2 cup water
1/8 teaspoon black pepper

Heat bacon drippings in a large skillet. Add onion to sauté. Cook sausage, covered, in another skillet with about 2 tablespoons water until sausage looks glazed. Add sausage and remaining ingredients to onion. Cook, covered, slowly for about 15 minutes or until apple is tender.

Yields: 4 servings

Saints Preserve Us Cookbook
St. Edward's Episcopal Church
Lawrenceville, Georgia

CHAMPAGNE BRUNCH

6 large eggs, beaten
4 cups milk
2 pounds sausage
4 slices day-old bread, torn up
2 cups shredded Cheddar
  cheese
1/2 teaspoon salt
2 teaspoons dry mustard

Mix all the ingredients in a large bowl. Pour into a 9 × 12-inch baking pan. Cover and refrigerate overnight. Bake at 350° for 1 hour and 20 minutes. Serve immediately.

Yields: 12 servings

Heavenly Tastes, Earthly Recipes
St. Andrew's Episcopal Church
Lake Worth, Florida

FESTIVAL BRUNCH DISH

9 slices white bread, cubed
1/2 pound sharp Cheddar
cheese, grated
1 (20-ounce) bag frozen cut
broccoli, slightly cooked and
drained
2 tablespoons dried minced
onion
2 cups diced, cooked ham
6 large eggs, beaten
3 1/2 cups milk
1/2 teaspoon salt
1/4 teaspoon dry mustard

Layer the bread and next 4 ingredients in a greased 9 × 12-inch baking pan. Combine the eggs, milk, salt, and dry mustard in a small bowl. Pour over layers in baking dish. Refrigerate overnight. Bake, covered, at 325° for 55 minutes. Let stand for 10 minutes before serving.
Yields: 12 servings

St. John the Baptist Centennial Cookbook
St. John the Baptist Episcopal Church
Seattle, Washington

RED BEANS AND RICE

1 pound dried red beans
3 quarts water
1/4 teaspoon Tabasco sauce
1 teaspoon Worcestershire
sauce
1 cup chopped celery
1 cup chopped onion
1/4 cup chopped fresh parsley
3 cloves garlic, minced
2 bay leaves
1/2 pound ham, cubed
1/4 pound hot sausage, sliced
1/2 pound smoked sausage,
sliced
3 tablespoons vegetable oil
Salt and black pepper to taste
Cooked rice

Wash and pick any pebbles, etc., out of red beans. Place beans and next 12 ingredients in a large pot; bring to a low boil. Cook, uncovered, for 2 hours or more until beans are soft. Add water if needed. To get a thick, creamy sauce, mash some of the beans against the side of the pot. Add salt and pepper to taste and cook 15 more minutes. Serve over rice in large bowls.
Yields: 4 to 6 servings

Cooking New Orleans Style!
All Saints' Episcopal Church
River Ridge, Louisiana

MEXICAN LASAGNA

1 large onion, chopped
1 red bell pepper, chopped
Olive oil
2 pounds Italian sausage or
   1 pound Italian sausage and
   1 pound ground beef
1 envelope taco seasoning
Cumin to taste
Black pepper to taste
2 cloves garlic, chopped
1 (10-ounce) can enchilada
   sauce
1 (10-ounce) can tomatoes with
   green chiles
1 (12-ounce) jar salsa with
   cilantro
2-3 packages shredded Mexican
   cheese
Soft taco shells
1 (16-ounce) can refried beans

Sauté onion and red pepper in small amount of olive oil in a large skillet. Add meat and cook until browned. Add taco seasoning and remaining spices. Then stir in enchilada sauce and next 2 ingredients. Allow to simmer for 5 to 10 minutes.

Ladle a small amount of sauce in a 9 × 13-inch baking pan. Add a layer of soft shells, then a layer of sauce and a layer of cheese. Add a second layer of shells, half of refried beans and cheese. Add shells, remaining refried beans, sauce, and cheese. Add shells and finish with sauce and cheese. Cover pan with foil. Bake at 350° for 30 to 45 minutes or until heated through and cheese is melted.
Yields: 8 to 10 servings

Parish Collection
Holy Trinity Episcopal Church
Iron Mountain, Michigan

BAVARIAN POT ROAST

1 (5-pound) chuck, rump, or
   bottom round roast
1 tablespoon cinnamon
2 teaspoons ginger
1 1/2 teaspoons salt
1 onion, chopped fine
1 cup water
1 1/2 cups apple juice
1 (8-ounce) can tomato sauce
1 tablespoon vinegar
1 bay leaf

Brown meat on all sides in Dutch oven. Mix cinnamon, ginger, and salt together in a bowl; add remaining ingredients and pour over browned meat. Cover and simmer 3 hours or until tender. Remove bay leaf. Thicken gravy with flour and serve over sliced meat.
Yields: 8 to 10 servings

Prize Recipes of Martinez
Grace Episcopal Church
Martinez, California

BEEF TENDERLOIN WITH ROASTED SHALLOTS, BACON, AND PORT

1 1/2 pounds large shallots
   (about 24), halved lengthwise
   and peeled
3 tablespoons olive oil
Salt and black pepper
6 cups canned beef broth
1 1/2 cups tawny port
1 tablespoon tomato paste
3–3 1/4 pounds beef
   tenderloins, large ends trimmed
2 teaspoons dried thyme
7 slices bacon, chopped
6 tablespoons butter
   (3/4 stick), divided
1 1/2 tablespoons all-purpose
   flour
1 large bunch watercress

Toss shallots with oil to coat in a 9-inch pie pan. Season with salt and pepper. Roast at 375° in the middle of the oven until shallots are deep brown and very tender, stirring occasionally, about 30 minutes. Boil broth and port in large saucepan until reduced to 3 3/4 cups, about 30 minutes. Whisk in tomato paste. (Shallots and broth mixture can be made 1 day ahead. Cover separately; chill.)

Pat beef dry. Sprinkle with thyme, salt, and pepper. Sauté bacon in a large roasting pan over medium heat until golden, about 4 minutes. Using slotted spoon, transfer bacon to paper towels. Add beef to pan; brown on all sides over medium-high heat, about 7 minutes. Transfer pan to oven; roast beef until meat thermometer inserted into center registers 125° for medium-rare, about 45 minutes. Transfer beef to platter. Tent loosely with foil.

Spoon fat off top of pan drippings in roasting pan. Place roasting pan over high heat. Add broth mixture and bring to a boil, scraping up any browned bits. Transfer to medium saucepan; bring to a simmer. Mix 3 tablespoons butter and flour in small bowl to form smooth paste; whisk into broth mixture and simmer until sauce thickens, about 2 minutes. Whisk in remaining 3 tablespoons butter; stir in roasted shallots and reserved bacon. Season sauce with salt and pepper. Cut beef into 1/2-inch-thick slices. Spoon some sauce over; garnish with watercress. Pass remaining sauce.
Yields: 6 to 8 servings

Favorite Recipes of St. Stephen's
St. Stephen's Episcopal Church
Spokane, Washington

ELEGANT BEEF WELLINGTON

1 (4- to 4 1/2-pound) beef filet
Salt and black pepper to taste
Pastry
Duxelles
1 large egg, beaten
1 tablespoon water
Sesame seeds

Place beef on a rack in a shallow baking pan; sprinkle with salt and pepper. Roast at 425° for 30 minutes. Let stand until cool. Trim off all fat. Prepare Pastry and Duxelles according to directions below. Roll pastry until it is 3 inches longer than the roast and 12 to 13 inches wide. Press duxelles into the pastry, leaving an inch uncovered on all edges. Place beef on the pastry. Moisten the pastry edges and enclose beef, pressing edges firmly together. Trim off excess pastry. Place, seam-side down, in shallow baking pan. If desired, cut decorations from excess pastry trimmings and place on top. Brush pastry with the beaten egg combined with 1 tablespoon water. Sprinkle with sesame seeds. Bake for 30 to 35 minutes at 400°. Let stand for 15 to 20 minutes before slicing to serve.
Yields: 8 to 10 servings

PASTRY
3 3/4 cups sifted all-purpose
   flour
1 teaspoon salt
1 cup cold butter
2 tablespoons shortening
3/4 cup cold water

Combine flour and salt in a bowl and cut in the butter and shortening until the particles are fine. Add the cold water, 1 tablespoon at a time, to make a stiff dough. Cover and chill.
Note: You can substitute prepared pastry or puff pastry.

DUXELLES
1 pound mushrooms, finely
   chopped
1/4 cup finely chopped green
   onions
1/4 cup butter
1/2 teaspoon salt
1/4 teaspoon marjoram
2 teaspoons all-purpose flour
Dash of black pepper
1/4 cup beef broth
2 tablespoons finely chopped
   parsley
1/2 cup finely chopped ham

Sauté mushrooms and green onions in butter until the liquid evaporates. Stir in salt, marjoram, flour, pepper, and broth. Cook, stirring constantly, until the mixture comes to a boil and thickens. Stir in the parsley and ham. Cool.

Another Touch of Basil
St. Basil's Episcopal Church
Tahlequah, Oklahoma

STEAK PAISANO STYLE

1 (1-pound) 1-inch-thick
  T-bone steak
Salt and black pepper to taste
Garlic powder
1 teaspoon chopped parsley
1/2 teaspoon oregano
1 medium tomato, sliced
1 tablespoon vegetable or
  olive oil

Place steak in baking pan. Sprinkle with salt, pepper, garlic powder, parsley, oregano, and tomato slices. Add oil. Broil for about 20 minutes.
Yields: 2 servings

St. Christopher's Cookbook
St. Christopher's Episcopal Church
El Paso, Texas

PEPPER STEAK AND RICE

1 (1-pound) boneless
  round steak
2 tablespoons butter
1 medium-size green bell
  pepper, cut into pieces
1 large onion, chopped
1/2 cup chopped celery
1/2 cup chopped fresh
  mushrooms or 1 (4-ounce)
  can, undrained
1/4 cup soy sauce
3 tablespoons water
1 teaspoon cornstarch
1 tablespoon water
Hot cooked rice

Trim fat from steak. Slice across grain into 1/4-inch strips. Melt butter in a large skillet. Sauté vegetables; set aside. Brown meat. Stir in vegetables, soy sauce, and 3 tablespoons water. Simmer, covered, for 30 minutes. Remove meat and vegetables. Combine cornstarch and 1 tablespoon water in a small bowl. Stir into pan drippings until smooth and thick. Return meat and vegetables to the skillet; mix well. Serve over rice.
Yields: 3 or 4 servings

The Vicar's Guild Cookbook
Episcopal Church of the Resurrection
Loudon, Tennessee

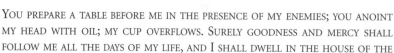

YOU PREPARE A TABLE BEFORE ME IN THE PRESENCE OF MY ENEMIES; YOU ANOINT MY HEAD WITH OIL; MY CUP OVERFLOWS. SURELY GOODNESS AND MERCY SHALL FOLLOW ME ALL THE DAYS OF MY LIFE, AND I SHALL DWELL IN THE HOUSE OF THE LORD MY WHOLE LIFE LONG.

PSALM 23:5–6

STUFFED FLANK STEAKS

1/3 cup chopped onion
2 tablespoons butter
4 cups dry bread cubes
1/2 teaspoon poultry seasoning
1 teaspoon salt, divided
Dash of black pepper
1/4 cup water
2 (1 1/2-pound) beef flank
  steaks, scored
All-purpose flour
Shortening for browning
Salt and black pepper to taste
1 (16-ounce) can tomatoes
1/4 cup chopped onion
1/4 cup ketchup
1/4 cup chopped green bell
  pepper
1 (3-ounce) can sliced
  mushrooms, drained

In skillet, cook 1/3 cup onion in butter until tender. Add bread cubes, poultry seasoning, 1/2 teaspoon salt, and dash of pepper; toss until bread is lightly toasted. Sprinkle with 1/4 cup water to moisten. Spread stuffing over steaks and roll up lengthwise as for jellyroll; fasten with wooden pick and lace with string. Roll in flour; brown all sides in skillet in small amount of hot shortening. Season with salt and pepper. Add tomatoes, 1/4 cup chopped onion, ketchup, and remaining 1/2 teaspoon salt. Simmer, covered, for 1 1/2 to 2 hours. Add green pepper and mushrooms during last 15 minutes of cooking. Remove steaks to warm platter. Mix 1 tablespoon flour with 2 tablespoons cold water until smooth. Stir into sauce; cook until thick and bubbly.
Yields: 6 to 8 servings

Shared Treasures
St. James Episcopal Church
Wichita, Kansas

CALDILLO

2 pounds cubed round steak
1 tablespoon vegetable oil
1 tablespoon all-purpose flour
1 onion, chopped
1/2 cup canned tomatoes
1/8 teaspoon cumin powder
1 clove garlic, minced
1 (4-ounce) can chopped
  green chiles
Salt to taste

Brown steak in oil in a large skillet. Add flour and brown well. Stir in remaining ingredients. Add water to desired consistency. Simmer until meat is tender. Serve with flour tortillas.
Yields: 4 to 6 servings

St. Christopher's Cookbook
St. Christopher's Episcopal Church
El Paso, Texas

SHREDDED BEEF

1 (5- to 7-pound) boneless
  beef roast
2–3 large cloves garlic, chopped
3 large onions, chopped
1/2–1 cup dry red wine
25–30 hamburger buns

Combine all ingredients in a large slow cooker. Cook, covered, on low for 18 to 20 hours. Beef is ready to serve when you can easily shred it with two forks. Shred beef and serve hot on buns.
Note: May substitute 2 beef bouillon cubes or tomato juice for the wine.
Yields: 25 to 30 servings

Keep the Feast
Church of the Ascension
Middletown, Ohio

CORNISH PASTY

1 cup lard (1/2 pound) or
  1 cup shortening
3 cups all-purpose flour
1 cup cold water
1 1/2 pounds boneless
  sirloin steak
1 pound pork steak
1/2 medium rutabaga,
  chipped into 1/2-inch pieces
5 potatoes, chopped
4 large yellow onions, finely cut
Salt and black pepper to taste

Cut lard into flour and then use a pastry blender to mix well. Add cold water, and mix well; form into a roll, wrap in foil, and refrigerate. Cut meat in strips and then at an angle into small pieces. Mix meat and divide into five portions. Roll 1/5 of pastry in circle the size of a dinner plate. Spread thin layer of rutabaga, then generous layer of potatoes, then 1 portion of meat, and finally a generous layer of onions. Season to taste.

Dip fingers in water and wet edge of pastry. Fold pastry edges up to top; seal and crimp. Cut off any excess pastry from ends of pasty. Slice a 1-inch hole in top with a sharp knife. Place on baking sheet. Repeat for other four pasties. Bake at 400° for 1/2 hour; reduce oven temperature to 350° and bake 1 hour. Remove from oven. Pour 1 tablespoon of water in hole of each pasty. Allow to sit for 10 minutes for juice to form inside.
Note: Pasties can be baked for the first half hour; then cooled. Wrap in foil and freeze. When ready to use, remove from oven and place frozen pasty in 350° oven for 1 1/2 hours. Add water and allow to sit for 10 minutes, as noted above.
Yields: 5 servings

Sharing Our Best
Trinity Episcopal Church
Houghton, Michigan

HUNGARIAN GOULASH

1 pound onion, sliced thin
3 tablespoons vegetable oil, divided
2 pounds lean chuck (beef), cut in 1-inch cubes
3 tablespoons Hungarian paprika
1 teaspoon caraway seed
2 cups chicken or beef broth or water
1 teaspoon salt
1/2 teaspoon fresh ground black pepper
1 pound tomatoes, peeled and cut up, or 1 (16-ounce) can
2 green bell peppers, chopped
3 large cloves garlic, minced
1 teaspoon marjoram
2 large potatoes, cut in 1-inch cubes

Brown onions in 2 tablespoons of oil in a large cast-iron skillet. Remove and set aside. Add the remaining tablespoon of oil and brown beef. Add paprika, caraway seed, broth, salt, and ground pepper; cook until meat is tender (1 hour or more). If pan is full, switch to pot to finish. Add onions, tomato, green pepper, garlic, marjoram, and potatoes. Boil 15 minutes or until potatoes are done. Should be a little soupy. If not, add a little water. Serve with bread or rolls and salad.
Yields: 4 to 6 servings

Potluck Favorites
St. Augustine's Episcopal Church
Kingston, Rhode Island

GRANDMA'S GOULASH

1/2 pound ground beef
1/2 cup chopped onion
1 teaspoon salt
1/4 teaspoon black pepper
Tabasco sauce to taste
4 cups cooked tomatoes
1 cup uncooked macaroni

Brown ground beef and onion in a large skillet. Add seasonings and tomatoes and bring to a boil. Add macaroni. Simmer until macaroni is tender, stirring often.
Yields: 4 servings

Butter 'n Love Recipes
St. Matthew's Episcopal Church
Unadilla, New York

TOUQUIERE
(French Meat Pie)
(This pie is traditionally served by all French people on New Year's Eve or Day.)

1/2 pound ground beef,
  lightly browned
1/2 pound ground pork,
  lightly browned
1 medium onion chopped,
  sautéed
1/4 teaspoon chives
1 teaspoon cinnamon
1 teaspoon celery salt
1 teaspoon black pepper
1/2 teaspoon poultry seasoning
1 cup bread crumbs
2 (9-inch) pie crusts

Mix all ingredients together in a bowl. Spoon into a pie crust; top with other crust. Bake at 400° for 30 minutes. *Note*: Serve with a medium cream sauce to which is added 1/2 cup grated sharp cheese.
Yields: 6 to 8 servings

Loaves & Fishes and Other Dishes
St. Andrew's Episcopal Church
Turners Falls, Massachusetts

GERMAN CARAWAY MEAT BALLS

1 pound lean ground meat
1/4 cup milk
1/4 cup dry fine bread crumbs
1 large egg
1 teaspoon salt
Dash of black pepper
1/4 teaspoon poultry seasoning
1 tablespoon snipped parsley
2 tablespoons shortening
1 (10-ounce) can beef broth
1 (3-ounce) can chopped
  mushrooms, drained
1/2 cup chopped onion
1 cup sour cream
1 tablespoon all-purpose flour
1/2 teaspoon caraway seed
Cooked wide noodles

Combine meat and next 7 ingredients in a bowl. Shape into about 24 (1 1/2-inch) balls. Brown slowly on all sides in the shortening in a large skillet, shaking frequently. Add broth, mushrooms, and onion. Simmer, covered, for 30 minutes. Blend sour cream, flour, and caraway seed in a small bowl; stir into broth. Cook and stir until mixture thickens. Toss with noodles and serve.
Yields: 4 servings

More Manna… and a Little Quail
St. Luke's on the Lake
Austin, Texas

SPAGHETTI SAUCE WITH MEAT BALLS

1 small onion, diced
2–3 cloves garlic
1 tablespoon olive oil
1 pound chuck or round steak,
  cut in chunks
1 pork chop
2–3 mild Italian sausages
  (optional)
2 (6-ounce) cans tomato paste
1 (4-ounce) can tomato sauce
2 cups water
1 (15-ounce) can Italian-style
  tomatoes
2 teaspoons salt
1 teaspoon black pepper
2 1/2 tablespoons basil
2 bay leaves
Parsley
1 1/2 tablespoons oregano
1–2 teaspoons sugar
1/2 cup red wine
Meat balls

Fry diced onion and garlic cloves in olive oil in a large skillet. Add beef, pork, and sausage (optional) and brown. Add tomato paste, tomato sauce, and 2 cups water (use it to rinse out cans and add to sauce). Strain Italian-style tomatoes through a sieve (discard pulp) and add tomatoes to the sauce. When sauce starts to boil, add salt, pepper, basil, bay leaves, and parsley. Add oregano by putting it in palm of hand and crumbling it into the cooking pot. Add a little sugar to cut the tart tomatoes and red wine for flavor. Simmer for 1 hour with lid partly covering the pot. Remove garlic cloves and bay leaves from pot and add Meat Balls; cook for another 1/2 hour.
Yields: 6 to 8 servings

MEAT BALLS
1 pound ground beef
  (chuck or round)
2 small garlic cloves,
  minced finely
3 large eggs
Salt and black pepper to taste
1/2 cup bread crumbs
1 teaspoon mint, crushed in the
  palm of your hand
1/4 cup grated Romano cheese
4–5 sprigs parsley, stems pulled
  off and added in whole pieces

Mix all ingredients in bowl by hand, adding a little water for texture. Wet hands and make meat balls. Put in pan in refrigerator until sauce is ready. Add to sauce.

Pohickory Cookbook
Pohick Church
Lorton, Virginia

MEAT BALLS IN CAPER SAUCE

4 tablespoons butter, divided
3 onions, chopped
6 slices white bread
1 cup light cream
1 1/2 pounds ground beef
1/2 pounds ground veal
1/2 pounds ground pork
4 anchovy fillets
3 large eggs
2 teaspoons salt, divided
1 teaspoon black pepper,
  divided
1/2 cup ice water
3 cups boiling water
1/4 teaspoon marjoram
3 sprigs parsley
3 stalks celery
Dash of nutmeg
2 tablespoons all-purpose flour
2 tablespoons lemon juice
1/4 cup capers, drained

Melt 2 tablespoons butter in a skillet and add onions. Sauté for 10 minutes, stirring occasionally. Soak the bread in cream for 10 minutes. Press excess liquid from it. Grind bread with the sautéed onions, ground meats, and anchovies in a food chopper. Add the eggs, 1 teaspoon salt, 1/2 teaspoon pepper, and ice water. Mix together and shape into 2-inch balls. Combine the boiling water, remaining salt and pepper, marjoram, parsley, and celery in a deep saucepan. Drop meat balls into it and boil for 20 minutes.

Add nutmeg to the gravy. Melt the remaining butter in a saucepan. Add the flour and mix to a smooth paste. Strain the liquid in which the meat balls were cooked, and add to the flour paste, stirring constantly, until the boiling point is reached. Cook over low heat for 5 minutes. Add the lemon juice and capers and stir well. Place meat balls on a platter and pour sauce over them.
Yields: 6 to 8 servings

Best of Bayou Cuisine
St. Stephen's Episcopal Church
Indianola, Mississippi

RUNZES

3 pounds lean ground beef
2 large onions, chopped
1 medium head cabbage,
  chopped
Tabasco sauce to taste
5 loaves frozen bread dough,
  thawed
Butter or margarine, melted
Salt

Brown beef and onions in large Dutch oven. Add chopped cabbage, and simmer for 5 to 7 minutes or until cabbage is tender. Drain excess fat. Add Tabasco sauce. Break each bread loaf into 5 or 6 pieces. Flatten each piece with heel of hand, making 4- to 5-inch rounds. Top each round with 2 or 3 tablespoons meat mixture. Bring sides of dough together, pinching to seal. Place seam down on ungreased baking sheet. Bake at 350° for 25 to 30 minutes or until golden brown. Brush tops with melted butter, and sprinkle lightly with salt.
Yields: 18 to 20 servings

Served with Love
Diocese of West Missouri

STUFFED GREEN PEPPERS

7 medium green bell peppers
1 tablespoon salt
3 quarts water
3/4 cup sliced onion
2 tablespoons margarine, divided
2 (8-ounce) cans tomato sauce, divided
1 (8-ounce) can stewed tomatoes
1/4 cup lemon juice
3 tablespoons honey
1 1/4 teaspoons salt, divided
1/2 cup chopped onion
1 pound lean ground beef
1 cup cooked rice
1/4 teaspoon black pepper
1 1/2 teaspoons Worcestershire sauce

Remove tops and seeds of peppers. Cook peppers and 1 tablespoon salt in a saucepan with 3 quarts boiling water for 5 minutes; drain. Meanwhile, sauté sliced onion in 1 tablespoon margarine over medium heat until tender. Combine with 1 can tomato sauce, stewed tomatoes, lemon juice, honey, and 1/4 teaspoon salt in a 2-quart baking dish. Melt remaining 1 tablespoon margarine in a skillet. Brown chopped onion and meat over medium-high heat; drain. Stir in remaining can of tomato sauce, rice, remaining salt, black pepper, and Worcestershire sauce. Spoon meat mixture evenly into peppers. Stand peppers, cut side up, in baking dish. Bake at 400° for 30 minutes. To serve, spoon tomato sauce over top of peppers.
Yields: 7 servings

Taste & See
St. Peter's Episcopal Church
Louisville, Kentucky

MEAT LOAF

2/3 cup dry bread crumbs
1 cup milk
1 1/2 pounds ground beef
2 large eggs, beaten
1/4 cup grated onion
1 teaspoon salt
1/8 teaspoon black pepper
1/2 teaspoon sage
Piquante sauce

PIQUANTE SAUCE
3 tablespoons brown sugar
1/4 cup ketchup
1 teaspoon dry mustard

Soak bread crumbs in milk. Add the ground beef and next 5 ingredients. Mold into loaf and place in roasting pan or loaf pan. Cover with Piquante Sauce before baking. Bake 1 hour at 350°.
Yields: 6 to 8 servings

Combine all three ingredients; mix well.

Trinity Episcopal Church Cookbook
Society of Mary and Friends
Gladstone, Michigan

EASY CHILI CON CARNE

1 1/2 pounds lean ground beef
1 onion, chopped
1 teaspoon salt
2 teaspoons chili powder
1 bay leaf
1 teaspoon Worcestershire
  sauce
2 (8-ounce) cans tomato sauce
2 (16-ounce) cans kidney
  beans, drained

Brown chopped meat in saucepan; drain excess fat. Combine all ingredients in an electric slow-cooker. Cover and cook on high for 3 hours. Remove bay leaf before serving.
Yields: 4 to 6 servings

St. Anne's Guild Cookbook
St. James the Less Church
Scarsdale, New York

SAUERBRATEN PATTIES

1 pound ground beef
3 slices stale bread softened
  in water
1 minced onion
1 large egg
1 1/2 teaspoons salt
2 tablespoons vegetable oil
1/2 cup vinegar
1 1/2 cups water
10 cloves
3–5 bay leaves
8 ginger snaps

Combine ground beef, bread, onion, egg and salt in a bowl; mix well. Shape into small patties. Brown the patties in a skillet in oil. Add vinegar, water, cloves, bay leaves, and ginger snaps. Simmer for 1 hour. Remove bay leaves before serving. Serve over egg noodles.
Yields: 6 to 8 servings

Parish Collection
St. Edward's Episcopal Church
Lawrenceville, Georgia

LEG OF LAMB

2 cups red wine
1/4 cup red wine vinegar
1 tablespoon rosemary
1 tablespoon basil
1 medium onion
2 cloves garlic
Salt to taste
Black pepper to taste
1 (6- to 8-pound) leg of lamb,
   boned and butterflied

Combine wine and next 7 ingredients in a bowl; mix well. Pour over lamb; marinate for 6 hours. Grill for 45 minutes. Slice like steak.
Yields: 8 to 10 servings

Cooking with Love
St. Timothy's Episcopal Church
Fairfield, Connecticut

LAMB CURRY

1 pound lamb shoulder or
   leftover lamb, cut in cubes
2 tablespoons butter or
   vegetable oil
1 cup water
1/2 teaspoon salt
1/4 teaspoon black pepper
1 tablespoon chopped onion
1/2 cup chopped celery
2 tablespoons chopped parsley
Curry powder

Brown lamb in butter or oil. Add water and next 5 ingredients. Cover and simmer for 20 minutes, stirring frequently. Thicken stock if necessary. Add curry powder to taste, and cook 2 minutes longer.
Note: Serve over rice with chopped nuts, flaked coconut, and chopped green onions.
Yields: 6 servings

Our Favorite Recipes
St. Thomas' Episcopal Church
Pittstown, New Jersey

GRILLED MARINATED LAMB CHOPS

1/4 cup olive oil
2 tablespoons red wine vinegar
2 teaspoons prepared mustard
1 teaspoon salt
1 teaspoon crumbled rosemary
   leaves
3/4 teaspoon powdered garlic
1/2 teaspoon minced onion
1/4 teaspoon ground black
   pepper
1/4 teaspoon ground ginger
6 lamb chops

Combine first 9 ingredients in a mixing bowl. Add lamb chops. Marinate, covered, at least 5 to 6 hours or overnight in refrigerator. Cook slowly over slow-burning charcoal fire or grill until well done and browned. Or, broil in oven for 15 to 20 minutes. Baste with marinade while cooking.
Yields: 4 to 6 servings

Taste & See
Trinity Episcopal Church
Red Bank, New Jersey

STUFFED GRAPE LEAVES

1 cup rice
1 pound ground lamb
2 tablespoons melted butter
1/4 teaspoon cinnamon
1 teaspoon allspice
1 teaspoon pepper
1 tablespoon salt
20–60 grape leaves
1/4 cup freshly squeezed
   lemon juice

Combine rice and next 6 ingredients in a bowl; mix well. Spoon about 1 tablespoon mixture on each leaf near the stem end. Roll up and place evenly in a saucepan that's lined with grape leaves. Add water to cover about 1/4 inch above the leaves. Place a plate, upside down, on top of leaves to keep them submerged. Cook, covered, on low heat for 20 minutes or so. Add lemon juice and simmer for 5 minutes. Serve immediately. Grape leaves can also be chilled and served with a dollop of yogurt.
Yields: 20 to 30 servings

St. Stephen's Parish Cookbook
St. Stephen's Parish
Schuylerville, New York

VEAL SUPREME

1 teaspoon sugar
1 small onion, sliced in rings
1/4 cup butter or margarine
1 1/2 pounds cubed veal,
  cut into 1/2-inch pieces
1 1/2 cups chicken stock
1/2 teaspoon salt
1/4 teaspoon black pepper
2 tablespoons soft butter mixed
  with 2 tablespoons flour
1/2 cup dry white wine
1/2 pound mushrooms, sliced
1 cup small white onions,
  cooked
1/2 cup heavy cream
1 tablespoon grated lemon rind

Cook the sugar and onion rings in a heavy skillet over low heat until sugar is caramelized and onion is limp, stirring constantly with wooden spoon. Add 1/4 cup butter, veal, chicken stock, salt, and pepper. Cover tightly. Simmer until veal is tender. Stir in the butter mixed with flour until blended. Add wine, mushrooms, and small onions. Cover; simmer until mushrooms are tender. Add heavy cream and grated lemon. Heat only to the boiling point. Spoon onto a hot platter. Serve with noodles.
Yields: 4 servings

What's Cooking?
St. John's Episcopal Church
Huntington, L.I., New York

BAKED VEAL PARMESAN

3 tablespoons bread crumbs
3 tablespoons grated Parmesan
  cheese
Dash of pepper
1 large egg, beaten
1 teaspoon water
2 veal cutlets
1/4 cup ketchup
2 teaspoons water
1/4 teaspoon oregano,
  dried and crushed
Dash of onion salt
Dash of black pepper
Mozzarella cheese, shredded

Combine bread crumbs, Parmesan cheese, and dash of pepper in a small bowl. Combine egg and water in a small bowl. Dip veal in egg mixture; then in crumb mixture. Place into baking dish. Bake at 400° for 20 minutes. Turn and bake an additional 20 minutes or until tender. Combine ketchup and next 4 ingredients in a small bowl. Spread over veal; top with mozzarella. Bake until cheese melts, about 1 to 2 minutes.
Yields: 2 servings

What's Cookin' at Epiphany?
Church of the Epiphany
Richmond, Virginia

VEAL WITH MUSHROOMS

1 1/2 pounds veal
1 clove garlic
1/4 cup all-purpose flour
1/2 teaspoon salt
1/4 cup butter or margarine
1/2 pound mushrooms, sliced
1/4 cup chicken broth
1/4 cup dry white wine

Pound veal to 1/4-inch thickness. Rub with cut garlic. Cut into 2-inch pieces. Dredge with flour and salt. Sauté veal in butter in a large skillet. Remove meat from pan. Sauté mushrooms. Add chicken broth and wine. Return veal to pan. Cover and simmer about 20 minutes.

Yields: 4 to 6 servings

Breaking Bread with St. Nicholas
St. Nicholas Episcopal Church
Midland, Texas

[Thus sayeth the Lord God] "On the banks, on both sides of the river, there will grow all kinds of trees

Poultry

for food. Their leaves will not wither nor their fruit fail, but they will bear fresh fruit every month, because the water for them flows from the sanctuary. Their fruit will be for food, and their leaves for healing."

Ezekiel 47:12

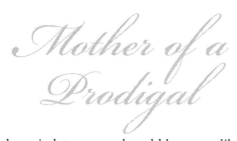

Mother of a Prodigal

Perhaps, in later years, she told her story like this:

They always talk about it as if I hadn't even been there. Yes, it was my husband who ran out in the street when Joshua came home. True, he was the one who ordered the best calf in the herd killed to celebrate our boy's return. But who do you think actually made the dish?

Joshua was a good boy, but he didn't have much respect for the family, really. What a slap in the face it was to my husband when he asked for the inheritance and walked out the door. I guess he thought he could make something more of himself, live it up in some far country. But things didn't work out, and back he came.

You know, we always loved Joshua. We never stopped loving him. My husband used to stand out front as the sun was setting, scanning the horizon, hoping someone would appear down the road with news of his boy. He wouldn't admit it to me, but I knew that was what he was doing.

We always loved Joshua, and we'll take him back, no questions asked. You say he made mistakes? Well, we all do. I agree with my husband: throw a party, share a meal, and start over. If there are things to talk about, they'll come up eventually. We'll deal with them. The important thing is that Joshua has come home.

Of course the meal needed to be something special for Joshua's sake. But I was worried about Reuben, who I knew was going to be jealous. I understand him, my boy Reuben, because he takes after me. I was a good girl, you know, always letting myself stay in the background, trying to do the right thing. I would watch Joshua talk about how the world ought to be, and I admired his ambition. But like Reuben, I'm the stay-at-home type. Let's not have so much drama, I thought. We're doing what we should; isn't that enough?

But that was then. Joshua has gone and come back now, and a homecoming deserves a feast. So I did roast that calf, just like my husband asked, rubbing it with oil and garlic to make the meat as savory as could be. That's an important thing to do, no? Everyone who tasted it raved about it. But the storytellers still never mention me.

That's why you probably haven't heard how the evening ended. I'm a mother and I know the table. I know my sons. It was good to celebrate with a special dish for Joshua, but I knew that we had to do something for Reuben, too, or else he would feel forgotten. He had already said so to my husband.

Well, I'm a mother and I know the table. I know my sons. So I'll tell you what I did. While the meat was cooking, I made Reuben's favorite side dish, the one with mint and lentils. I set it down at the center of the banqueting table, in our best serving platter, right next to the fatted calf. And when he saw it he understood: he wasn't forgotten.

That meal kept both my sons, as different as they are, at the table together. It was nothing special, just a woman's way to help us feel like a family again. But the next time you see the storytellers, you can smile to yourself and think of me, because you'll never hear about it from them.

CHICKEN BREASTS GORDON

1 (15-ounce) can whole
   cranberry sauce
1/2 cup medium dry sherry
1 1/2 cups chicken stock
1/4 teaspoon ground ginger
1/4 teaspoon grated nutmeg
1/4 teaspoon ground cloves
1/4 teaspoon black pepper
2 whole star anise (optional)
1/2 teaspoon dry mustard
2 tablespoons dark brown
   sugar
8 boneless, skinless half
   chicken breasts
1/4 cup all-purpose flour
   seasoned with salt and black
   pepper
1/4 cup unsalted butter

Combine cranberry sauce, sherry, chicken stock, ginger, nutmeg, cloves, pepper, anise, mustard, and brown sugar in a steel or enameled saucepan. Simmer mixture, stirring for 10 minutes. Discard anise, if used. Pound chicken breasts lightly between sheets of waxed paper. Dust with seasoned flour. Heat butter in a large skillet over moderate heat until foamy. Sauté chicken breasts for 1 minute on each side. Transfer to oven-proof serving dish. Pour cranberry mixture into skillet; reduce by half over high heat. Spoon sauce over chicken and bake at 350° for 15 minutes, or until chicken springs to touch and sauce is bubbly.
Yields: 6 to 8 servings

Suppers in Season
All Saints' Episcopal Church
Wolfeboro, New Hampshire

ONO (SWEET) MICROWAVE CHICKEN

1 (3-pound) whole fryer
   chicken
1 tablespoon Hawaiian or
   kosher salt
2 tablespoons soy sauce
2 tablespoons rice wine
1 tablespoon sugar
1 teaspoon Five-Spice powder
   (optional)

Rinse chicken and pat dry. Mix remaining ingredients together and rub them on the outside and inside of the chicken. Place seasoned chicken in a glass baking dish and cover. Marinate chicken for an hour, turning it over once to marinate the other side. Microwave on high for 25 minutes. Let stand for a few minutes. Chop chicken into bite-size pieces and serve with its sauce.
Note: Cool and shred chicken as garnishment for salad or use as sandwich filling.
Yields: 4 to 6 servings

...and Sew We Eat!
Diocese of Hawaii
Honolulu, Hawaii

ORANGE CHICKEN

3 pounds chicken pieces
Salt and black pepper to taste
1/4 teaspoon garlic power or
  fresh garlic
1/4 cup butter, melted
1 (6-ounce) can frozen orange
  juice concentrate, thawed

Place chicken in flat pan; add salt, pepper, and garlic powder. Bake, uncovered, at 350° for 30 minutes. Blend butter and orange juice concentrate. Pour over chicken, covering each piece. Continue baking another 45 minutes, basting frequently until chicken is very tender. Serve chicken with orange gravy over rice, mashed potatoes, or noodles.
Yields: 6 servings

Diocese of Central Pennsylvania
Diocese Board Collection

HONEY-CURRY CHICKEN

1 (4- to 6-pound) chicken,
  cut into pieces
1/4 cup margarine, melted
1/4 cup honey
1/4 cup prepared mustard
1/2–1 teaspoon curry
1/4 teaspoon salt

Brown chicken pieces in butter in a large skillet. Combine remaining ingredients in a bowl. Place chicken in baking dish; pour curry-honey sauce over chicken. Cover dish with foil. Bake in oven at 350° for 1 hour. Serve with rice.
Yields: 4 to 6 servings

Potluck Sunday
St. Mary's Episcopal Church
Madisonville, Kentucky

BAKED LEMON CHICKEN

4 chicken breast halves,
  skinned
1/4 cup plus 2 tablespoons
  lemon juice
1/2 cup butter or margarine,
  melted
1 teaspoon garlic powder
1 teaspoon poultry seasoning
1/2 teaspoon salt
1/4 teaspoon black pepper
Hot cooked rice, optional

Place chicken in a lightly greased 12 × 7-inch baking dish. Combine juice, butter, garlic powder, poultry seasoning, salt, and pepper; pour over chicken. Bake, uncovered, at 350° for 1 hour or until chicken is tender, basting frequently. Serve with rice, if desired.
Yields: 4 servings

St. Philip's Cooks
St. Philip's Episcopal Church
Brevard, North Carolina

CHICKEN DIJON

6 chicken breast halves
Salt, black pepper, garlic
  powder to taste
3/4 cup sour cream
1/2–3/4 cup Dijon mustard
Italian bread crumbs
Parsley

Sprinkle chicken with salt, pepper, and garlic powder. Mix sour cream and mustard in a small bowl. Coat chicken well and roll in bread crumbs. Cover lightly and bake at 350° for about 45 to 50 minutes. Sprinkle with parsley.
Yields: 6 servings

Parish Collection
St. Peter's Episcopal Church
Altavista, Virginia

BARBECUED CHICKEN

1 (3- to 4-pound) chicken,
  cut up
1 (18-ounce) bottle hickory-
  smoked barbecue sauce
1 (8-ounce) can crushed
  pineapple
1 cup firmly packed brown
  sugar

Lay chicken pieces in a baking pan. Combine barbecue sauce, pineapple, and brown sugar in a bowl; mix well. Pour over chicken. Bake at 350° for 2 hours or until chicken is well done.
Yields: 6 to 8 servings

Parish Collection
St. Mary's Episcopal Church
Mitchell, South Dakota

FETA-STUFFED CHICKEN

4 whole chicken breasts, boned
1 (10-ounce) package frozen
  chopped spinach, thawed
  and drained
Minced garlic
1 cup pine nuts
Salt and black pepper
Olive oil
1 cup feta cheese
1 large egg, beaten with
  1 tablespoon water
Italian bread crumbs

Halve chicken breasts and pound flat. Sauté spinach, garlic, pine nuts, salt, and pepper in olive oil in a large skillet. Place 1/8 cup cheese and 1/8 cup spinach mixture on each breast. Roll and secure with a wooden pick. Dip each breast in egg mixture, then roll in bread crumbs. Brown in olive oil. Place breasts, seam side down, in baking dish. Bake at 350° for 20 to 30 minutes or until done.
Yields: 8 servings

Angels in the Kitchen
Holy Trinity Episcopal Church
Gainesville, Florida

APPLE-STUFFED CHICKEN BREASTS

6 whole chicken breasts,
  skinned, boned, and split
2 medium apples, peeled
  and cored
6 tablespoons butter or
  margarine, divided
1 medium onion, finely
  chopped
1 clove garlic, minced
1 cup soft bread crumbs
1 teaspoon salt
1–2 teaspoons rosemary
1–2 teaspoons basil
All-purpose flour
3–4 cups apple juice
2 tablespoons cognac or sherry
Cornstarch, optional

Pound chicken breast until thin. Grate apples and set aside. Melt 3 tablespoons butter in a large skillet and sauté onion and garlic until tender. Stir in apple, bread crumbs, salt, rosemary, and basil. Stir over low heat until thoroughly mixed. Spoon 2 to 3 tablespoons apple mixture on boned side of each breast. Roll up, tucking in ends, and secure well. Coat with flour. Heat remaining 3 tablespoons butter in the skillet and brown rolls on all sides. Add apple juice and cognac. Simmer, covered, 25 to 30 minutes or until tender. Thicken pan juices with cornstarch and water, if desired. Serve sauce over rolls.
Yields: 10 to 12 servings

St. Uriel's Guild Cookbook
Church of St. Uriel the Archangel
Sea Girt, New Jersey

CHICKEN WINGS ORIENTAL

2 cloves garlic
1 tablespoon dry sherry
1 teaspoon ginger
1/2 cup soy sauce
1 tablespoon sesame seed oil
1/2 teaspoon black pepper
2 1/2 pounds chicken wings

Combine garlic and next 5 ingredients in a bowl; mix well. Marinate chicken wings in the garlic mixture for several hours or overnight. Place wings and marinade in broiler pan and broil until the chicken skin is crisp and meat is done. Serve with rice and Oriental vegetables.
Yields: 4 to 6 servings

Another Touch of Basil
St. Basil's Episcopal Church
Tahlequah, Oklahoma

CHICKEN CASSEROLE

2 cups diced baked chicken
1 cup chicken broth
1 cup bread crumbs or noodles
1 cup sour cream
1/2 cup green olives, chopped
1/2 cup chopped fresh
   mushrooms
1 cup grated cheese

Arrange chicken and next 5 ingredients in a baking dish. Top with cheese. Bake at 350° for 25 to 30 minutes.
Yields: 4 to 6 servings

Parish Recipes
Emmanuel Episcopal Church
Staunton, Virginia

CHICKEN ENCHILADA CASSEROLE

1/2 cup chopped onion
1 cup chopped green bell
   pepper
6 tablespoons butter or
   margarine, divided
2 cups chopped cooked chicken
1 (4-ounce) can chopped
   green chiles
1/4 cup all-purpose flour
1 teaspoon ground coriander
   seeds
1/2 teaspoon salt
1 (20-ounce) can chicken broth
1 cup sour cream
8 ounces Monterey Jack cheese,
   shredded and divided
12 (6-inch) flour tortillas

Cook onion and green pepper in skillet in 3 tablespoons butter until tender. Combine in bowl with chicken and chiles; set aside. Melt remaining 3 tablespoons butter in skillet; stir in flour, coriander seeds, and salt. Stir in chicken broth, stirring mixture well until thickened and bubbly. Remove from heat. Stir in sour cream and one-third of cheese. Stir 1/2 cup into chicken mixture. Place tortillas, one at a time, into hot sauce to soften. Fill each with about 2 tablespoons chicken mixture. Roll up and arrange in 9 × 13-inch baking dish. Pour remaining sauce over tortillas and sprinkle with remaining cheese. Bake, uncovered, at 350° for about 25 minutes or until lightly browned and bubbly.
Yields: 6 servings

Recipes from St. Paul's 1981
St. Paul's Episcopal Church
Naples, Florida

HOT BROWN

8 slices white bread,
  crusts removed
Chicken or turkey slices
Bechamel Sauce
Mornay Sauce
Sautéed mushrooms
Grated Parmesan cheese
8 slices bacon, fried
Sliced tomatoes

Toast white bread. Put 2 slices toast on oven-proof platter. Put slices of chicken or turkey on slices of toast. Cover with some Bechamel Sauce and then Mornay Sauce. Top with mushrooms, then a little Parmesan cheese. Place in hot oven until pale tan. Top with bacon and sliced tomatoes; cut into triangles if desired. Broil until hot and bubbly.
Yields: 4 servings

BECHAMEL SAUCE
1/3 cup butter
1/2 medium onion, minced
1/3 cup all-purpose flour
3 cups hot milk
1 teaspoon salt
Dash of cayenne pepper
Dash of nutmeg

Sauté onion in butter until clear. Add flour to make smooth paste. Add hot milk and seasonings. Stir constantly until thick, about 20 to 25 minutes, then strain.

MORNAY SAUCE
2 cups bechamel sauce
2 large egg yolks
1/2 cup grated Parmesan
  cheese
1 tablespoon butter
4 tablespoons whipping cream

Combine bechamel sauce with egg yolks in saucepan; simmer, stirring constantly. When hot and thick, remove from heat and add cheese and butter. Fold in whipping cream.

Gifts from the Kitchen
Church of the Advent
Cynthiana, Kentucky

❖

On the first day of Unleavened Bread, when the Passover lamb is sacrificed, his disciples said to him, "Where do you want us to go and make the preparations for you to eat the Passover?" So he sent two of his disciples, saying to them, "Go into the city, and a man carrying a jar of water will meet you; follow him, and wherever he enters, say to the owner of the house, 'The Teacher asks, Where is my guest room where I may eat the Passover with my disciples?' He will show you a large room upstairs, furnished and ready. Make preparations for us there." So the disciples set out and went to the city, and found everything as he had told them; and they prepared the Passover meal.

Mark 14:12–16
(Disciples prepare for the Passover)

ROAST GINGERED TURKEY BREAST

1 (1 1/2- to 2-pound) turkey
  breast, skinned and boned
4 cloves garlic, chopped
3/4 teaspoon ground cinnamon
2 tablespoons fresh ginger,
  peeled and chopped
2 teaspoons sugar
1 1/2 tablespoons balsamic
  vinegar
1/4 cup chicken stock
1 teaspoon sesame oil
1 teaspoon black sesame seeds
1 tablespoon soy sauce
1 green onion, chopped

Cut several 1/2-inch-deep slits in the thick part of the turkey meat. Combine the garlic and remaining ingredients in a large bowl; mix well. Place the turkey breast into the marinade, turning to coat it. Cover and refrigerate for up the 24 hours, turning occasionally. Remove turkey from marinade; reserve marinade. Allow turkey to come to room temperature. Place on a rack in a roasting pan. Roast at 350° for 15 to 20 minutes, or until it feels firm but springy to the touch. Baste once with reserved marinade while roasting. Allow turkey to stand for 5 minutes before slicing. Serve hot or cold.

Yields: about 4 servings

St. Philip's Cooks
St. Philip's Episcopal Church
Brevard, North Carolina

PICANTE TURKEY PIE

1 pound ground raw turkey
1 large onion, chopped
1 clove garlic, minced
3/4 cups picante sauce
1 teaspoon ground cumin
1/2 teaspoon salt
1 large tomato, seeded and
  chopped
1 1/2 cups chopped carrots
1/3 cup sliced olives
2 cups shredded Cheddar or
  Monterey Jack cheese, divided
2 tablespoons cornstarch
2 (9-inch) unbaked pie crusts

Brown turkey with onion and garlic in a 12-inch skillet; drain. Stir in picante sauce, cumin, and salt; simmer 5 minutes or until most of liquid has evaporated. Remove from heat; stir in tomato, carrots, olives, 1 1/2 cups cheese, and cornstarch. Sprinkle remaining 1/2 cup cheese over bottom of 1 pie crust fitted into a 9-inch pie plate. Spoon turkey mixture over cheese. Top with second crust, seal and flute edge. Cut slits in center of top crust to allow steam to escape. If desired, brush with heavy cream or beaten egg. Bake at 400° for 30 to 35 minutes or until golden brown. Let stand 5 minutes. Cut into wedges and serve with additional picante sauce.

Yields: 6 to 8 servings

The Loaves and Fishes, Act III
St. Stephen's Episcopal Church
Oak Ridge, Tennessee

ITALIAN-STYLE TURKEY BURGERS

1 pound lean ground turkey
1 tablespoon Worcestershire
  sauce
1/2 cup finely chopped onion
1/2 teaspoon garlic powder
1/4 cup seasoned bread crumbs
1/2 teaspoon Italian seasoning
Oatmeal
1/2 teaspoon black pepper

Combine all ingredients. Form into 4 (1/2-inch-thick) patties. Broil or grill for 4 minutes on each side or until they turn from pink to gray.
Yields: 4 servings

The Culinary Key
St. Peter's Episcopal Church
Cheshire, Connecticut

DAY-AFTER-THANKSGIVING QUICHE

1 (9-inch) pie crust
3/4 cup leftover turkey
1/2 cup diced ham
1/2 cup diced onion
1 cup diced mushrooms
1 cup grated mozzarella cheese
1/2 cup chopped broccoli,
  uncooked
4 large eggs
1/2 cup milk
1 teaspoon ground cloves
1 tablespoon chopped parsley
1 tablespoon chopped oregano
Dash of coarse ground black
  pepper
Additional cheese for garnish

Arrange turkey and next 5 ingredients in the pie crust. Combine the eggs, milk, and spices in a bowl; stir well. Pour egg mixture over dry ingredients. Sprinkle additional cheese on top. Bake for 1 hour at 350°. Test with knife in the center to check doneness.
Yields: 6 servings

Parish Collection
Stras Memorial Episcopal Church
Tazewell, Virginia

FEASTS ARE MADE FOR LAUGHTER; WINE GLADDENS LIFE, AND MONEY MEETS EVERY NEED.

ECCLESIASTES 10:19

ROCK CORNISH HENS

4 Cornish game hens
1 cup orange marmalade
1/2 teaspoon ginger
1/4 cup firmly packed brown
  sugar
3 tablespoons wine vinegar
Dash of cayenne pepper
2 tablespoons Worcestershire
  sauce
Salt and black pepper to taste
1/2 teaspoon curry powder

Cut hens in half. Place skin side down in baking dish. Combine remaining ingredients in a saucepan. Heat for 2 minutes. Pour over hens; let stand in refrigerator for 1/2 hour. Turn and baste. Baste again after 1/2 hour. Bake at 350° for 1 hour. Serve with wild rice and vegetables.
Yields: 4 servings

Heavenly Scents
Christ Episcopal Church
Toms River, New Jersey

DUCK WITH SAUERKRAUT AND APPLE STUFFING

6 ounces salt pork
1 large onion, coarsely chopped
3 tart green apples, peeled
  and diced
3 tablespoons brown sugar
Salt and freshly ground black
  pepper
Thyme, to taste
1–2 teaspoons caraway seeds
1 1/2 pounds sauerkraut,
  drained and minced
1 (3- to 4-pound) duck

Dice salt pork and heat in frying pan until transparent. Add onion and fry. Add apple, and toss with onion and salt pork. When golden, add brown sugar, salt, pepper, thyme, and caraway seeds. Remove from heat. Toss sauerkraut with apple and onion mixture. Wash duck inside and out. Rub cavity with salt and pepper. Stuff with apple/sauerkraut mixture and truss. Prick well with sharp fork and place duck on rack in roasting pan. Roast at 350° for 2 1/2 to 3 hours. Prick duck frequently to allow fat to escape.
Yields: 4 servings

Saint Peter's Recipes
St. Peter's Episcopal Church
Rockland, Maine

DUCK BREASTS ROYALE

1/2 pound butter
2/3 cup sherry
1/3 cup bourbon or brandy
1 tablespoon currant jelly
1 tablespoon Worcestershire
  sauce
4 duck breasts

Combine the butter and next 4 ingredients in a large skillet; bring to a boil. Add the duck breasts; cover and reduce heat. Cook for 12 minutes, turning once. Place the breasts on a platter, pour the sauce over them and serve immediately.
Yields: 4 servings

Entertaining Grace-fully
Grace Episcopal Church
Hutchinson, Kansas

PHEASANT IN GOURMET SAUCE

1/2 cup all-purpose flour
1 teaspoon salt
1 teaspoon paprika
1/8 teaspoon black pepper
1/8 teaspoon powdered
  sweet basil
2 pheasants, cut into pieces
1/4 cup shortening
1 clove garlic, crushed
1/4 cup chopped ripe olives
1/2 cup water
1/2 teaspoon Worcestershire
  sauce
1/2 cup white wine
Dash of all-purpose Greek
  seasoning

Combine flour, salt, paprika, pepper, and basil in a small bowl. Coat pheasant with seasoned flour; brown on all sides in shortening in large skillet. Add garlic, olives, water, and Worcestershire sauce. Cover tightly and simmer 45 minutes. Turn pheasant and add wine and Greek seasoning; cover and simmer 45 minutes or until tender. Add additional water if necessary to make sauce.
Yields: 6 to 8 servings

Episcopal Churchwomen Cookbook
Church of the Transfiguration
Ironwood, Michigan

DOVE BREASTS

2 dozen dove breasts
Seasoned all-purpose flour
1 stick butter
1 1/2 cups chopped celery
1/4 cup chopped onion
1/4 cup chopped green bell
   pepper
1 (14 1/2-ounce) can chicken
   broth
1/2 carton frozen chives
Mushrooms
4 ounces cooking wine
Salt and black pepper to taste
Pinch of curry

Flour dove breast with seasoned flour; melt butter in an electric skillet and brown breasts; remove breasts. Put celery, onion, and bell pepper into skillet, and cook until the onion is transparent. Put doves back in, turn skillet to simmer, add chicken broth, and simmer, covered, for 3 hours, adding more broth if necessary. A half hour before doves are done, add chives, mushrooms, wine, salt, pepper, and curry.

Yields: 6 to 8 servings

Best of Bayou Cuisine
St. Stephen's Episcopal Church
Indianola, Mississippi

THEN JESUS WAS LED UP BY THE SPIRIT

INTO THE WILDERNESS TO BE TEMPTED BY

THE DEVIL. HE FASTED FORTY DAYS AND

FORTY NIGHTS, AND AFTERWARDS HE WAS

FAMISHED. THE TEMPTER CAME AND SAID

Fish & Seafood

TO HIM, "IF YOU ARE THE SON OF GOD,

COMMAND THESE STONES TO BECOME

LOAVES OF BREAD." BUT HE ANSWERED, "IT

IS WRITTEN, 'ONE DOES NOT LIVE BY

BREAD ALONE, BUT BY EVERY WORD THAT

COMES FROM THE MOUTH OF GOD.'"

MATTHEW 4:1–4
(JESUS IS TEMPTED)

133

The Holy Table

Even as a little girl, Catherine Benincasa (who grew up to become Doctor of the Church St. Catherine of Siena) was extraordinarily devout. Later in life, this fourteenth-century woman spent herself in service to the marginalized and helped thousands by her writing and teaching. But it was at age six that she had a vision of Jesus in full vestments giving her his blessing; a year later, she made a total consecration of herself to God.

The extravagance of her devotion expressed itself in extravagant acts: at meals she used to pass her portion under the table to the family dog, for example, and offer up her hunger as a sacrifice. Having refused all offers of marriage, Catherine lived in her family's home in Siena. Throughout her life she had the habit of remaining in her bedroom for hours in contemplation, and she reported that sometimes, as she recited the Daily Office, Jesus himself would arrive to say the Psalms with her.

One evening, apparently, Catherine was in prayer at around the time for the evening meal. She was experiencing so much spiritual consolation that she would have preferred to remain in her room and ignore her family. After all, her parents, Jacobo and Lapa, had more often than not put roadblocks in her way, trying to dissuade her from concentrating so exclusively on God. Perhaps they had hoped for her to emulate her brothers and sisters, who had made more conventional choices to go into business or become skilled in housework. Or perhaps they just thought the intensity of her devotion a little overdone; saints are, after all, not always easy to live with.

So Catherine thought she would skip supper that day. But Jesus' voice spoke within her: no, go downstairs and sit at table. Your family needs you at the common meal. You can return and pray later.

Some may find this surprising: aren't prayer and worship by definition the highest possible activities, superior to anything else? Or if not prayer, then activism (in which Catherine certainly also took part)—going out into the world and changing things for the better in God's name? What spiritual value could a homely little thing like showing up for dinner with Mom and Dad have? It doesn't sound religious to me.

Yet it is religious. In a faith that tells us that God took on flesh, ate and drank with us, and left us a meal to remember him by, we cannot allow ourselves to label only a select few of our activities as spiritual and all the others as secular. Any separation between the two is artificial.

Catherine of Siena did not walk downstairs and take her place at family dinner because she needed to stop doing something sacred and give a half-hour to the secular. She heard Jesus calling her to join her family at the evening meal because she apparently needed a reminder that the spiritual life took place just as much there as within her private bedroom sanctuary.

Sometimes, as we sit down to dinner, we may need that same reminder. The sacred can always be found within the secular, for by his presence on earth Jesus has infused everything from the pits to the Pleiades with holiness. It is not that the altar is no more holy than a table: it's that if you pay attention, every table can be as holy as the altar.

BAKED ROUGHY

2 pounds orange roughy fillets
Salt and black pepper to taste
3/4 cup sour cream
1/4 cup bread crumbs,
    finely crumbled
1/4 teaspoon minced garlic
2 small green onions, chopped
1/3 cup Parmesan cheese
1 teaspoon paprika

Clean fish and wipe dry. Grease shallow baking pan and arrange fish in a single layer. Season lightly. In a bowl, mix sour cream, bread crumbs, garlic, and green onions. Spread sauce over fish. Sprinkle with the Parmesan and paprika. Bake at 400° for about 10 minutes or until fish flakes easily with a fork.

Yields: 4 servings

Grace Cooks
Grace Episcopal Church
Chattanooga, Tennessee

BAKED RED SNAPPER

4 large onions, chopped,
    divided
1/2 cup butter, divided
4 cups bread cubes
1/4 cup white wine
Salt and black pepper to taste
1 (6–8 pound) red snapper
1 tablespoon olive oil
1 clove garlic, minced
2 1/2 cups canned tomatoes
6 cups water
3 sprigs parsley
1 bay leaf
1/4 teaspoon thyme leaves
1 whole clove
2 cups chopped celery

In a large skillet sauté half of the onions in half of the butter until they are brown around the edges. Add the bread cubes and wine. Fry the mixture for 10 minutes, stirring. Add the salt and pepper. Remove the mixture from the heat and allow it to cool. Wash the fish and dry it with paper towels. Rub the cavity with the olive oil, salt, and pepper. Stuff the cavity with the bread mixture and place it in a generously buttered, large baking pan. In a large skillet, sauté the remaining onions and the garlic in the remaining butter. Add the tomatoes, water, parsley, bay leaf, thyme, clove, and celery and mix well. Pour the sauce over the fish and bake it at 350° for 20 minutes. Increase oven temperature to 450° and continue baking for 20 minutes or until done. Transfer the fish to a warm serving platter. Remove bay leaf from the sauce. Serve the fish with the sauce spooned over it.

Yields: 4 to 6 servings

La Bonne Cuisine
All Saints' Episcopal Church
River Ridge, Louisiana

BAKED FILLET OF HADDOCK WITH SESAME SEED CRUMBS

1 1/2 pounds haddock
1 teaspoon salt
6 pats margarine
3 cups fresh bread crumbs
1/4 teaspoon black pepper
2 tablespoons toasted sesame
  seeds
1/3 cup margarine

Cut fish into six pieces. Place in a greased 9-inch square baking pan. Rub salt on each piece of fish and top each with margarine pat. Combine bread crumbs and remaining ingredients in a bowl; spread over fish, covering completely. Bake at 350° for 25 to 30 minutes or until brown.
Yields: 4 to 6 servings

St. Uriel's Guild Cookbook
Church of St. Uriel the Archangel
Sea Girt, New Jersey

BAKED STUFFED FLOUNDER

1/2 cup chopped celery
1/2 cup chopped green onions
1 clove garlic, minced
1 stick butter, divided
1 1/2 cups moistened bread
  cubes
1/2 pound boiled shrimp,
  chopped
1/2 pound crabmeat
2 tablespoons chopped parsley
1 large egg, slightly beaten
Salt, black pepper, and cayenne
  pepper
4 flounder fillets

Sauté celery, onion, and garlic in large skillet in 1/2 stick butter over low heat. Add bread, shrimp, crabmeat, parsley, and egg; mix well. Season with salt, pepper, and cayenne. Place stuffing between each 2 fillets. Melt remaining 1/2 stick butter in a shallow baking pan. Place fish in pan. Bake, covered, at 375° for 25 minutes or until fish flakes very easily with a fork. Remove cover; bake for another 5 minutes.
Yields: 2 servings

The Culinary Key
St. Peter's Episcopal Church
Cheshire, Connecticut

As Jesus was walking along, he saw a man called Matthew sitting at the tax booth; and he said to him, "Follow me." And he got up and followed him.

And as he sat at dinner in the house, many tax collectors and sinners came and were sitting with him and his disciples. When the Pharisees saw this, they said to his disciples, "Why does your teacher eat with tax collectors and sinners?" But when he heard this, he said, "Those who are well have no need of a physician, but those who are sick. Go and learn what this means, 'I desire mercy, not sacrifice.' For I have come to call not the righteous but sinners."

Matthew 9:9–13
(Jesus eats with sinners at Matthew's house)

LEMON BUTTER MAHI MAHI

3 pounds mahi mahi fillets,
    wedged
Garlic salt
Black pepper
1 stick butter
1–2 cloves garlic, crushed
Juice of 1 lemon
Vegetable oil
Capers and/or sliced
    mushrooms

Season fish with garlic salt and black pepper and place evenly in a baking dish. Melt butter in a saucepan and sauté garlic. Add the lemon juice and a few drops of cooking oil. Stir in capers and mushrooms, if desired. Pour sauce over fillets. Bake at 400° for 20 minutes or until fish flakes when tested with a fork.
Yields: 6 servings

All Saints' Cook
All Saints' Episcopal Church
Kapaa, Kauai, Hawaii

SWORDFISH TERIYAKI

1 1/4 pounds swordfish fillets
1/3 cup soy sauce
2 tablespoons light brown
    sugar
1 teaspoon grated fresh ginger
1 clove garlic, pressed
2 tablespoons bourbon
2 medium sweet potatoes
1 small red bell pepper
1 small yellow bell pepper
1 small green bell pepper
4 cherry tomatoes
1 fresh pineapple
Pineapple juice

Slice fish crosswise to make 12 slices. Thread onto bamboo skewers. In a rectangular baking dish, combine soy sauce, brown sugar, ginger, garlic, and bourbon. Add skewered fish. Rotate to coat on all sides. Cover and refrigerate 1 hour. Peel sweet potatoes; cut into 12 chunks. Simmer in boiling water until just tender, about 15 minutes; drain well. Wash peppers; remove seeds and cut into 8 squares. Wash and drain tomatoes and pineapple; slice pineapple in half and crosswise. Remove and save fronds. Peel top half of pineapple. Cut crosswise into 1/3-inch-thick slices. Cut each in half and remove core. Hollow out bottom of pineapple. Refrigerate pineapple meat from center for another use. Place pineapple bowl on serving platter garnished with fronds. Thread fruit and vegetables onto 4 skewers.

Heat broiler. Arrange fish on broiler pan; brush with the soy sauce marinade. Broil 3 inches from heat until just brown, about 3 minutes. Turn fish. Add skewered fruit and vegetables. Brush with marinade and broil until just browned, about 3 minutes. Arrange on platter over fronds. Add pineapple juice to marinade; bring to a boil in a saucepan. Pour into pineapple bowl for dipping sauce.
Yields: 4 servings

Memories from the Kitchen
St. Paul's Episcopal Church
Mount Lebanon, Pennsylvania

FISH FILLETS WITH TARRAGON BUTTER

2 tablespoons white wine
 vinegar or tarragon vinegar
1/2 teaspoon dried tarragon or
 1 teaspoon fresh, chopped
1/2 cup butter, cut into 8 pieces
1 1/2 pounds fish fillets, such as
 red snapper, scrod, sea bass,
 or sea trout
2 tablespoons vegetable oil
Salt and black pepper to taste
Paprika
2–3 tablespoons chopped fresh
 parsley

Put vinegar and tarragon in small pan and boil until reduced to one-third. Over very low heat whisk in butter, one piece at a time, letting each piece dissolve before adding next piece. Chill mixture in small bowl until able to roll into cylinder 1 inch thick, about 1/2 hour. Wrap cylinder in plastic wrap and chill at least 15 minutes. With sharp knife dipped in hot water, slice into pieces 1/8 inch thick. Refrigerate.

Brush fish with oil and scant salt, pepper, and paprika. Broil or grill 4 inches from heat for 6 to 8 minutes or bake at 450° for 8 to 10 minutes. Top fillets with tarragon butter discs, sprinkle lightly with paprika and serve immediately.
Yields: 4 to 6 servings

Heavenly Delights
St. Paul's Episcopal Church
Waterloo, New York

FISH PUDDING

1 2/3 pounds pollock, red
 snapper, or cod, cooked and
 deboned
2 tablespoons grated onion
2 tablespoons plus 2 teaspoons
 lemon juice
1/3 stick butter, melted
3 tablespoons cracker crumbs
1 teaspoon salt
1/3 cup milk
Light dash of Tabasco sauce
1/4 teaspoon baking soda
1/4 cup chopped parsley
1 tablespoon dry sherry
4 large eggs, well beaten
Cracker crumbs to cover
Butter pats

Combine fish and next 10 ingredients in a two-quart casserole. Stir in well-beaten eggs. Smooth mixture, cover with cracker crumbs, and dot with butter. Bake at 450° for 15 minutes; reduce heat to 350° and bake for 30 minutes or until set. Serve with potatoes and slaw.
Yields: 4 to 6 servings

The Shrimp Mousse and Other Waffle Shop Recipes
Calvary Episcopal Church
Memphis, Tennessee

PENNE WITH TUNA, CAPERS, AND TOMATO SAUCE

Olive oil
2 cloves garlic, minced
2 pounds fresh tuna
2 cups tomato sauce
1/2 cup white wine
2 tablespoons capers
1 pound penne pasta

In a large sauté pan, heat olive oil; sauté the garlic until golden brown; remove from the pan, and discard. Add the fresh tuna to the garlic oil; sauté until white. Remove the tuna from the pan. Add tomato sauce and white wine; simmer for 15 minutes. While the sauce is simmering, break up the cooked tuna into pieces; add to the sauce. Add the capers; simmer for 15 minutes. Taste for seasoning and caper flavor; add more capers if desired. Turn heat to low while pasta is cooking. Cook pasta according to package directions; drain; place on a warm serving platter. Pour tuna sauce over pasta. Serve immediately.
Yields: 6 servings

Holy Cow, Chicago's Cooking!
Church of the Holy Comforter
Kenilworth, Illinois

SALMON CHEESE LOAF

2 cups flaked cooked or
  canned salmon
1 1/2 cups grated cheese
1 large egg, beaten
3 tablespoons milk
1/2 teaspoon salt
Dash of black pepper
Cracker or bread crumbs
1 tablespoon melted butter

Combine salmon and next 5 ingredients in a bowl. Add enough cracker crumbs to make a stiff mixture. Press into a loaf pan. Cover with melted butter and additional cracker crumbs. Bake at 375° for 45 minutes or until golden brown.
Yields: 4 servings

St. Stephen's Parish Cookbook
St. Stephen's Episcopal Church
Schuylerville, New York

SALMON SOUFFLÉ

2 tablespoons margarine
2 tablespoons all-purpose flour
3/4 cup milk
Salt and black pepper to taste
1 large egg, separated
1 cup shredded Cheddar cheese
1 (16-ounce) can salmon,
  drained and flaked
12 saltine crackers, rolled fine
Butter

Melt margarine and add flour. Slowly add the milk, stirring until the sauce thickens (more milk may be needed if sauce seems too thick). Season to taste. Remove from heat; add beaten egg yolk, then add beaten egg white. Stir well. Place a layer of cheese in baking dish, then salmon, then cracker crumbs, alternating until all ingredients are used. Pour sauce over top. Dot the top with butter, and bake at 375° for about 20 minutes.
Yields: 2 servings

What's Cooking?
St. John's Episcopal Church
Huntington, L.I., New York

POACHED SALMON WITH DILL SAUCE

1 shallot, chopped
1/2 cup dry white wine
1 sprig fresh thyme
12 whole peppercorns
1 cup bottled clam juice
1/2 cup heavy cream
1/2 bunch dill, chopped
Salt and black pepper to taste
1 salmon fillet (with skin),
  about 3 pounds
2 quarts water
1/2 cup distilled vinegar
1 carrot, peeled and chopped
1 red onion, peeled and
  chopped
1 leek, chopped
12 allspice berries
1 tablespoon peppercorns
6 dill sprigs (for garnish)
18–24 cooked red new potatoes
  (with skins)

Place the chopped shallot, wine, thyme, and 12 peppercorns in a saucepan. Bring to a boil; continue boiling until liquid is reduced to 4 tablespoons. Add clam juice and cream; return to a boil. Reduce heat and simmer about 5 to 8 minutes. Strain and season with chopped dill, salt, and pepper.

Cut salmon into 6 portions with skin on. Place the water, vinegar, carrot, onion, leek, allspice, and peppercorns in a heavy pot; bring to a boil. Add salmon. Reduce to a simmer and poach 6 to 8 minutes, or until fish is done but still a little soft inside. Remove salmon from liquid and divide among 6 plates. Strain vegetables and spices from liquid and arrange over salmon. Spoon 1 tablespoon sauce on each fish portion, garnish with dill sprigs, if desired, and serve immediately with the red potatoes.
Yields: 6 servings

Celebrating Our Roots
St. Thomas' Episcopal Church
Knoxville, Tennessee

SCALLOPED SCALLOPS

1/2 cup butter
1/2 cup soft bread crumbs
1 cup cracker crumbs
1 pint scallops, cut up
3/4 cup medium cream or
  top milk
Salt and black pepper to taste

Melt butter in a small skillet and add bread and cracker crumbs; mix well. Butter baking dish and alternate layers of scallops and crumbs. Pour cream over top; season with salt and pepper. Bake at 400° for 25 minutes.
Yields: 4 servings

Treasure of Personal Recipes
Church of Our Fathers
Hulls Cove, Maine

SEAFOOD CASSEROLE

1/2 cup chopped onion
1/2 cup chopped green bell
  pepper
1/2 cup vegetable oil
1/2 cup all-purpose flour
1 teaspoon dry mustard
1 cup milk
1 cup plus 1 tablespoon
  shredded sharp cheese
1 (6-ounce) can crabmeat
2 cups cooked lobster meat,
  cut up
1 pound cooked shrimp
1 1/2 cups canned tomatoes
2 teaspoons Worcestershire
  sauce
1/2 teaspoon salt

Sauté onion and pepper in oil for 10 minutes in a large skillet. Blend in flour, mustard, milk, and 1 cup cheese. Add crabmeat, lobster, and shrimp. Blend in tomatoes, Worcestershire sauce, and salt. Spoon into casserole; sprinkle with 1 tablespoon cheese. Bake at 450° for 15 to 20 minutes. Serve over rice.
Yields: 4 to 6 servings

Loaves and Fishes
St. Mark's Episcopal Church
Chenango Bridge, New York

HE TOLD THEM ANOTHER PARABLE: "THE KINGDOM OF HEAVEN IS LIKE YEAST THAT A WOMAN TOOK AND MIXED IN WITH THREE MEASURES OF FLOUR UNTIL ALL OF IT WAS LEAVENED."

MATTHEW 13:33
(JESUS TELLS THE PARABLE OF THE YEAST)

DOWN EAST LOBSTER AND CLAM BAKE

3 bushels seaweed (rook weed),
  fresh and wet, divided
25 pounds steamer clams,
  washed
25 live Maine lobsters
  (1 to 1 1/2 pounds)
25 ears fresh corn-on-the-cob,
  husked
2 pounds butter, melted

You will need 3 armfuls hardwood, paper, and kindling. Place 2 bushels of wet seaweed on a 3 × 3-inch sheet iron over outdoor fireplace. Cover with cheesecloth. Place clams in center of pile (make a depression). Place live lobsters on top of and about the clams. Place husked corn on top of lobsters (add any kind of vegetables, seafood, or meat in tinfoil or net bags). Cover all with more cheesecloth. Cover entire bake with heavy (red/orange) builder's paper (available in rolls at building supply outlets). It will take 2 or more sheets to cover bake. Place fist-sized rocks or bricks along edges of paper, keeping paper back from edge of sheet metal to prevent flames from setting it afire. It is important to make paper snug to trap the steam inside. Take care not to rip holes in paper as this will allow the steam to escape. Place remaining bushel of seaweed on top of paper to hold down seams and moisten paper.

Use hardwood to build a medium heat fire in fireplace. Use 3- to 4-inch round or split logs as this will allow you to regulate the heat more easily. Keep fire burning evenly to create steam but not to burn the seaweed. (Feel top of paper and watch for steam as you cook to ascertain that the bake is cooking along.) A medium fire should cook lobsters thoroughly in 1 hour. Open a corner of bake (carefully, so as not to rip paper) and check the doneness of lobsters after about 45 minutes. Butter for dipping can be melted on top of bake.
Yields: 25 servings

Favorite Recipes Home-Style
St. Andrew's Episcopal Church
Readfield, Maine

ANGEL HAIR PASTA WITH LOBSTER SAUCE

1/2 cup chopped sun-dried
   tomatoes
4–5 green onions
6–8 fresh mushrooms
3/4 cup sliced mixed red and
   green peppers
1 tablespoon olive oil
2 tablespoons unsalted butter
4–6 slices of bacon, fried and
   drained
1–2 cups chopped cooked
   lobster meat (may substitute
   shrimp)
1 (16-ounce) package angel
   hair pasta
2 cups heavy cream
1 tablespoon lemon juice
Freshly ground black pepper
Lemon slices for garnish
4–5 fresh basil leaves, chopped
Fresh spinach (optional)

Sauté vegetables with olive oil and butter in skillet until tender. Do not overcook. Crumble bacon. Add bacon and lobster to vegetables; stir to coat and mix. Cook pasta according to package directions and drain. Combine drained pasta with vegetables, cream, lemon juice and pepper to taste. Heat until hot; do not boil. Garnish with lemon slices and fresh basil leaf. Serve on bed of fresh spinach, if desired.

Yields: 6 servings

Holy Cow, Chicago's Cooking!
Church of the Holy Comforter
Kenilworth, Illinois

STIR-FRIED GARLIC SHRIMP

2 large cloves garlic,
   finely chopped
2 teaspoons vegetable oil
1 pound peeled fresh or
   frozen shrimp
3 cups mushrooms, sliced
   (about 8 ounces)
1 cup green onions, cut in
   1-inch sections
1/4 cup dry white wine
2 cups hot cooked rice

Sauté garlic in oil for about 1 minute in a 10-inch nonstick skillet. Add shrimp; stir fry for 1 minute. Add mushrooms, onions, and wine. Continue to cook until shrimp are just pink and vegetables are hot, about 2 to 4 minutes. Serve over rice.

Yields: 4 servings

Angel Food
St. Timothy's Episcopal Church
Signal Mountain, Tennessee

SAVANNAH SHRIMP CASSEROLE

3 tablespoons butter or
  margarine
3 tablespoons all-purpose flour
1 pint half-and-half
1 teaspoon Worcestershire
  sauce
1/2 teaspoon paprika
2 tablespoons ketchup
2 tablespoons sherry
1 cup grated cheese
1 pound fresh shrimp, cooked
1 pound crabmeat
1 (16-ounce) can artichoke
  hearts, drained and thinly
  sliced
Buttered bread crumbs

Melt butter in a large skillet. Stir in flour. Add half-and-half, stirring constantly until thickened. Stir in Worcestershire sauce, paprika, and ketchup. Add sherry and cheese; blend well until cheese melts. Layer shrimp, crabmeat, artichokes, and sauce in a baking dish. Sprinkle with bread crumbs. Bake at 400° for 20 minutes.
Yields: 8 servings

St. David's Cookbook
St. David's Episcopal Church
Nashville, Tennessee

SHRIMP MOUSSE

10 pounds cooked salad shrimp
Cooking spray
2 large cans tomato soup
4 (10-ounce) cans tomato soup
6 (8-ounce) packages cream
  cheese
1 cup plus 2 tablespoons
  gelatin dissolved in
  4 1/3 cups water
2 cups lemon juice
1 cup Worcestershire sauce
1/2 teaspoon Tabasco sauce
12 cups finely chopped celery
4 cups finely chopped green
  bell pepper
1/2 cup pureed onion
1 jar Durkees mustard
12 cups homemade mayonnaise

Cook shrimp and distribute evenly in 10 × 18-inch pans coated with cooking spray. Place tomato soup in a large kettle over low heat. Add cream cheese in small lumps. Heat to dissolve, stirring often with a wire whisk until mixture is hot and cheese has disappeared. Turn off heat. Add gelatin and stir until dissolved. Add remaining ingredients; stir well. Pour over shrimp. Cover with plastic wrap so that wrap is touching the surface of the mousse. Refrigerate. Cut into squares to serve.
Yields: about 40 servings

The Shrimp Mousse and Other Waffle Shop Recipes
Calvary Episcopal Church
Memphis, Tennessee

CRAB IMPERIAL

1 pound crabmeat
3 tablespoons melted butter
1 teaspoon prepared mustard
1 large onion, chopped
1 tablespoon Worcestershire
   sauce
3 tablespoons mayonnaise
1 large egg, beaten
1 cup bread crumbs, divided
Butter

Combine all ingredients, except 1/2 cup bread crumbs and butter, in a large bowl. Spoon evenly into individual dishes or into 1 large baking dish. Cover with remaining 1/2 cup bread crumbs and dot with butter. Bake at 375° for 30 minutes or until bubbly.
Yields: 4 to 6 servings

St. Mary's Favorite Recipes
St. Mary's Episcopal Church, Fleeton
Reedville, Virginia

OUTER BANKS CRAB CAKES

1 large egg
1/4 cup finely chopped green
   bell pepper
1/8 cup finely chopped onion
2 tablespoons mayonnaise
1 tablespoon Worcestershire
   sauce
1 teaspoon fresh horseradish
1 teaspoon dry mustard
1 dash lemon juice
1/2 teaspoon Old Bay seasoning
1/2 teaspoon salt
1/4 teaspoon black pepper
1/4 teaspoon paprika
1/8 teaspoon cayenne pepper
Dash of thyme
Dash of oregano
4 slices dry bread, finely
   crumbled
1 pound crabmeat (at least half
   back fin), steamed

Beat egg in large bowl until yellow. Add all ingredients except bread crumbs and crabmeat. Mix well until mayonnaise is blended. Add bread crumbs and mix well. Add crabmeat last (and carefully so as not to bruise meat). Use hands to mix well. If mixture is a bit "soupy," add another slice of crumbled bread. The mixture has to cohere so it does not separate while frying. Refrigerate for 1/2 hour. Shape into 6 cakes. Fry in heavy skillet filled with 1/3 inch vegetable oil until bottom is browned. Turn carefully and brown the other side. Use medium frying heat (high heat will cause the cakes to brown too fast and burn on the outside). Serve with cocktail sauce.
Yields: 4 servings

Pohickory Cookbook
Pohick Church
Lorton, Virginia

CRAB-SAUCED LASAGNA

2 tablespoons butter
1/4 cup minced onion
1 (4-ounce) can sliced
  mushrooms
1/4 teaspoon garlic powder
2 (8-ounce) cans tomato sauce
  with tomato bits
1 tablespoon parsley
1/4 teaspoon dill
1 teaspoon salt
1/4 teaspoon oregano
1/4 teaspoon dried basil
2 (7-ounce) cans crabmeat
1 (16-ounce) package lasagna
  noodles
1 cup sour cream
3/4 cup grated mozzarella
  cheese
2 cups grated Cheddar cheese

Melt butter in a large skillet; sauté onion, mushrooms, and garlic powder until onion is golden. Stir in tomato sauce, parsley, and spices. Simmer for 20 minutes. Add crabmeat. Cook noodles according to package directions; drain. Layer noodles, crab sauce, sour cream, and cheeses in large baking dish in order listed. Repeat layers. Bake at 350° for 30 minutes or until bubbly and cheese is melted.
Yields: 8 servings

Parish Collection
St. Hilary's Church
Fort Myers, Florida

CRABMEAT, SOUTH CAROLINA STYLE

1 stalk celery, chopped
1 green bell pepper, chopped
2 tablespoons chopped onion
1 clove garlic, chopped
2 tablespoons vegetable oil
1 teaspoon Worcestershire
  sauce
1 tablespoon A-1 Sauce
1/2 teaspoon Tabasco sauce
1/2 cup ketchup
1/2 cup mayonnaise
1 tablespoon chopped parsley
1 pound crabmeat
8 teaspoons Parmesan cheese
Melted butter
Paprika

Sauté celery, green pepper, onion, and garlic in oil in a large skillet until tender but not brown; remove from heat. Stir in Worcestershire sauce and next 5 ingredients; mix well. Divide the crabmeat among 8 cooking shells. Top each with equal amounts of sauce, 1 teaspoon Parmesan cheese, a little melted butter, and paprika. Bake at 450° for 12 to 15 minutes, or until nicely browned.
Yields: 8 servings

The Way to a Man's Heart
All Saints' Episcopal Church
Norton, Virginia

CRABBY POTATOES

2 large baking potatoes
1 cup light sour cream
1/4 cup fresh chives, chopped
2 tablespoons fresh basil,
  chopped
1/2 teaspoon seasoned salt
1 cup cooked crabmeat
2 dashes cayenne pepper
1/4 cup parsley, chopped
Paprika

Roast potatoes in oven. Mix together sour cream, chives, basil, salt, crabmeat, and cayenne pepper; blend well. Split hot baked potatoes and spoon crab mixture over each. Sprinkle with parsley and paprika.
Yields: 2 servings

Parish Collection
Church of the Cross
Bluffton, South Carolina

CRAB OPEN-FACED SANDWICHES

1 (7-ounce) can crabmeat or
  1/2 pound fresh crabmeat,
  drained
1/4 cup mayonnaise
1 (3-ounce) package softened
  cream cheese
1 large egg yolk
1 teaspoon finely chopped
  onion
1/4 teaspoon prepared mustard
1 tablespoon sour cream
Dash of salt
3 English muffins, split and
  toasted
2 tablespoons butter or
  margarine, softened
Paprika

Stir together crabmeat and mayonnaise in a small bowl; set aside. Beat together cream cheese, egg yolk, onion, mustard, sour cream, and salt until creamy and smooth. Spread toasted muffin halves with butter, then with crabmeat mixture. Top with cream cheese mixture. Sprinkle with paprika. Place on baking sheet; broil 5 to 6 inches from heat for 2 to 3 minutes or until tops are bubbly and golden. Ingredients may be prepared ahead, but do not top muffins until ready to broil.
Yields: 3 to 6 servings

Cooking with Grace
Grace Church
Bath, Maine

OYSTER QUICHE

12 ounces oysters
4 large eggs
3/4 cup table cream
2 tablespoons minced shallots
  or green onions
1/2 cup shredded Swiss cheese
1 1/2 tablespoons melted butter
1/2 teaspoon salt
Pinch cayenne
Pinch nutmeg
5 slices cooked bacon
1 (9-inch) baked pie crust
Butter

Heat oysters in a small skillet until edges just begin to curl. Place eggs, cream, shallots, cheese, butter, salt, cayenne, and nutmeg in a mixing bowl; blend with a whisk. Place bacon in bottom of pie crust, then oysters. Add cheese mixture in middle of pie. Dot top with butter. Bake at 375° for 30 minutes.
Yields: 6 servings

Not by Bread Alone
Trinity Episcopal Church
Oak Ridge, Virginia

MAINE MUSSELS MARINARA

3–4 pounds mussels
8 ounces salsa
1/4 cup butter
3 tablespoons olive oil
1 1/2 cup red onion, grated
4 garlic cloves, minced
1 teaspoon dried rosemary
1 teaspoon dried oregano
1 tablespoon fresh parsley,
  chopped
1 cup dry white wine

Place the mussels in a large kettle and cover with cold water. Inspect each and discard any that do not close when tapped gently with a knife. Scrub each. Scrape off any barnacles with a knife, and debeard. In another large kettle, combine the remaining ingredients and simmer for 30 seconds. Add the scrubbed mussels, and more wine if desired, and continue simmering until all the shells are open. Serve as a main course over your favorite pasta or as an appetizer with crusty bread.
Yields: 4 to 6 main course servings

Cooking with St. Francis by the Sea II
St. Francis by the Sea Episcopal Church
Blue Hill, Maine

NEW ORLEANS CREOLE CRAWFISH

3/4 cup finely chopped onion
3/4 cup finely chopped celery
1 teaspoon garlic, minced
4 teaspoons butter
1 (16-ounce) can whole
  tomatoes
1 (8-ounce) can tomato sauce
2 teaspoons salt
1 teaspoon sugar
1 teaspoon Worcestershire sauce
1 teaspoon chili powder
1 teaspoon Tabasco sauce
1 pound crawfish tails
1/2 cup chopped green bell
  pepper
2 teaspoons cornstarch
2 teaspoons water

Sauté onion, celery, and garlic in butter in a large skillet until tender. Add tomatoes, tomato sauce, salt, sugar, Worcestershire sauce, chili powder, and Tabasco sauce. Simmer, uncovered, 45 minutes. Add crawfish and bell pepper. Cover and simmer 5 minutes. Mix cornstarch with 2 teaspoons water and add to crawfish mixture. Simmer until mixture thickens. Serve with hot rice.
Yields: 2 to 4 servings

A Book of Favorite Recipes
Church of the Redeemer
Ruston, Louisiana

AND YOU, TAKE WHEAT AND BARLEY, BEANS

AND LENTILS, MILLET AND SPELT; PUT

THEM INTO ONE VESSEL, AND MAKE BREAD

Vegetables & Side Dishes

FOR YOURSELF. DURING THE NUMBER OF

DAYS THAT YOU LIE ON YOUR SIDE,

THREE HUNDRED AND NINETY DAYS, YOU

SHALL EAT IT.

EZEKIEL 4:9

God's Economy

"Let's take some of that zucchini to church," a family member triumphantly blurts out in late August. It sounds pretty good to you, despairing as you are at the piles of squash that have been building up in your kitchen like something out of *The Sorcerer's Apprentice*. Squash soup, ratatouille, zucchini boats, zucchini bread—at home it feels like the parade will never end.

You take your place in a venerable, if informal and uncelebrated, tradition, when it first occurs to you to carry the extra zucchini to the Sunday service. Everyone does it. At the same season the truly generous bring their tomatoes, juicy and red. Some of them have little flaws: the skin has burst or there is a scar of some sort. But nobody minds. We are not the vegetable police; we are your church family.

Sometimes it is anonymous zucchini, left out on a table in the narthex. "Who brought this?" someone from the singles' group will ask, hefting a bag in his hand and contemplating a quick stir-fry; but the usher will just shrug. At other times, the gardener takes a more hands-on route, circulating during coffee hour. "Tomatoes, anybody; who wants some fresh tomatoes? I picked them this morning."

Among any congregation are a few people one could call the vegetable-poor—families with no refrigerators who need help to meet the food budget, or college students cooking on a hot plate, or city dwellers in apartments with asphalt backyards. The vegetable-poor love August in churches. Since I have been one of them, I understand why. I remember the forced nonchalance with which I'd linger at coffee hour, accept someone's brown bag and peek inside, cheering silently at the anticipation of tasting real garden produce. I have even bitten right into a small, juicy, doubtless unwashed tomato right in the church parking lot.

I wonder where we would bring our excess vegetables if not to our parish? The habit of sharing them with the neighborhood is no longer that common, and for many of us our extended family is far away. Maybe we could donate them to a feeding program, but the quantity is so small it doesn't make sense. An institution can't really use three cucumbers or one bell pepper. So we take our modest little bags to church, where we know they will be welcomed.

We bring our own offering, as small and perhaps flawed as it may be, to our parish community. Our amateurish loaves and unprepared fish, our seven zucchini—yes, even the one that grew wrong and curved in on itself. Such gifts are always welcome in church. Someone can use them. That's God's economy. Someone in the community of the baptized needs what you have and think is ordinary.

And you doubtless need something each one of them has to offer, as well. Maybe, say, a good recipe for zucchini.

BROCCOLI PUFF

2 (10-ounce) packages frozen
 chopped broccoli
1 cup all-purpose baking mix
1 cup milk
2 large eggs
1/2 teaspoon salt
1 cup shredded Cheddar cheese

Cook broccoli according to package directions; drain.
Combine baking mix, milk, eggs, and salt in a bowl; mix
until smooth. Stir in broccoli and cheese. Spoon into a
greased 5 1/2-cup soufflé dish or 1/2-quart baking dish.
Bake at 325° for 1 hour or until knife inserted in center
comes out clean.
Yields: 6 servings

Keep the Feast
Church of the Ascension
Middletown, Ohio

SWEET AND SOUR GREEN BEANS

4 slices bacon
1/3 cup sugar
1/3 cup vinegar
1/3 cup water
2 pounds fresh green beans,
 cooked, or 2 (16-ounce) cans
 cut green beans, drained
2 tablespoons minced onion

Fry bacon in a skillet until crisp; drain, reserving 1/4 cup
drippings. Crumble bacon and set aside. Combine sugar,
vinegar, and water with reserved drippings in the skillet;
stir well. Combine beans and onion in a saucepan; pour
sugar mixture over top and stir well. Let stand for 2 hours.
Heat before serving. Top with crumbled bacon.
Yields: 4 to 6 servings

The Vicar's Guild Cookbook
Episcopal Church of the Resurrection
Loudon, Tennessee

RANCH HOUSE BEANS

2 (10-ounce) packages frozen
 lima beans
1/4 cup dark brown sugar
1 1/2–2 pounds canned tomatoes
1/2 cup chopped onion
1 teaspoon chili powder
1 teaspoon salt
1/2 teaspoon garlic powder
1/4 teaspoon cayenne pepper
1/8 teaspoon black pepper
6 slices bacon

Combine all ingredients except bacon in a baking dish;
mix well. Place bacon on top of mixture. Bake, covered, at
350° for 2 1/2 hours.
Yields: 6 to 8 servings

Food and Gladness
St. Francis Episcopal Church
Norris, Tennessee

BAKED BEANS

1 quart dry beans
3 teaspoons salt
5 tablespoons sugar
4 tablespoons molasses
1 teaspoon mustard
1/4 teaspoon ginger
1/4 teaspoon black pepper
1 small onion
1 small piece salt pork

Soak beans overnight; then drain and cover with cold water in a large saucepan. Bring to a boil, and cook just until the skins begin to come off. Drain and spoon into a bean pot. Combine the salt and next 5 ingredients with a little water; mix well and pour over beans. Add the small onion near the top of the pot. Fill bean pot with water. Make several cuts in top of salt pork and place on top. Bake, covered, at 300° for 1 hour; reduce heat to 250° and cook for 4 hours or until beans are brown. Add water at intervals if needed.
Yields: 6 to 8 servings

Miracles in the Kitchen
St. Luke's Episcopal Church
Farmington, Maine

CREAMED CABBAGE CASSEROLE

1 small head cabbage
6 tablespoons butter
4 tablespoons all-purpose flour
2 cups milk
1/2 teaspoon salt
1/2 cup bread crumbs
4 tablespoons melted butter
Grated Parmesan cheese,
  optional

Chop cabbage into fourths. Parboil in salted water in a saucepan for 10 minutes; drain. Melt 6 tablespoons butter in a skillet. Stir in flour; cook until bubbly. Slowly add milk and salt. Cook, stirring constantly, until sauce thickens. Layer cabbage then sauce in a baking dish; repeat layers until ingredients are used. Combine bread crumbs and 4 tablespoons melted butter in a small bowl. Sprinkle over cabbage. Top with grated cheese, if desired. Bake at 350° for 30 to 35 minutes.
Yields: 4 to 6 servings

Our Daily Bread
Church of the Incarnation
Mineral, Virginia

SWEET-AND-SOUR RED CABBAGE

8 slices bacon
1 small garlic clove, chopped
1 small onion, chopped
1 medium head red cabbage
  (about 1 1/2 pounds),
  finely chopped
1/4 cup firmly packed
  brown sugar
1 medium apple (red or green)
1/2 cup water
1 tablespoon cornstarch
Salt and black pepper to taste
1/4 cup red wine vinegar

In an electric skillet, cook bacon until crisp; remove from pan and drain on paper towels. Discard bacon drippings except for 4 tablespoons. Add garlic and onion and cook until tender but not brown. Add red cabbage; stir and cook, covered, at 350° for about 5 minutes, stirring frequently. Sprinkle cabbage with brown sugar and continue cooking. Core and dice apple, and add to cabbage; stir well. Mix water and cornstarch together; add salt and pepper. Stir into cabbage, then add wine vinegar. Cook, covered, until cabbage is done. Sprinkle bacon throughout.
Yields: 4 to 6 servings

Treasured Recipes
St. Mark's Episcopal Church
Prattville, Alabama

BAKED CARROTS

3 cups sliced carrots
3/4 cup bread crumbs
2 teaspoons minced onion
2 tablespoons melted butter
1/4 teaspoon black pepper
4 tablespoons grated Cheddar
  cheese

Boil carrots in salted water until tender; drain and reserve 1/2 cup liquid. Mash carrots and stir in bread crumbs, onion, butter, and pepper. Spoon into greased baking dish. Sprinkle with cheese. Bake at 350° for 15 minutes or until cheese melts.
Yields: 6 to 8 servings

Parish Collection
St. Edward's Episcopal Church
Lawrenceville, Georgia

SCALLOPED CORN

1/2 cup chopped green bell
  pepper
2 tablespoons butter
1 (17-ounce) can cream-style
  corn
1 cup milk
2 large eggs
1 (16-ounce) can whole kernel
  corn, drained
20 soda crackers, crushed

Sauté green pepper in butter in a small skillet. Combine with the remaining ingredients in a large bowl; mix well. Spoon into a greased baking dish. Bake at 350° for 45 minutes to 1 hour.
Yields: 4 to 6 servings

Parish Collection
St. Luke's Episcopal Church
Delta, Colorado

CORN PUDDING

2 cups cream-style corn
2 tablespoons melted butter
1 teaspoon salt
2 large eggs, beaten
1 (2-ounce) jar pimiento
1 cup grated cheese, divided
1/2 cup milk
2 tablespoons sugar
2 tablespoons all-purpose flour

Combine corn, butter, salt, eggs, pimiento, half the cheese, and milk and place in a greased 2-quart baking dish. Mix the sugar and flour. Stir into the corn mixture. Top with remaining cheese. Bake at 375° for about 40 minutes or until corn mixture is firm.
Yields: 4 servings

Parish Recipes
Emmanuel Episcopal Church
Staunton, Virginia

LENTEN "CORN OYSTERS"

8 tablespoons all-purpose flour
1 teaspoon salt
2 large eggs
1 cup milk
2 cups fresh or canned corn
1 tablespoon butter

Sift flour and salt and mix to a batter with egg and milk. Stir corn into batter. Melt butter on a hot griddle and add spoonfuls of corn batter. Brown on both sides.
Yields: 4 to 6 servings

Food and Gladness
St. Francis Episcopal Church
Norris, Tennessee

CORN FRITTERS

2 large eggs, beaten
2/3 cup milk
1/2 (17-ounce) can cream-style corn
1 tablespoon vegetable oil
2 cups all-purpose flour
2 teaspoons baking powder
Pinch of salt
Vegetable oil for deep frying

Combine eggs, milk, cream-style corn, and oil in a large bowl. Add flour, sifted with baking powder and salt; mix well. Drop into hot oil in deep fryer by teaspoon. Fry until golden brown. Drain on paper towels. Serve with warmed maple syrup.
Note: Dip spoon in hot oil, then fill with batter. Batter will then fall cleanly from spoon. Fritters may be frozen and then warmed in oven.
Yields: 4 to 6 servings

Family Collections
St. Matthew's Episcopal Church
Snellville, Georgia

EGGPLANT WITH SESAME

1 large eggplant
1 large clove garlic, crushed
3 tablespoons sesame paste
  (tahini)
Juice of 2 lemons
Salt to taste
Dash freshly ground black
  pepper
Olive oil
1/2 cup parsley and/or
  pomegranate seeds

Roast eggplant at 450° for 1/2 hour or until the pulp feels soft under the skin. Peel and mash pulp until smooth. Combine the garlic, sesame paste, lemon juice, salt, and pepper; stir until blended. Add to the mashed eggplant pulp. Adjust seasonings and chill thoroughly. Place in shallow dish and drizzle olive oil over top; garnish with parsley and/or pomegranate seeds. Serve with pita bread.
Note: Tahini is available in health food stores and some markets.
Yields: 4 servings

Cooking with Love
St. Timothy's Episcopal Church
Fairfield, Connecticut

STIR-FRIED EGGPLANT PARMESAN

1 medium eggplant, peeled and
  cut in 1/2-inch cubes
1 teaspoon salt
1/4 cup olive oil
1/4 cup minced onion
2 tablespoons chopped green
  bell pepper
3 tablespoons chopped fresh
  basil
1 clove garlic, minced
1/4 teaspoon rosemary
4 medium tomatoes, seeded
  and cubed
1/2 pound shredded mozzarella
  cheese
1/2 cup grated imported
  Romano cheese

Place eggplant in a colander and sprinkle with salt. Let stand 30 minutes to drain. Pat dry with paper towels. Add oil to coat the bottom of a large skillet. Heat before adding onion, green pepper, basil, garlic, and rosemary. Stir for 3 minutes. Add eggplant, and continue to stir-fry until lightly browned. Add tomatoes, and stir-fry 1 minute more. Remove from heat and add cheeses, stirring to incorporate. Turn onto heated platter and serve.
Yields: 4 servings

Holy Cow, Chicago's Cooking!
Church of the Holy Comforter
Kenilworth, Illinois

RATATOUILLE

3/4 pound eggplant, cubed
3/4 pound zucchini, sliced
2 teaspoons salt, divided
6 tablespoons olive oil, divided
1 cup thinly sliced onions
1 large clove garlic
2 green bell peppers,
    thinly sliced
4 cups coarsely chopped
    tomatoes, peeled, seeded
2 teaspoons minced parsley,
    divided
1 teaspoon fresh basil
1/4 teaspoon black pepper

Toss eggplant and zucchini with 1 teaspoon salt. Allow to sit for 30 minutes. Rinse and drain. Heat 4 tablespoons olive oil in skillet; add eggplant and zucchini. Sauté over medium high heat, stirring frequently until coated with oil and lightly browned. In a Dutch oven, heat remaining 2 tablespoons olive oil and add onions; sauté until soft. Add garlic and cook 1 to 2 minutes; add peppers and cook another 5 minutes. Add tomatoes, remaining 1 teaspoon salt, 1 teaspoon parsley, basil, and pepper; continue to cook until tomatoes have rendered their juices, about 5 to 8 minutes. Add eggplant and zucchini; cover and simmer for 20 minutes. Uncover and raise temperature; continue cooking 15 to 20 minutes until most of liquid has evaporated. Watch carefully. Sprinkle with remaining parsley and serve.

Note: May also be served cold with addition of 1 tablespoon olive oil and 1 tablespoon capers. Garnish with lemon wedges and Greek olives.

Yields: 6 to 8 servings

What's Cooking?
St. John's Episcopal Church
Huntington, L.I., New York

❖

NOW WHEN JESUS HEARD THIS, HE WITHDREW FROM THERE IN A BOAT TO A DESERTED PLACE BY HIMSELF. BUT WHEN THE CROWDS HEARD IT, THEY FOLLOWED HIM ON FOOT FROM THE TOWNS. WHEN HE WENT ASHORE, HE SAW A GREAT CROWD; AND HE HAD COMPASSION FOR THEM AND CURED THEIR SICK. WHEN IT WAS EVENING, THE DISCIPLES CAME TO HIM AND SAID, "THIS IS A DESERTED PLACE, AND THE HOUR IS NOW LATE; SEND THE CROWDS AWAY SO THAT THEY MAY GO INTO THE VILLAGES AND BUY FOOD FOR THEMSELVES." JESUS SAID TO THEM, "THEY NEED NOT GO AWAY; YOU GIVE THEM SOMETHING TO EAT." THEY REPLIED, "WE HAVE NOTHING HERE BUT FIVE LOAVES AND TWO FISH." THEN HE SAID, "BRING THEM HERE TO ME." THEN HE ORDERED THE CROWDS TO SIT DOWN ON THE GRASS. TAKING THE FIVE LOAVES AND TWO FISH, HE LOOKED UP TO HEAVEN, AND BLESSED AND BROKE THE LOAVES, AND GAVE THEM TO THE DISCIPLES, AND THE DISCIPLES GAVE THEM TO THE CROWDS. AND ALL ATE AND WERE FILLED; AND THEY TOOK UP WHAT WAS LEFT OVER OF THE BROKEN PIECES, TWELVE BASKETS FULL. AND THOSE WHO ATE WERE ABOUT FIVE THOUSAND MEN, BESIDES WOMEN AND CHILDREN.

MATTHEW 14:13–21
(JESUS FEEDS FIVE THOUSAND)

ROASTED SUMMER VEGETABLES

3 medium zucchini,
  thinly sliced
4 medium red potatoes,
  thinly sliced
2 medium eggplants,
  thinly sliced
1 large red bell pepper,
  thinly sliced
1 large onion, thinly sliced
3 cloves garlic, finely chopped
1 teaspoon dried oregano
1 teaspoon dried marjoram
1/2 teaspoon dried thyme
4 tablespoons chopped fresh
  parsley
Salt
Freshly ground black pepper
Olive oil
Red wine vinegar (optional)

Layer the vegetables and herbs in a large roasting pan. Season with salt and pepper. Drizzle oil on vegetables and toss thoroughly. Roast at 350° for about 45 minutes or until tender and edges are crisply browned. Sprinkle with red wine vinegar, if desired, before serving.
Yields: 8 to 10 servings

Angels' Food
St. Mary's Episcopal Church
Napa, California

MUCH MORE THAN MUSHROOMS

1 pound mushrooms
4 tablespoons butter
1 cup chopped green onions
1 cup chopped green bell
  pepper
1 cup chopped celery
1/2 teaspoon black pepper
2 tablespoons parsley
1/2 cup mayonnaise
6 slices crustless bread
3 large eggs
2 cups milk
1/4 cup Parmesan cheese

Sauté mushrooms in butter in large skillet for 5 minutes. Add green onion, green bell pepper, and celery. Simmer 5 minutes. Add pepper, parsley, and mayonnaise; set aside. Cut bread into cubes. Place half the cubes in a buttered casserole. Spoon mushroom mixture over the cubes and cover with remaining cubes. Whip the eggs and milk in a bowl until foamy. Pour over casserole. Bake at 350° for 50 minutes. Sprinkle with Parmesan cheese and return to oven for 10 minutes or until golden brown.
Note: Chopped ham may be added.
Yields: 6 to 8 servings

St. John the Baptist Centennial Cookbook
St. John the Baptist Episcopal Church
Seattle, Washington

GRILLED PORTABELLO MUSHROOMS AND RED PEPPERS

2–3 red bell peppers, sliced
10 ounces portabello
  mushrooms, sliced
2 tablespoons olive oil
1 tablespoon minced garlic
4 ounces feta cheese, crumbled

Toss peppers, mushrooms, olive oil, and garlic together in a bowl; mix well. Spoon into aluminum foil; sprinkle with feta cheese, then wrap tightly. Grill on low heat to taste.
Yields: 4 servings

Loaves & Fishes and Other Dishes
St. Andrew's Episcopal Church
Turners Falls, Massachusetts

BLACK-EYED PEAS AND RICE

1 1/2 cups dried black-eyed
  peas (field peas)
1 teaspoon salt
1 1/2 cups onion, diced
1 bay leaf
1 minced clove garlic
1 ham hock
1/2 teaspoon black pepper
Dash of cayenne pepper
Hot cooked rice

Pick over and wash peas. Soak overnight in 3 to 5 cups of water. Drain, saving the water. Remove any peas that float. Heat saved water in a large saucepan; add soaked peas and remaining ingredients except rice. Cover and bring to boiling point; reduce heat and simmer for about 1 1/4 hours or until peas are tender and only a small amount of liquid is left. Pick meat from the ham hock. Discard ham bone and bay leaf, and add meat to the peas. Mix cooked rice lightly with the peas. Cook for 2 or 3 minutes for flavors to blend.
Yields: 12 servings

Keeping the Feast
St. Thomas Episcopal Church
Abingdon, Virginia

CURRIED PECAN AND GREEN PEA SHORTCAKES

2 cups prepared biscuit mix
1/4 cup soft butter
2/3 cup milk
2 tablespoons chopped onion
1 tablespoon butter
3 tablespoons water
1 (10-ounce) package frozen
  green peas, partially thawed
1/2 teaspoon salt
1 cup shelled pecans, halved
2 tablespoons butter
2 tablespoons all-purpose flour
1/2 teaspoon salt
1/2 teaspoon paprika
1/2–1 teaspoon curry powder
1/2 cup half-and-half
3/4 cup milk

Combine biscuit mix and 1/4 cup butter in a bowl; stir in 2/3 cup milk. Roll out dough to 1/4 inch thick on floured board. Cut with 3-inch biscuit cutter. Cut center from half the rounds. Stack 2 biscuits, one with hole on top of one without, on baking sheet. Bake according to biscuit mix directions. Cook onion in 1 tablespoon butter in a large skillet until tender. Add water, peas, and 1/2 teaspoon salt. Cook, covered, over low heat until peas are tender. Stir in pecans and heat through. Spoon pea-pecan mixture into biscuit centers. Combine 2 tablespoons butter and flour in skillet. Add remaining ingredients, stirring well. When sauce thickens, pour over filled biscuits.
Yields: 4 to 6 servings

St. David's Cookbook
St. David's Episcopal Church
Nashville, Tennessee

FRIED BANANA PEPPERS

1 large jar (10) hot banana
  peppers, drained
1 cup milk
1 1/4 pound cracker meal,
  unseasoned
1/4 cup all-purpose flour
1 1/4 teaspoon cayenne pepper
Vegetable oil for deep frying

Cut peppers in half; soak in milk. Combine cracker meal, flour, and cayenne pepper to make breading mixture. Remove peppers from milk and roll in breading. Deep fry at 350° until golden brown.
Yields: 4 to 6 servings

Heavenly Tastes, Earthly Recipes
St. Andrews Episcopal Church
Lake Worth, Florida

JALAPEÑO PIE

2–3 jalapeño peppers, seeded
  and chopped
1 pound sharp Cheddar cheese
6 large eggs, beaten

Place peppers in a well-greased 9-inch square pan; cover with cheese. Pour eggs over cheese. Bake at 350° for 30 minutes or until firm. Cool and cut into 1-inch squares.
Yields: about 6 1/2 dozen

Christ Episcopal Church Cookbook
Christ Episcopal Church
Pearisburg, Virginia

PINEAPPLE CASSEROLE

3 (20-ounce) cans pineapple
  chunks, drained
3 tablespoons all-purpose flour
3 tablespoons sugar
1 1/2 cups grated sharp
  Cheddar cheese
1 stack buttery round crackers,
  crumbled
1 stick butter, melted

Place pineapple in baking dish. Mix flour and sugar together and sprinkle over pineapple. Combine cheese and cracker crumbs, and sprinkle on top of pineapple. Pour butter on top. Bake at 350° for 30 minutes.
Yields: 4 to 6 servings

Parish Collection
St. Peter's Episcopal Church
Altavista, Virginia

BAKED PLANTAINS

3 ripe plantains (or bananas),
  sliced
Juice of 1 key lime
2/3 cup firmly packed brown
  sugar, divided
3 tablespoons sherry
1 teaspoon cinnamon
2 whole cloves
1/4 cup butter

Arrange sliced plantains in buttered baking dish. Sprinkle with lime juice. Cover with 1/3 cup brown sugar, then sherry, cinnamon, and cloves. End with remaining brown sugar. Cut butter in pieces and dab over ingredients. Bake at 375° for 1 hour.
Yields: 6 servings

St. Simons ECW Cookbook
St. Simons Episcopal Church
Miami, Florida

SQUASH CASSEROLE

1 small onion, chopped
2 cups sliced squash
1/2 teaspoon salt
1 cup water
20 butter-flavored round
  crackers
1 large egg
1/2 cup cubed cheese
1 tablespoon butter
1 tablespoon cream

Cook onion, squash, and salt in water in a saucepan until vegetables are tender; mash. Crumble 16 crackers into squash; add egg and beat. Add cheese and butter; mix well. Place in greased casserole. Crumble remaining crackers and cream over top. Bake at 350° for 30 minutes.
Yields: 4 servings

Potluck Sunday
St. Mary's Episcopal Church
Madisonville, Kentucky

SPINACH RING

3 tablespoons butter
3 tablespoons all-purpose flour
1 cup milk, warmed
1/3 teaspoon ground nutmeg
1 teaspoon grated onion
1 teaspoon lemon juice
2 large eggs, well beaten
1 teaspoon salt
2 1/2 cups chopped, cooked
  fresh spinach

Melt butter in a large skillet; stir in flour and cook for 1 minute. Add warmed milk and stir until thickened. Add remaining ingredients. Pour into well-greased 1-quart ring mold. Place in a pan of hot water and bake until firm, at least 40 minutes. Unmold and fill center with buttered cauliflower florets, artichoke hearts or other vegetable desired.
Yields: 8 to 10 servings

Parish Collection
Christ Episcopal Church
Bradenton, Florida

SPINACH CASSEROLE

2 (10-ounce) packages frozen
  chopped spinach, thawed and
  drained
1/4 cup cooked onion
1 pound sautéed mushrooms
1 cup grated Cheddar cheese

Combine spinach with onion and mushrooms in a baking dish. Top with cheese. Bake at 350° for 20 to 25 minutes.
Yields: 8 servings

Cooking with Grace
Grace Church
Bath, Maine

GINGERED SPINACH IN TOMATO CUP

4 medium tomatoes
Salt
2 teaspoons finely chopped
    ginger root
1 small clove garlic, crushed
1 teaspoon soy sauce
1 (12-ounce) package fresh
    spinach, divided
1/2 cup chopped water
    chestnuts

Remove 1/4 inch from top of a tomato; scoop out seeds and lightly sprinkle with salt; set aside. Cook and stir ginger root in oil in 10-inch skillet over medium heat; stir in garlic, soy sauce, and half of spinach. Cook and stir until spinach begins to wilt. Stir in remaining spinach and water chestnuts. Cook and stir until spinach is wilted, about 2 minutes. Fill tomatoes with spinach mixture. Place in shallow baking dish. Bake tomato cups at 375° for 10 to 15 minutes.
Yields: 4 servings

Holy Tidbits
St. Christopher's Episcopal Church
Fairborn, Ohio

STUFFED BAKED TOMATOES

1 (10-ounce) package frozen
    chopped spinach
1/2 cup mayonnaise
1 (3-ounce) package cream
    cheese
1 clove garlic, pressed
1 teaspoon nutmeg
Salt and black pepper to taste
6 medium firm, ripe tomatoes
1/4 cup pine nuts
Pat of butter

Cook spinach according to package directions; squeeze dry. Combine in a bowl with mayonnaise, cream cheese, garlic, nutmeg, salt, and pepper. Scoop out tomatoes and fill with spinach mixture. Top with pine nuts and butter. Bake at 325° for 35 minutes.
Yields: 6 to 8 servings

The Book of Common Fare
Grace-St. Luke's Church
Memphis, Tennessee

TOMATO PIE

1 single (8-inch) pie crust, rolled out 1/2 inch larger than pie plate
4 medium ripe tomatoes, cored, seeded, and sliced
1 small onion, chopped and sautéed
1 small green bell pepper, chopped and sautéed
2 slices crisp bacon
Grated Cheddar cheese
Parsley, sage, thyme, and rosemary

Place crust loosely in pie plate. Layer tomato, onion, pepper, bacon, cheese, and seasonings, ending with cheese. Bring crust to center leaving a 2- to 3-inch opening. Bake at 400° for 20–30 minutes or until crust is browned and tomatoes tender.

Yields: 6 servings

Cooks of St. Barnabas
St. Barnabas Episcopal Church
Augusta, Maine

❖

ONCE MORE JESUS SPOKE TO THEM IN PARABLES, SAYING; "THE KINGDOM OF HEAVEN MAY BE COMPARED TO A KING WHO GAVE A WEDDING BANQUET FOR HIS SON. HE SENT HIS SLAVES TO CALL THOSE WHO HAD BEEN INVITED TO THE WEDDING BANQUET, BUT THEY WOULD NOT COME. AGAIN HE SENT OTHER SLAVES, SAYING, 'TELL THOSE WHO HAVE BEEN INVITED: LOOK, I HAVE PREPARED MY DINNER, MY OXEN AND MY FAT CALVES HAVE BEEN SLAUGHTERED, AND EVERYTHING IS READY; COME TO THE WEDDING BANQUET.' BUT THEY MADE LIGHT OF IT AND WENT AWAY, ONE TO HIS FARM, ANOTHER TO HIS BUSINESS, WHILE THE REST SEIZED HIS SLAVES, MISTREATED THEM, AND KILLED THEM. THE KING WAS ENRAGED. HE SENT HIS TROOPS, DESTROYED THOSE MURDERERS, AND BURNED THEIR CITY. THEN HE SAID TO HIS SLAVES, 'THE WEDDING IS READY, BUT THOSE INVITED WERE NOT WORTHY. GO THEREFORE INTO THE MAIN STREETS, AND INVITE EVERYONE YOU FIND TO THE WEDDING BANQUET.' THOSE SLAVES WENT OUT INTO THE STREETS AND GATHERED ALL WHOM THEY FOUND, BOTH GOOD AND BAD; SO THE WEDDING HALL WAS FILLED WITH GUESTS.

"BUT WHEN THE KING CAME IN TO SEE THE GUESTS, HE NOTICED A MAN THERE WHO WAS NOT WEARING A WEDDING ROBE, AND HE SAID TO HIM, 'FRIEND, HOW DID YOU GET IN HERE WITHOUT A WEDDING ROBE?' AND HE WAS SPEECHLESS. THEN THE KING SAID TO THE ATTENDANTS, 'BIND HIM HAND AND FOOT, AND THROW HIM INTO THE OUTER DARKNESS, WHERE THERE WILL BE WEEPING AND GNASHING OF TEETH.' FOR MANY ARE CALLED, BUT FEW ARE CHOSEN."

MATTHEW 22:1–14
(PARABLE OF THE WEDDING FEAST)

VIDALIA ONION PIE

Cooking spray
4 cups chopped Vidalia onions
1 tablespoon bacon drippings
1 tablespoon margarine
1/2 teaspoon salt
1/2 teaspoon black pepper
2 cups shredded Swiss cheese,
    divided
1 (9-inch) pie crust, baked
2 tablespoons capers
3 tablespoons sliced olives
2 tablespoons Parmesan cheese

Spray large skillet with cooking spray and sauté onions in bacon drippings and margarine just until tender. Season with salt and pepper. Place half of Swiss cheese in bottom of pastry shell. Top with half of onions. Repeat layers. Sprinkle capers, olives, and Parmesan cheese over top. Bake at 350° for 20 minutes.

Yields: 6 servings

Pohickory Cookbook
Pohick Church
Lorton, Virginia

MASHED POTATO CASSEROLE

10–12 potatoes
1 (8-ounce) package cream
    cheese
2 large eggs, beaten
2 tablespoons all-purpose flour
2 tablespoons chopped onion
2 tablespoons fresh parsley
Salt and black pepper
1 (6-ounce) can French-fried
    onions

Boil potatoes in salted water; drain and mash until smooth. Beat in cream cheese. Stir in eggs, flour, chopped onion, parsley, salt, and pepper. Spoon into a greased baking dish. (May refrigerate for up to 24 hours ahead of baking time.) Top with onions before baking. Bake at 350° for 30 minutes.

Yields: 8 to 10 servings

Not by Bread Alone
Christ Church, the Episcopal Parish
Shrewsbury, New Jersey

CREAMED GARDEN POTATOES AND PEAS

1 pound small early red-skin
    potatoes
2 tablespoons butter or
    margarine
1 tablespoon chopped onion
2 tablespoons all-purpose flour
1 1/4 teaspoons salt
1/2 teaspoon dillweed
1/8 teaspoon black pepper
1 1/2 cups milk
1 1/2 cups fresh peas or
    1 (10-ounce) package frozen
    peas, cooked

Cook unpeeled potatoes in boiling water in a saucepan until tender, about 20 to 25 minutes; drain and cool. Peel, if desired, and set aside. Combine butter and onion in saucepan; cook until onion is tender. Blend in flour, salt, dillweed, and pepper. Stir in milk, mixing well. Cook until mixture boils, stirring constantly. Add potatoes and peas; heat through.

Yields: 4 to 5 servings

Christ Church Classics
Christ Church
Lexington, Kentucky

POTATO CROQUETTES, ITALIAN STYLE

6 medium potatoes
Dash black pepper
1 tablespoon Romano cheese, grated
1 teaspoon basil
1 large egg white, beaten
1 teaspoon parsley
1/2 teaspoon garlic powder
1 large egg yolk, beaten
2 cups bread crumbs, seasoned

Boil potatoes; peel and mash with fork in a large bowl. Add pepper, cheese, basil, egg white, parsley, and garlic powder. Fold with a fork. Form into 1-inch rolls and flatten. Dip in egg yolk and bread crumbs. Fry in very hot oil on both sides until golden brown. Can be frozen.
Yields: 6 servings

St. Raphael's Cookbook
St. Raphael's Episcopal Church
Brick, New Jersey

BOURBON SWEET POTATOES

4 pounds sweet potatoes
1/2 cup butter, softened
1/2 cup bourbon
1/3 cup orange juice
1/4 cup firmly packed light brown sugar
1 teaspoon salt
1/2 teaspoon apple pie spice
1/3 cup chopped pecans

Scrub potatoes and cook in salted boiling water until tender. Peel and mash; stir in remaining ingredients, except pecans, and mix well. Place in baking dish. Sprinkle with pecans. Bake at 350° for 45 minutes.
Yields: 10 servings

Cooking with Grace
Grace Church
Bath, Maine

FRIED RICE

6 tablespoons vegetable oil
2 large eggs, beaten
6 slices bacon
6 green onions, chopped
1 (8-ounce) can sliced water chestnuts
1/2 cup frozen green peas, cooked
Dash of garlic powder
3 cups cooked rice
1–2 tablespoons soy sauce

Heat oil in small skillet. Add eggs and cook, stirring constantly until firm but still moist; set aside. Cook bacon; reserve drippings. Crumble bacon and set aside. Add onions, water chestnuts, peas, and garlic powder to bacon drippings; cook until onions are tender. Stir in rice, soy sauce, eggs, and bacon. Cook until thoroughly heated.
Yields: 6 servings

Christ Episcopal Church Cookbook
Christ Episcopal Church
Pearisburg, Virginia

GREEN RICE FOR LENT

1 medium bunch parsley
1 green bell pepper
1 medium onion
1 clove garlic
1/4 pound pimiento cheese
1 (5-ounce) can evaporated milk
2 tablespoons butter or
   margarine
2 large eggs, beaten
Salt and black pepper to taste
2 cups cooked rice

Grind first 4 ingredients in a food processor. Melt cheese in milk in a medium saucepan. Add butter, beaten eggs, salt, and pepper. Combine the chopped vegetables, cheese mixture, and the cooked rice in a large baking dish. Bake at 350° just until browned. Add more milk if necessary.
Yields: 4 servings

Food and Gladness
St. Francis Episcopal Church
Norris, Tennessee

SPINACH AND DILL RICE

1 pound fresh spinach
3 tablespoons olive oil
2 cloves garlic, minced
2 teaspoons salt, divided
1 teaspoon dried dillweed
2 teaspoons white wine
Dash of vinegar
Black pepper to taste
4 cups water
1 1/2 cups long-grain white rice
1/2 cup finely crumbled feta
   cheese
1/2 cup fresh-grated Parmesan
   cheese

Wash and trim the spinach; mince it. Heat the olive oil in a medium skillet and add the minced spinach and minced garlic to it. Season the spinach with 1/2 teaspoon of the salt, the dillweed, wine, vinegar, and black pepper. Cook the mixture over medium heat, stirring often, for about 10 minutes or until all the excess liquid evaporates, leaving a thick puree. Bring the water to a boil in a large saucepan and stir in the remaining 1 1/2 teaspoons salt. Add the rice and lower the heat to a simmer. Cook, covered, over very low heat for 25 minutes. The rice will absorb all the water.

Add the spinach mixture and toss lightly with two spoons until the rice and spinach are well-blended. Cook, covered, over low heat for 3 or 4 minutes. Toss together the cheeses. Spoon the green rice onto a warm platter; sprinkle with cheeses and serve immediately.
Yields: 8 servings

Cook Book
St. Anne's Episcopal School
Denver, Colorado

VEGETABLE RICE RING

2 cups cooked rice
1/2 cup Italian salad dressing
1/2 cup mayonnaise or
  salad dressing
2 small tomatoes,
  seeded and diced
1 medium green bell pepper,
  chopped
1/2 cup chopped celery
1 cup sliced radishes
1/4 cup chopped green onions
1 medium cucumber,
  seeded and diced
Lettuce leaves
1 pint cherry tomatoes,
  for garnish

Combine cooked rice and Italian dressing in a large bowl; cover and chill overnight. Add mayonnaise to undrained rice and stir well. Fold in tomatoes and next 5 vegetables. Press into 5 1/2-cup ring mold. Cover and refrigerate at least 3 hours. To serve, unmold onto lettuce-lined platter; fill center with cherry tomatoes.

Yields: 8 to 10 servings

Memories from the Kitchen
St. Paul's Episcopal Church
Mount Lebanon, Pennsylvania

BROWN RICE WITH SUNFLOWER SEEDS & RED GRAPES

1 medium onion,
  finely chopped
1 stalk celery, finely chopped
1 tablespoon vegetable oil
1 cup uncooked brown rice
1–2 tablespoons finely chopped
  fresh thyme or 1 teaspoon
  crushed
2 1/2 cups chicken broth
1/2 cup unsalted, shelled,
  toasted sunflower seeds
3/4 cup halved seedless red
  grapes

Cook onion and celery in oil in 10-inch skillet until onion is translucent. Stir in rice and thyme. Add chicken broth and bring to a boil; reduce heat and simmer, covered, for 45 to 50 minutes or until liquid has been absorbed and rice is tender. Stir in seeds and grapes.

Yields: 8 servings

Cooking with Love
St. Andrew's Episcopal Church
Downers Grove, Illinois

BRAZILIAN RICE

1 (10-ounce) package frozen
   chopped spinach, cooked
   without seasoning
1 cup raw rice, cooked
   without salt
1/4 cup butter
4 large eggs, beaten
1 pound grated cheese
1 cup milk
1 tablespoon chopped onion
1 tablespoon Worcestershire
   sauce
2 teaspoons salt
1/2 teaspoon each of marjoram,
   thyme, and rosemary

Combine all ingredients in a large bowl; mix well. Spoon into a greased baking dish and bake at 350° for 30 minutes. Cut into squares and serve.

Yields: 6 to 8 servings

Not by Bread Alone
Trinity Episcopal Church
Oak Ridge, Virginia

BULGHUR PILAF

1/2 cup butter
1 medium onion, chopped
1/2 pound fresh mushrooms,
   sliced
2 cups coarse-ground
   bulghur wheat
3 cups chicken stock, bouillon,
   or consommé
1 cup light cream
1 teaspoon salt
1/4 teaspoon freshly ground
   black pepper

Melt butter in 2-quart baking dish (one that has a cover) and sauté onions and mushrooms until crisp-tender; add the bulghur and sauté briefly. Heat chicken stock and cream, and add to bulghur mixture with salt and pepper to taste. Cover and bake in a preheated 350° oven for 30 minutes. Stir with a fork and bake for 15 minutes longer.

Yields: 8 servings

Cooking with Love
St. Timothy's Episcopal Church
Fairfield, Connecticut

RICH NOODLE PUDDING

1/2 pound medium egg noodles
3 tablespoons butter
1 (8-ounce) package cream
  cheese
1/2 pound cottage cheese
1/2 cup dairy sour cream
3 large eggs, separated
1/2 teaspoon salt
1/2 cup sugar
1 teaspoon cinnamon
1 cup sliced apples
1/4 cup broken walnuts
1 teaspoon grated lemon rind
1/2 cup white raisins

Cook noodles according to package directions; drain. Toss with butter in bowl. Mix cream cheese, cottage cheese, and sour cream until light. Add egg yolks; beat well. Pour over noodles in bowl. Add remaining ingredients, except egg whites; mix well. Beat egg whites until stiff; fold into noodle mixture. Pour into a greased baking dish. Bake, uncovered, at 350° for 45 minutes.
Yields: 8 servings

Canterbury Feasts
Canterbury School of Florida
St. Petersburg, Florida

BAKED MACARONI AND CHEESE

2 tablespoons margarine
1/4 cup all-purpose flour
1 teaspoon salt
1/2 teaspoon dry mustard
1/4 teaspoon black pepper
2 1/2 cups milk
2 cups grated Cheddar cheese,
  divided
8 ounces macaroni noodles or
  pasta, uncooked
1/4 cup fresh bread crumbs
Ham (optional)

Melt margarine in a large skillet; stir in flour, salt, mustard, and pepper until smooth. Remove from heat. Gradually stir in milk until smooth. Cook over medium heat about 10 minutes or until thickened, stirring constantly. Remove from heat. Stir in 1 1/2 cups cheese until melted. Cook macaroni according to directions; drain. Place in greased baking dish. Pour cheese sauce over macaroni; mix well. Mix remaining cheese and bread crumbs. Sprinkle over top. Bake at 375° for 25 minutes or until topping is slightly browned.
Yields: 6 servings

Our Favorite Recipes
St. Thomas' Episcopal Church
Pittstown, New Jersey

MEXICAN GRITS

1 1/2 cups grits, uncooked
6 cups water
2 teaspoons salt
1 pound American cheese,
  shredded
2 tablespoons margarine
2 (4-ounce) cans green chiles,
  chopped
1 (2- to 4-ounce) jar pimiento,
  chopped
3 large eggs, beaten

Cook grits in salted water according to package directions. Add cheese, margarine, chiles, and pimiento; mix well. Add eggs; mix well. Pour into large baking dish. Do not cover. Bake at 350° for 1 hour.
Yields: 8 servings

Parish Collection
Christ Episcopal Church
Bradenton, Florida

CORNBREAD DRESSING

1 large onion
1 stick butter
2 tablespoons sage
1 teaspoon salt
1 teaspoon black pepper
Cornbread
6 slices dry hard white toast
  (broken into pieces)
4 large eggs, lightly beaten
2 cups chopped celery
2 cans chopped water chestnuts
Giblet and turkey stock
Paprika

Glaze the onion in butter in a skillet; add sage, salt, and pepper. In a bowl, mix Cornbread, toast, and eggs. Add the seasoned and glazed onion, celery, and water chestnuts. Add enough stock from giblets for a soft mixture. Stir; do not pack down. Place in a buttered 9 × 13-inch baking dish. (May be frozen at this point or will keep in refrigerator for several days before cooking. If frozen, thaw and add stock from pan of cooking turkey.) Add paprika on top and bake at 350° for about 45 minutes.
Yields: 8 to 10 servings

CORNBREAD
1 cup white cornmeal
1 1/4 cups all-purpose flour
1 teaspoon salt
3 teaspoons baking powder
1/4 cup shortening
3 tablespoons sugar
2 large eggs
1 3/4 cups milk

Sift together cornmeal and next 3 ingredients; set aside. Cream shortening and sugar; add eggs and milk. Combine dry and wet ingredients. Pour into greased and floured pan. Cook at 400° for about 30 minutes.

Parish Collection
Christ Episcopal Church
Bradenton, Florida

GRANDMA'S DRESSING

2 small loaves white bread
2 teaspoons salt
1/4 teaspoon black pepper
1 teaspoon poultry seasoning
2/3 cup butter
3/4 cup boiling water
1 medium onion, chopped
2 stalks celery, chopped
2 large eggs, lightly beaten

Break bread into cubes in a large bowl. Add seasonings. Melt butter in boiling water in a saucepan; pour over bread. Add onion, celery, and eggs; toss lightly. Stuff turkey or chicken lightly. Extra stuffing can be baked in a baking dish.

Yields: enough for 1 (16- to 18-pound) turkey

Feed My Sheep
St. Peter's Episcopal Church
Lebanon, Indiana

RAISIN-NUT STUFFING

1 pound ground chuck
6 stalks celery, chopped
2 medium onions, chopped
2 boiled potatoes, mashed
3 cups unseasoned croutons
1 cup raisins
1 cup chopped walnuts
Salt, black pepper, and poultry
  seasoning to taste

Brown meat in a large skillet. Add celery and onion and simmer for 20 minutes. Add potatoes, croutons, raisins, and nuts. Simmer with enough water to keep moist. Season with salt, pepper, and poultry seasoning. Cool and stuff into turkey.

Yields: enough for 1 (12- to 14-pound) turkey

Parish Collection
Holy Trinity Episcopal Church
Iron Mountain, Michigan

HE SAID ALSO TO THE ONE WHO HAD INVITED HIM, "WHEN YOU GIVE A LUNCHEON OR A DINNER, DO NOT INVITE YOUR FRIENDS OR YOUR BROTHERS OR YOUR RELATIVES OR RICH NEIGHBORS, IN CASE THEY

Sauces

MAY INVITE YOU IN RETURN, AND YOU WOULD BE REPAID. BUT WHEN YOU GIVE A BANQUET, INVITE THE POOR, THE CRIPPLED, THE LAME, AND THE BLIND. AND YOU WILL BE BLESSED, BECAUSE THEY CANNOT REPAY YOU, FOR YOU WILL BE REPAID AT THE RESURRECTION OF THE RIGHTEOUS."

LUKE 14:12–14
(JESUS TEACHES ABOUT PARTY-GIVING)

Cooking in Instructions for Life

My memory must be wrong. It couldn't possibly have been every Friday that Ann and Susan and I would spend the night at Susan's house. It feels to me now as if our junior high slumber parties happened that often, but probably we really only got together about once a month.

At these gatherings we behaved, of course, like teenage girls, giggling and getting into things we shouldn't have. But whatever else we did, there was one ritual that had to be carried out, without which the sleepover didn't count at all: we had to make our own pizza

Funnily, I have only vague memories of any other part of these slumber parties. Surely we must have talked about boys. I expect we watched TV or listened to the latest hits on the radio. What did we do while we were waiting for the pizza to bake? Again, I have no idea.

But the cooking, I remember in detail. It was our gathering ritual, as important as a church's processional hymn or a recovery meeting's review of the twelve steps. Susan's mom would buy a little pizza kit and graciously vacate the house, or at least hide herself somewhere. As soon as we'd dumped our sleeping bags in the TV room, we would tear open the kit and go to work.

The meaning of our shared cooking changed over the months. The first few times, we felt only the amateurish thrill of doing it ourselves. We would pore over the directions and try to make the movements of our hands, the measurements, and the spreading, duplicate the words printed on the side of the box.

Scatter the cheese. What was scattering, exactly? Did you push it down, or leave it the way it fell? Was there some official way to deploy the sauce? Preheat, the box warned us: well, for how long?

As Ann and Susan and I gradually learned, cooking instructions are clearest to those who have already had the experience. The first time you try to get an onion "translucent," for example, you will not know what to look for. But after you have lived with onions in the pan, you know how they can crisp on the edges too quickly, how the larger pieces can look ready before they are, and how, yes, they do kind of relax in the heat so that they are no longer opaque. Then you understand what the line in the cookbook means.

At first we assumed that there was some external, scientific reality hidden behind the instructions, which we had to achieve. Later, we came to discover a more flexible, more narrative thing: making a meal happen. To that, the instructions were just signposts.

So our confidence grew. We would divide the labor and spread out the dough, shaking and scattering and topping our creations with abandon. Ann checked the temperature. Susan set the timer. Soon, our pizza came out of the oven and we divided it into pieces with a knife, since the kitchen lacked a rolling pizza cutter.

The slices never looked that pretty, and the pizza itself had often assumed some crazy shape. The crust usually came out too soft, a casualty of the necessarily low baking temperature. But much more important than these predictable glitches was the knowledge that we had made the pizza and along with it shaped our friendship and that now we were going to sit down and eat.

Of course, we could have had objectively better pizza by ordering in. But we didn't want objectively better pizza. We wanted the chance to cook together, rehearsing creation, rehearsing community, rehearsing our lives as women. Maybe I'm still rehearsing, because I never make a pizza without remembering it all.

EPISCOPADES REMOULADE SAUCE

1 cup mayonnaise
l tablespoon wine vinegar
2 tablespoons chopped parsley
1/2 teaspoon tarragon
1 teaspoon chives
1 teaspoon Dijon mustard
2 tablespoons chopped sweet
   pickle
1 teaspoon chopped capers
1 clove garlic, crushed
1 teaspoon anchovy paste

Mix all ingredients together well in a small bowl; chill until ready to use on salad or shrimp.
Yields: 1 1/2 cups

Canterbury Feasts
Canterbury School of Florida
St. Petersburg, Florida

HOLLANDAISE SAUCE

1/4 cup butter or margarine
1 cup sour cream
2 tablespoons lemon juice
   (use less if real lemon)
4 large egg yolks

From 10 minutes to 2 weeks in advance, melt butter in small saucepan over medium to low heat. With wire whisk, beat in sour cream and lemon juice. Beat in egg yolks and heat, beating constantly, for about 5 minutes, until slightly thickened. (If it coats a spoon, it's done.) Use warm right away or refrigerate and then reheat over low heat, stirring constantly.
Yields: 1 2/3 cups

All Saints' Cookbook
All Saints' Episcopal Church
Morristown, Tennessee

TARTAR SAUCE

1 cup mayonnaise
1/2 tablespoon chopped parsley
1/2 tablespoon capers
1/2 teaspoon horseradish
1/2 teaspoon onion juice
2 tablespoons chili sauce
1/2 tablespoon chopped dill or
   sour pickle
1 tablespoon Durkees salad
   dressing

Combine all ingredients; mix well. Store in refrigerator. Serve on salad or fish.
Yields: about 1 1/2 cups

Down Plantation Road
St. Philip Episcopal Church
Bartlett, Tennessee

TANGY BARBECUE SAUCE

2 tablespoons vegetable oil
1 onion, chopped
2 stalks celery, chopped
1 green bell pepper, chopped
3 (4-ounce) cans tomato sauce
1 (8-ounce) can crushed
  pineapple
1/4 cup molasses
1 teaspoon ginger
1/2 teaspoon cinnamon
1 teaspoon Worcestershire
  sauce
Salt and black pepper to taste

Combine all ingredients and cook over low heat for 15 minutes. Brush the sauce on meat that's at room temperature. Barbecue over a charcoal fire or broil in the oven.
Yields: enough for 3 pounds meat

Best of Bayou Cuisine
St. Stephen's Episcopal Church
Indianola, Mississippi

BARBECUE SAUCE FOR CHICKEN

2 quarts water
2 quarts vegetable oil
2 quarts cider vinegar
  (white or wine vinegar may
  be substituted)

Mix together water, oil, and vinegar in a large container. Pour into pump-type sprayer (reserve some to soak chicken prior to placing on rack, bone side down). Cook for 10 minutes. Spray before turning and after turning each time. Cook meat side for 5 minutes. Spray before and after turning to prevent blistering. To test for thorough cooking, grasp end of leg bone and twist. When the bone turns freely, chicken is done. On smaller grills, a small spray bottle may be used, but do not have more than one layer of charcoal. This reduces the chance of burning the chicken. Takes about 45 minutes to cook tasty chicken halves.
Yields: enough for 100 chicken halves

Favorite Recipes Home-Style
St. Andrew's Episcopal Church
Readfield, Maine

MUSTARD SAUCE

1/2 cup butter or margarine
1/2 cup sugar
1/2 cup prepared mustard
2 large eggs, beaten
1/2 cup vinegar
1/2 cup tomato soup

Melt butter in a saucepan; blend in other ingredients until smooth. This sauce keeps well in the refrigerator. An excellent sauce for ham.
Yields: about 2 1/2 cups

The Parish Pantry
St. John's Episcopal Church
Thomaston, Maine

RAISIN SAUCE

2/3 cup firmly packed brown
   sugar
3 tablespoons all-purpose flour
   or 1 1/2 tablespoons cornstarch
1 teaspoon cinnamon
1/4 teaspoon ground cloves
1/8 teaspoon salt
1/4 cup vinegar
1 cup raisins
1/2 cup orange juice
1/2 cup water

Blend sugar, flour, and spices in a medium saucepan. Add vinegar, raisins, orange juice, and water. Simmer, covered, until thickened. Serve warm with ham or pork chops.
Yields: about 1 1/2 cups

The Culinary Key
St. Peter's Episcopal Church
Cheshire, Connecticut

HOT GARLIC AND PEPPER SAUCE

6 cups fresh tomatoes, pureed
2 whole garlic pods, chopped
2 green bell peppers, chopped
2 onions, chopped
2 cups Datil or jalapeño
   peppers, chopped
1 quart red wine vinegar
3 cups sugar

Combine all ingredients in a large saucepan; bring to a boil. Reduce heat and simmer, uncovered, for 1 hour or until thickened. This hot sauce is good on beans and peas, among other things.
Yields: 8 to 10 cups sauce

Food for the Flock
St. Catherine's Episcopal Church
Jacksonville, Florida

HORSERADISH SAUCE

4 tablespoons prepared
  horseradish
1/2 cup mayonnaise
1 cup sour cream
1 tablespoon Dijon mustard

Combine all ingredients in a small bowl; mix thoroughly. Serve with roast beef.

Yields: about 1 3/4 cups

Parish Collection
St. John's Episcopal Church
Homestead, Florida

BROWN SAUCE

1/2 cup beef, veal, or pork fat
1/4 cup chopped carrot
1/2 cup finely chopped onion
1/2 cup all-purpose flour
2 quarts beef stock
8 peppercorns
1 clove garlic
1 bay leaf
1 tablespoon chopped parsley
1/4 cup chopped celery
1/2 cup tomato paste

Melt fat; add carrot and onion, cooking until tender. Add flour and cook slowly until vegetables brown, stirring frequently. Add stock, peppercorns, garlic, bay leaf, parsley, celery, and tomato paste. Cook slowly until reduced to 4 cups. Strain and use as base for sauces.

Yields: 4 cups

A Book of Favorite Recipes
Grace Episcopal Church and Grace Day School
Massapequa, New York

❖

WHEN IT WAS EVENING, HE CAME WITH THE TWELVE. AND WHEN THEY HAD TAKEN THEIR PLACES AND WERE EATING, JESUS SAID, "TRULY I TELL YOU, ONE OF YOU WILL BETRAY ME, ONE WHO IS EATING WITH ME." THEY BEGAN TO BE DISTRESSED AND TO SAY TO HIM ONE AFTER ANOTHER, "SURELY, NOT I?" HE SAID TO THEM, "IT IS ONE OF THE TWELVE, ONE WHO IS DIPPING BREAD INTO THE BOWL WITH ME. FOR THE SON OF MAN GOES AS IT IS WRITTEN OF HIM, BUT WOE TO THAT ONE BY WHOM THE SON OF MAN IS BETRAYED! IT WOULD HAVE BEEN BETTER FOR THAT ONE NOT TO HAVE BEEN BORN." WHILE THEY WERE EATING, HE TOOK A LOAF OF BREAD, AND AFTER BLESSING IT HE BROKE IT, GAVE IT TO THEM, AND SAID, "TAKE; THIS IS MY BODY." THEN HE TOOK A CUP AND AFTER GIVING THANKS HE GAVE IT TO THEM, AND ALL OF THEM DRANK FROM IT. HE SAID TO THEM, "THIS IS MY BLOOD OF THE COVENANT, WHICH IS POURED OUT FOR MANY. TRULY I TELL YOU, I WILL NEVER AGAIN DRINK OF THE FRUIT OF THE VINE UNTIL THAT DAY WHEN I DRINK IT NEW IN THE KINGDOM OF GOD."

MARK 14:17–25
(THE LAST SUPPER)

MARINADE FOR STEAK

2 tablespoons soy sauce
1 tablespoon lemon zest or
   juice
2 teaspoons sesame oil
1 tablespoon ginger
1 clove garlic, minced
1 teaspoon black pepper
1 teaspoon brown sugar

Combine all ingredients in a small bowl; mix well. Rub mixture into surface of steak. Cover and refrigerate overnight. Grill to your liking.
Yields: about 1/4 cup

Taste & See
Trinity Episcopal Church
Red Bank, New Jersey

MARINADE FOR FRUIT

1/2 cup orange or other
   fruit juice
Grated rind and juice of
   1/2 lemon
1/4 cup maple or corn syrup
1 vanilla bean or 5 to 6
   crushed coriander seeds
1/4 cup brandy

Combine all ingredients. Pour over freshly peeled and sliced fruits, mixing gently. Cover and refrigerate for 4 to 6 hours.
Yields: about 1 cup

Feeding Our Flock
St. Andrew's Episcopal Church
Longmeadow, Massachusetts

ENGLISH LEMON BUTTER

1 cup sugar
1/4 cup butter or margarine
3 large eggs, well beaten
1/3 cup lemon juice
Grated rind of 1 lemon

Melt butter in top of double boiler. Add sugar, stirring well. Add butter mixture to eggs in a bowl. Return to pan. Add lemon juice and rind. Cook, stirring constantly, until thickened. Refrigerate in jar until ready to use.
Yields: about 1 cup

Diocese Board Collection
ECW Diocese of New Jersey

STRAWBERRY BUTTER

1 pound (4 sticks) sweet butter, softened
3–5 tablespoons confectioners' sugar
3/4 cup finely chopped fresh strawberries

Combine all ingredients in blender or food processor with steel knife. Whip until light.
Yields: 2 1/2 cups

Heavenly Scents
Christ Episcopal Church
Toms River, New Jersey

CHOCOLATE SAUCE

1 stick plus 3 tablespoons butter
4 squares unsweetened chocolate
4 squares semisweet chocolate
2 cups sugar
1 pint heavy cream
1/4 teaspoon salt
4 teaspoons vanilla

Melt butter and chocolates in top of a double boiler. Add sugar, cream, and salt. Cook, stirring constantly, until sugar is dissolved. Remove from heat and stir in vanilla. Serve warm with pound cake or ice cream. Store in glass jars and refrigerate.
Yields: about 4 cups

The Shrimp Mousse and Other Waffle Shop Recipes
Calvary Episcopal Church
Memphis, Tennessee

❖

HE WAS PRAYING IN A CERTAIN PLACE, AND AFTER HE HAD FINISHED, ONE OF HIS DISCIPLES SAID TO HIM, "LORD, TEACH US TO PRAY, AS JOHN TAUGHT HIS DISCIPLES." HE SAID TO THEM, "WHEN YOU PRAY, SAY: FATHER, HALLOWED BE YOUR NAME. YOUR KINGDOM COME. GIVE US EACH DAY, OUR DAILY BREAD. AND FORGIVE US OUR SINS, FOR WE OURSELVES FORGIVE EVERYONE INDEBTED TO US. AND DO NOT BRING US TO THE TIME OF TRIAL."

AND HE SAID TO THEM, "SUPPOSE ONE OF YOU HAS A FRIEND, AND YOU GO TO HIM AT MIDNIGHT AND SAY TO HIM, 'FRIEND, LEND ME THREE LOAVES OF BREAD; FOR A FRIEND OF MINE HAS ARRIVED, AND I HAVE NOTHING TO SET BEFORE HIM.' AND HE ANSWERS FROM WITHIN, 'DO NOT BOTHER ME; THE DOOR HAS ALREADY BEEN LOCKED, AND MY CHILDREN ARE WITH ME IN BED; I CANNOT GET UP AND GIVE YOU ANYTHING.' I TELL YOU, EVEN THOUGH HE WILL NOT GET UP AND GIVE HIM ANYTHING BECAUSE HE IS HIS FRIEND, AT LEAST BECAUSE OF HIS PERSISTENCE HE WILL GET UP AND GIVE HIM WHATEVER HE NEEDS."

LUKE 11:1–8
(JESUS TEACHES HIS DISCIPLES ABOUT PRAYER)

LEMON SAUCE

1 cup sugar
1 teaspoon lemon rind
1/4 cup butter
3 tablespoons lemon juice
1 large egg, slightly beaten
1/2 cup water

Combine all ingredients in top of double boiler; cook, stirring constantly, until thick and smooth.
Yields: about 1 1/4 cups

Down Plantation Road
St. Philip Episcopal Church
Bartlett, Tennessee

BUTTERSCOTCH SAUCE

1/2 cup unsalted butter,
  softened
1 cup dark brown sugar
2/3 cup light corn syrup
1/2 cup whipping cream

Boil the butter, sugar, and corn syrup gently in a saucepan for 8 to 10 minutes, stirring occasionally. Let cool. Stir in cream and mix until smooth and silky. Store in refrigerator.
Yields: about 2 cups

Cooking with Love
St. Andrew's Episcopal Church
Downers Grove, Illinois

"But the father said to his slaves, 'Quickly, bring out a robe—the best one—and put it on him; put a ring on his finger and sandals on his feet. And get the fatted calf and kill it,

and let us eat and celebrate; for this son of mine was dead and is alive again; he was lost and is found!' And they began to celebrate."

Luke 15:22–24
(Return of the Prodigal Son)

185

Slow Food

There are four fastfood outlets within two blocks just down the road from my house, and I rarely go by without seeing cars lined up outside. Commuters on the way to work, getting a doughnut inserted through their car window; mothers passing little bags of French fries into the back seat to be grabbed by waiting children's hands; teenagers ordering a 99-cent taco apiece on the way home from senior high.

All this convenience has its merits. For one thing, it's, well, convenient. No need to perk the coffee or heat up the oven; just run by the drive-in and kill your hunger with something packed in cardboard. After all, think how much time you'll save by eating while you commute: that counts, in our efficiency-idolizing society, as accomplishing two things at once. If you have the radio on for today's news, you can make it three.

Even my local grocery store has several fastfood outlets now; not national chains, but sandwich areas, a pizza stand, and a bin of pre-roasted whole chickens immediately in front of the checkout counters. I guess I would rather look at chicken than tabloid news. But I often wonder what Carlo Petrini would think of it all.

Petrini, an Italian food critic, founded the International Slow Food Movement in 1986 after the first McDonald's opened in Rome. Slow Food's symbol, appropriately, is the snail. By 1998, the movement had grown to forty thousand adherents in thirty-five countries, all of them dedicated to leisurely meals and good company. While they host an international conference, the Salone del Gusto, a more essential part of their commitment is to local groups called "Convivia."

Whether or not you would ever join such a club, the experience of taking time for a relaxed, joyous meal with people you love feeds you in a lot more ways than just the nutrients you all share. Fast food in the car will never give you that. Always just grabbing something or other on the run may satisfy your body, but it will leave your soul undernourished.

Good shared meals play a mysterious role in human wholeness. Perhaps they function somewhat like REM sleep, the phase of sleep characterized by rapid eye movement during dreaming. You can lie in bed passed out for quite some time, but if your sleep is interrupted every time you begin to dream, your rest will not ultimately be satisfying and you will show symptoms of sleep deprivation. REM sleep is uniquely important to human well-being.

In the same way, we miss the heart of our meals, the part that truly satisfies spiritual as well as physical hunger, when we eat without ever sharing the table. And we end up community-starved. (Not to mention the fact that fast food's calories and fat are often much higher, so that the food that takes a toll on our spirits can take a toll on our bodies as well.)

If that's true, an alternative is right here at our fingertips. Could we begin by sitting down together and asking one another how things are? Could we put something easy on the table while the conversation continues? Sharing meals won't solve all our problems, but it might be a first step toward simply slowing down, paying attention, and letting ourselves be nourished—not just by food, but by each other.

A WORD OF CAUTION

Time and temperatures have to be worked out very carefully for canning. Too little time or too low a temperature means you are not protecting the food against bacteria, enzymes, molds, and yeasts. Too much time or too high a temperature may mean you are needlessly destroying nutrients in the food. Several different methods should be followed to the letter, such as *boiling water, bath canning,* or *steam pressure canning.* We suggest you use the professional guidance of *Mrs. Wages® New Home Canning Guide* or another reputable book in preparing the recipes in this section.

SPICED PEAR JAM WITH PINEAPPLE

3 pounds firm cooking pears
1 orange, seeded
1 lemon, seeded
1 cup crushed pineapple
4–5 cups sugar
5–6 whole cloves
1 (6-inch) stick cinnamon
1 (1-inch) piece ginger

Peel and core pears. Coarsely grind pears, orange, and lemon with a blender, food processor, or grinder. Combine with remaining ingredients in a large stockpot. Boil 30 to 45 minutes. Spoon into pint jars and cover with paraffin.
Yields: 8 to 10 pints

What's Cookin' at Epiphany?
Church of the Epiphany
Richmond, Virginia

BANANA BERRY JAM

12 ounces fresh cranberries,
  chopped (3 cups)
1 1/2 cups water
7 cups sugar
2 cups mashed bananas
1/2 (6-ounce) package liquid
  fruit pectin

Combine cranberries and water in 5-quart kettle. Simmer, covered, for 10 minutes. Add sugar and bananas; stir. Bring to boil. Boil hard 1 minute. Remove from heat. Stir in pectin. Spoon into hot half-pint jars. Adjust lids; process in boiling water for 15 minutes.
Yields: 8 half-pints

Wholly Cookery
Trinity Episcopal Church
Tulsa, Oklahoma

CALAMONDIN MARMALADE
(Florida calamondin is outstanding for marmalade.)

Calamondin
Water
Sugar

Wash, cut in half and then seed the calamondin. Cut into strips. Measure and add half as much water as fruit. Bring to a boil and boil for 10 minutes, then let mixture cool 10 minutes off the heat. Measure pulp and add an equal amount of sugar. Cover pan and let it rest overnight. Next day, boil to jelly stage and seal into sterile jars. Process in hot water bath for 10 minutes.

Grandma's Pantry Cookbook
St. Mark's Episcopal Church
Marco Island, Florida

CHAMPAGNE JELLY

1 (4/5-pint) bottle champagne (about 1 2/3 cups)
1 1/3 cups reconstituted frozen tangerine juice
4 1/2 cups sugar
1 (8-ounce) bottle liquid fruit pectin

Combine champagne, tangerine juice, and sugar in top of double boiler. Place over boiling water; cook, stirring constantly, until sugar is dissolved. Continue cooking until very hot, about 5 minutes; skim foam off top. Remove from heat; stir in liquid fruit pectin and mix well. Ladle jelly into hot, sterilized jars. Seal following manufacturer's directions. Label and date.
Yields: about 2 pints

All Saints' Cookbook
All Saints' Episcopal Church
Morristown, Tennessee

❖

AS THEY CAME NEAR THE VILLAGE TO WHICH THEY WERE GOING, HE WALKED AHEAD AS IF HE WERE GOING ON. BUT THEY URGED HIM STRONGLY, SAYING, "STAY WITH US, BECAUSE IT IS ALMOST EVENING AND THE DAY IS NOW NEARLY OVER."

SO HE WENT IN TO STAY WITH THEM. WHEN HE WAS AT THE TABLE WITH THEM, HE TOOK BREAD, BLESSED AND BROKE IT, AND GAVE IT TO THEM. THEN THEIR EYES WERE OPENED, AND THEY RECOGNIZED HIM; AND HE VANISHED FROM THEIR SIGHT.

LUKE 24:28–31
(JESUS APPEARS TO TWO TRAVELERS ALONG THE ROAD)

CRANBERRY COVE SAUCE

1 pound fresh cranberries
2 cups sugar
1 cup port wine

Wash and pick over berries. Place in large pot with sugar and wine. Bring to a boil and boil for 10 minutes, stirring occasionally. Cool a little, then force mixture through a coarse sieve into a bowl. Spoon into sterile jars and process for 10 minutes in a water bath.
Note: Can be frozen rather than canned.
Yields: 1 pint

Grandma's Pantry Cookbook
St. Mark's Episcopal Church
Marco Island, Florida

BREAD AND BUTTER PICKLES

6 quarts cucumbers, sliced
6 medium onions, sliced
1 cup salt
1 1/4 quarts vinegar
6 cups sugar
1/2 cup mustard seed
1 tablespoon celery seed

Place cucumbers and onions in layers with salt. Let stand for 3 hours, then drain. Boil vinegar, sugar, and seasonings; add cucumbers and onions. Simmer but do not boil. Pack hot in jars and seal.
Yields: 10 to 12 pints

Treasure of Personal Recipes
Church of Our Fathers
Hulls Cove, Maine

PICKLED SQUASH

1 gallon squash, sliced
10 medium onion, sliced
1/2 cup salt
5 cups sugar
5 cups vinegar
1 1/2 teaspoons mustard seed
1 1/2 teaspoons celery seed

Layer squash, onion, and salt in a large bowl. Refrigerate for about 3 hours. Wash off salt and drain for 15 minutes. Pack in pint jars. Bring sugar, vinegar, mustard seed, and celery seed to a boil in a saucepan. Pour over squash and onion in jars. Seal jars and process.
Yields: 6 to 8 pints

Kitchen Confessions
St. Edward's Episcopal Church
Lawrenceville, Georgia

PICKLED OKRA

5–7 cloves garlic
5–7 hot peppers
About 4 to 5 pounds okra,
  with part of stem removed
5–7 teaspoons dill seeds
1 quart white vinegar
1 cup water
1/2 cup salt

Place a garlic clove and hot pepper in each hot sterilized jar. Pack firmly with clean, young okra pods. Top each jar with 1 teaspoon dill seeds. Bring vinegar, water, and salt to a boil in a saucepan; reduce heat and simmer for 5 minutes. Pour hot mixture over okra; seal jars immediately.
Yields: 5 to 7 pints

What's Cookin' at Epiphany?
Church of the Epiphany
Richmond, Virginia

ARTICHOKE PICKLE

4 quarts Jerusalem artichokes,
  diced
2 quarts onions, chopped
6 red and green bell peppers,
  chopped
1 large head cauliflower,
  broken into florets
1 gallon water
2 cups salt
2 quarts vinegar
4 cups sugar
1 cup all-purpose flour
1 teaspoon turmeric
2 teaspoons dry mustard
1/4–1/3 cup cold water

Soak vegetables overnight in 1 gallon water and 2 cups salt; drain. Boil vinegar and sugar together. Make paste of flour, turmeric, dry mustard, and 1/4 to 1/3 cup cold water. Add paste to boiling vinegar. Cook until entire mixture is thickened. Add all vegetables and simmer a few minutes. Seal in sterilized pint jars while still hot.
Yields: 16 pints

Holy Cow, Chicago's Cooking!
Church of the Holy Comforter
Kenilworth, Illinois

FRESH CRANBERRY-ORANGE RELISH

4 cups fresh cranberries
2 unpeeled oranges, quartered
  and seeded
2 apples, cored and quartered
1 lemon, quartered and seeded
2 1/2 cups sugar

Wash and stem cranberries. Grind cranberries, oranges, apples, and lemon with medium blade of chopper. Add sugar and mix well. Chill 24 hours before serving.
Yields: about 1 quart

Cooks of St. Barnabas
St. Barnabas Episcopal Church
Augusta, Maine

JALAPEÑO TOMATO RELISH

1 (16-ounce) can tomatoes
4–5 jalapeño peppers
1/2 medium onion
1/2 small green pepper
  (optional)
5–6 tablespoons jalapeño juice

Pour tomatoes in bowl and chop fairly coarse. Seed and wash jalapeños and chop fairly fine. Chop onions fine; chop green pepper fine. Mix all together and add jalapeño juice. Store in glass jar in refrigerator.
Yields: 1 pint

Lunches & Brunches
St. Mark's Episcopal Church
Plainview, Texas

CORN RELISH

12 ears corn
12 onions
3 green bell peppers
3 red bell peppers
1 tablespoon ground mustard
1 tablespoon celery seed
1/4 teaspoon turmeric
1 quart vinegar
Salt to taste

Cook the corn in a large stockpot for 3 to 5 minutes; cool and cut from cob. Finely chop onion and peppers. Mix with corn and other ingredients in a large saucepan. Cook for 25 minutes. Pour into sterilized jars and seal immediately.
Yields: 3 or 4 pints

Sharing Our Best
Trinity Episcopal Church
Houghton, Michigan

QUICK-AND-EASY CORN RELISH

2 (12-ounce) cans whole kernel
  corn with sweet peppers,
  drained
3 tablespoons vegetable oil
1/2 cup sugar
1/2 cup vinegar
2 teaspoons minced dried
  onion
1/2 teaspoon salt
1/4 teaspoon celery seed

Combine corn and cooking oil in a bowl. In a small saucepan, combine sugar, vinegar, onion, salt, and celery seed. Cover and bring to boiling. Reduce heat and simmer for 2 minutes. Add sugar mixture to corn mixture; cover and cool. Refrigerate for several hours or until chilled.
Yields: about 3 cups

Grace Cooks
Grace Episcopal Church
Chattanooga, Tennessee

HOT DOG RELISH

8 quarts green tomatoes
6 large green peppers
2 hot red peppers
2 red bell peppers
8 large onions
1/2 cup canning salt
1 quart cider vinegar
2 teaspoons allspice
6 cups sugar
1 1/2 teaspoon dry mustard

Eight hours before canning or the night before, grind the green tomatoes, green peppers, hot red peppers, red peppers, and onions in food processor. Mix thoroughly with the salt in a big bowl and let stand overnight, or for 8 hours covered; drain well. Wash and sterilize 13 pint jars and keep hot. Place the vinegar, allspice, sugar, and dry mustard in a large pot and boil for 10 minutes. Blend hot liquid with the ground vegetables and cook 10 minutes. Pack into sterilized jars and process in boiling hot water bath for 5 minutes. Remove and cool on racks. Label when cooled.
Yields: 13 pints

Favorite Recipes Home-Style
St. Andrew's Episcopal Church
Readfield, Maine

❖

ONE OF THE DINNER GUESTS, ON HEARING THIS, SAID TO HIM, "BLESSED IS ANYONE WHO WILL EAT BREAD IN THE KINGDOM OF GOD!" THEN JESUS SAID TO HIM, "SOMEONE GAVE A GREAT DINNER AND INVITED MANY. AT THE TIME FOR THE DINNER HE SENT HIS SLAVE TO SAY TO THOSE WHO HAD BEEN INVITED, 'COME, FOR EVERYTHING IS READY NOW.' BUT THEY ALL ALIKE BEGAN TO MAKE EXCUSES. THE FIRST SAID TO HIM, 'I HAVE BOUGHT A PIECE OF LAND, AND I MUST GO OUT AND SEE IT; PLEASE ACCEPT MY REGRETS.' ANOTHER SAID, 'I HAVE BOUGHT FIVE YOKE OF OXEN, AND I AM GOING TO TRY THEM OUT; PLEASE ACCEPT MY REGRETS.' ANOTHER SAID, 'I HAVE JUST BEEN MARRIED, AND THEREFORE I CANNOT COME.' SO THE SLAVE RETURNED AND REPORTED THIS TO HIS MASTER. THEN THE OWNER OF THE HOUSE BECAME ANGRY AND SAID TO HIS SLAVE, 'GO OUT AT ONCE INTO THE STREETS AND LANES OF THE TOWN AND BRING IN THE POOR, THE CRIPPLED, THE BLIND, AND THE LAME.' AND THE SLAVE SAID, 'SIR, WHAT YOU ORDERED HAS BEEN DONE, AND THERE IS STILL ROOM.' THEN THE MASTER SAID TO THE SLAVE, 'GO OUT INTO THE ROADS AND LANES, AND COMPEL PEOPLE TO COME IN, SO THAT MY HOUSE MAY BE FILLED. FOR I TELL YOU, NONE OF THOSE WHO WERE INVITED WILL TASTE MY DINNER.'"
LUKE 14:15–24
(JESUS TELLS THE PARABLE OF THE GREAT FEAST)

CHOW CHOW

1 peck green tomatoes
1/2 cup salt
1 large head cabbage
6 large onions
6 green bell peppers
6 red bell peppers or
  1 (4-ounce) jar pimientos
3 cups sugar
1 quart vinegar
1 tablespoon mixed spiced
1 teaspoon celery seed
1 teaspoon turmeric (optional)

Coarsely grind the tomatoes and place in a large bowl; add salt and let stand overnight. Drain off juice in the morning. Grind cabbage, onions, and peppers; add to tomatoes. Dissolve sugar in vinegar; add spices and pour over vegetables. (Add more sugar as needed.) Cook in a large stockpot over low heat until tender but not mushy. Seal in pint jars.
Yields: 8 to 10 pints

Cook Book
Church of the Transfiguration
Bennington, Kansas

CRANBERRY CHUTNEY

1 pound cranberries
2 cups sugar
1 cup water
1 cup orange juice
1 cup raisins
1 cup chopped nuts
1 cup chopped celery
1 cup chopped apple
1 teaspoon grated orange peel
1 teaspoon grated ginger

Combine cranberries, sugar, and water in a large saucepan. Bring to a boil; reduce heat and simmer 15 minutes. Remove from heat. Add remaining ingredients; mix well. Refrigerate.
Yields: about 8 cups

Prize Recipes of Martinez
Grace Episcopal Church
Martinez, California

MANGO CHUTNEY

4 pounds green mangos, peeled
2 onions, peeled
2 cloves garlic
2 pounds raisins
2 pounds currants
1 quart vinegar
3 pounds brown sugar
1 teaspoon salt
1 tablespoon powdered ginger

Slice mangos. Chop or grind with onions and garlic. Combine with remaining ingredients and let stand overnight. Cook in a large saucepan until thickened. Pack into hot pint jars, leaving 1/2-inch head space. Wipe jar mouths and adjust lids. Process in boiling water bath canner for 5 minutes.
Yields: 4 to 6 pints

St. Simons ECW Cookbook
St. Simons Episcopal Church
Miami, Florida

SEE TO IT THAT NO ONE FAILS TO OBTAIN

THE GRACE OF GOD; THAT NO ROOT OF BIT-

TERNESS SPRINGS UP AND CAUSES TROUBLE,

AND THROUGH IT MANY BECOME DEFILED.

SEE TO IT THAT NO ONE BECOMES LIKE

ESAU, AN IMMORTAL AND GODLESS PER-

SON, WHO SOLD HIS BIRTHRIGHT FOR A

SINGLE MEAL.

HEBREWS 12:15–16

Proclaiming a Fast

When Lent comes around and I point out the fast days during our Sunday service's announcement time, I always wonder if anyone is planning to observe them. Sometimes I suspect that the whole thing is a charade, that the congregation is looking at me thinking, "Surely everyone knows nobody fasts anymore," while I look at them thinking, "Surely they're not actually going to do this." I go through the temptation every year to ignore the fast days myself; but I always end up observing them personally as well as promoting them, because in spite of it all, the concept is one we need.

All kinds of religions fast, of course; there is nothing uniquely Christian about it. Some people may be drawn to special seasons of abstinence, and others have individually undertaken long fasts, or controlled eating programs, for health or for spiritual reasons. But when we ask people to join in the traditional fast on Good Friday, we are talking about something different: a communal practice whose value is as much symbolic as literal.

Most of us will take part in fasting only in that traditional sense, as part of a rhythm dictated by the liturgical calendar; these days we are not likely to believe that long-term, grueling self-denial is particularly healthy. But if that is so, neither, then, can long-term, incessant self-indulgence be. Even in the modern world, we need to hear a note of sacrifice, of emptiness, to offset the cacophony of our too-full lives.

We need a rhythm that draws us apart now and again, and the few fast days (Ash Wednesday and Good Friday) mentioned in the Book of Common Prayer are surely not excessive. Nor, certainly, would it be dangerously austere to make some little gesture on the days "observed by special acts of discipline" (Lenten weekdays and all Fridays outside of festival seasons).

Fasting is something undertaken in community and as an expression of community. In this sense, it fulfills basically the same function as eating together. Both partaking of food in community and abstaining from food in community have this in common: it isn't the food itself that's the most important. It's the symbolic and experiential value of letting what we do with food shape us. Many people have commented how much more cohesive a community is when it has clearly understood dietary practices: fish on Fridays, no pork, no caffeine, whatever. Every time you sit at table you have a reminder: this is who I am. I am part of a "We."

Those "We's" and their rules have been used to instill fear, of course. On one level, it is probably a moral advance to realize that God is not automatically obligated to punish us if we violate a particular dietary regulation. Having a hamburger on a fast day will not irreparably rupture our relationship with Christ.

But if we do go on and skip the fast days completely, we have lost something in surrendering that which sets us apart. When "we" behave at table exactly like "they" do, we lose one more of those reminders that we are God's people. Yes, it may feel awkward and unusual to follow an ancient dietary restriction based on a calendar the secular world isn't even using. But think of it this way: isn't that precisely the point?

FRENCH APPLE PIE

6–7 cooking apples, sliced thin
1/4 cup sugar
1/4 teaspoon cinnamon
2 tablespoons lemon juice
1 (9-inch) unbaked pie crust
1/4 cup firmly packed brown
  sugar
1/2 cup all-purpose flour
1/4 cup butter or margarine
1/2 cup broken nuts

Mix apples with sugar, cinnamon, and lemon juice; arrange in pie crust. Mix brown sugar and flour in a medium bowl. Cut in butter until mixture is like cornmeal. Add nuts and sprinkle mixture over apples. Bake at 400° for 30 minutes. Reduce to 375° and cook 30 minutes longer.
Yields: 8 servings

St. Andrew's 75th Celebration
St. Andrew's Episcopal Church
Maryville, Tennessee

MILLIONAIRE PIE

1 (8-ounce) container frozen
  whipped topping
1 (4-ounce) jar maraschino
  cherries, chopped
1/4 cup lemon juice
1/2 cup chopped pecans
1 (14-ounce) can sweetened
  condensed milk
1 (8-ounce) can crushed
  pineapple, drained
2 (8-inch) graham cracker
  crusts

Mix the first 6 ingredients in a large bowl. Spoon into the graham cracker crusts. Refrigerate several hours before serving.
Yields: 12 to 16 pieces

Angels in the Kitchen, II
Emmanuel Episcopal Church
Bristol, Virginia

SODA CRACKER PIE

3 large egg whites
1 teaspoon baking powder
1 cup sugar
1 teaspoon vanilla
12–14 soda crackers,
  coarsely broken
3/4 cups pecans, chopped
1 1/2 cups whipped cream

Combine egg whites and baking powder; beat until stiff. Add sugar slowly; add vanilla and beat until creamy. Add crackers and nuts. Pour into greased pie plate. Bake at 350° for 30 minutes; cool. An hour before serving, cover with whipped cream and return to refrigerator.
Yields: 6 servings

Gracing Your Table
Christ Episcopal Church
Hudson, Ohio

STRAWBERRY-RHUBARB PIE

4 cups chopped rhubarb
1 pint chopped strawberries
1 1/4 cup sugar
1/3 cup orange juice
2 tablespoons tapioca
1/4 teaspoon salt
2 tablespoons butter
1 (3-ounce) package
  strawberry gelatin
Pastry for two (9-inch) pies

Combine rhubarb, strawberries, sugar, orange juice, tapioca, salt, butter, and gelatin. Let stand 15 minutes or longer. Prepare crusts and line two (9-inch) pie pans. Divide filling for each and cover with top crusts. Bake at 375° for 40 minutes.
Yields: 2 (9-inch) pies

Butter 'n Love Recipes
St. Matthew's Episcopal Church
Unadilla, New York

CREAMY PEACH PIE

1 regular or deep-dish pie crust
3 cups fresh or frozen
  unsweetened peaches,
  drained and chopped
1/4 cup sugar
1 (8-ounce) package cream
  cheese, softened
1 cup confectioners' sugar
1 teaspoon vanilla
2 cups frozen whipped topping,
  thawed

Bake pie crust according to directions; cool. Combine 1 1/2 cups peaches and sugar in a small saucepan. Bring to a boil, stirring occasionally, and continue to cook 4 to 5 minutes, or until peaches are soft; cool. Beat cream cheese, confectioners' sugar, and vanilla in a medium bowl. Fold in whipped topping and remaining peaches. Spoon into pie crust. Arrange cooked peaches evenly over top of cream cheese mixture. Chill several hours, until set.
Yields: 6 to 8 servings

Family Collections
St. Matthew's Episcopal Church
Snellville, Georgia

GRAPE PIE

1 cup seeded Concord grapes
3 large egg yolks
1 1/2 cups sugar
1/2 cup melted butter
3 heaping tablespoons
  all-purpose flour
1 tablespoon water
1 (9-inch) pie crust
3 large egg whites
6 tablespoons sugar

Snip grape peels with scissors until fine. Combine grapes and next 5 ingredients in a bowl; mix well and pour into pie crust. Bake at 350° for 1 hour. Beat egg whites with sugar until stiff peaks form. Spoon over pie. Bake 10 minutes longer or until brown.
Yields: 6 to 8 servings

Gifts from the Kitchen
Church of the Advent
Cynthiana, Kentucky

KUMQUAT REFRIGERATOR PIE

1 (14-ounce) can sweetened
  condensed milk
1 (8-ounce) container frozen
  whipped topping, thawed
1/2 cup lemon juice
1/3 cup pureed kumquats
1 (9-inch) baked pie crust
Mint leaves and kumquats for
  garnish

Beat together condensed milk and whipped topping in a large bowl. Add lemon juice and beat until thickened. Fold in kumquats. Pour into baked pie crust; chill for several hours. Garnish with mint leaves and kumquats, if desired.
Yields: 6 to 8 servings

The Garden of Eatin' Cook Book
Diocese of Southwest Florida

STRAWBERRY TART

1/2 cup currant or guava jelly,
  melted
1 tablespoon rum
1 (9-inch) baked pie crust
1 quart ripe strawberries
Crème Chantilly

CRÈME CHANTILLY
1 cup heavy cream
2 tablespoons sugar
1 teaspoon vanilla or 1
  tablespoon rum

Combine the jelly and rum and paint the bottom and sides of the shell. Wash the berries and remove the stems. Arrange berries cut side down in the shell and brush with melted jelly. Serve with Créme Chantilly.
Note: This tart has more flavor if not refrigerated.
Yields: 6 to 8 servings

Beat the cream until stiff; stir in the sugar and the flavoring. Refrigerate until ready to serve.

Suppers in Season
All Saints' Episcopal Church
Wolfeboro, New Hampshire

SOUR CREAM RAISIN PIE

1 cup sour cream
1 cup sugar
1 cup raisins, chopped
3 large egg yolks, beaten
1/8 teaspoon cinnamon
1/8 teaspoon cloves
1/8 teaspoon nutmeg
1 (9-inch) pie crust
3 large egg whites
Sugar to taste

Combine first 7 ingredients and pour into unbaked pie crust. Bake at 350° for 30 minutes. Beat egg whites and sugar until stiff peaks form. Cover pie with meringue and bake 20 minutes more. Chill before serving.
Yields: 6 to 8 servings

Our Daily Bread and More
St. Christopher's Episcopal Church
Kingsport, Tennessee

PINK GRAPEFRUIT PIE

4 grapefruits
1 cup sugar
1 (3-ounce) package unflavored
  gelatin
1/4 cup cold water
2 cups frozen whipped topping,
  thawed
1 (10-inch) graham cracker
  crust

Cut grapefruits in half, remove segments, set aside. Squeeze shells to obtain 1 cup grapefruit juice. Combine sugar and 1 cup grapefruit juice in a saucepan and bring to a boil. Sprinkle gelatin over cold water. Add to hot juice. Stir until dissolved. Place in freezer; chill until thickened then fold in whipped topping and grapefruit sections (with skins removed). Spoon into pie crust and refrigerate until ready to serve.
Yields: 6 to 8 servings

Diocese Board Collection
Diocese of Central Pennsylvania

TEXAS PECAN PIE

8 tablespoons all-purpose flour
1 cup firmly packed light
  brown sugar
2 cups warm milk
2 large egg yolks, beaten
1/2 teaspoon salt
2 tablespoons butter
1 teaspoon vanilla
1 cup coarsely broken pecans
1 (9-inch) baked pie crust

Combine flour and sugar in a large saucepan. Stir in warm milk, egg yolks, and salt. Cook over medium heat until thick, stirring constantly. Remove from heat and add butter, vanilla, and pecans. Cool and pour into the baked shell. Serve warm or cold.
Yields: 6 to 8 servings

The Galveston Island Cookbook
Trinity Episcopal Church
Galveston, Texas

PIE CRUST

3 cups all-purpose flour
1 teaspoon salt
1 cup shortening
1 large egg, beaten
1 tablespoon vinegar
1/3 cup cold water

Sift flour and salt; add shortening and cut in until mixture resembles cornmeal. Combine egg, vinegar, and water; add to flour mixture. Stir lightly with fork until dough follows fork in the bowl. Form into a ball. Chill until ready to roll into crusts. Will keep in refrigerator for 1 week.
Yields: 2 (9-inch) double crusts

Angels in the Kitchen, II
Emmanuel Episcopal Church
Bristol, Virginia

CRUSTLESS COCONUT MACAROON PIE

2 large eggs, lightly beaten
1 cup sugar
1/2 cup water
1/4 cup all-purpose flour
1/4 teaspoon almond extract
1/4 teaspoon salt
1 1/3 cups coconut
1/3 cup butter, melted

Combine eggs, sugar, water, flour, almond extract, and salt in a large bowl until well blended. Stir in coconut and melted butter. Pour into well-buttered 9-inch pie pan. Bake at 350° for about 35 minutes or until lightly browned. Serve at room temperature but refrigerate any leftovers (covered with plastic wrap).
Yields: 8 servings

Heavenly Hosts
St. John's Episcopal Church
Naples, Florida

POUND CAKE
(A family recipe that's more than 100 years old)

2 cups sugar
2 sticks butter or margarine
5 large eggs
2 cups all-purpose flour
3 tablespoons bourbon

Cream sugar and butter in a large bowl; add eggs, one at a time, mixing well after each addition. Add flour, a tablespoon at a time. Add bourbon. Pour batter into a greased tube pan. Bake at 325° for 50 to 60 minutes.
Yields: 10 to 12 servings

St. David's Cookbook
St. David's Episcopal Church
Nashville, Tennessee

RUSSIAN EASTER CAKE (PASHKA)

3 (24-ounce) packages large
  curd cottage cheese
16 large egg yolks
3 tablespoons vanilla
1 1/4 cups sugar
1 cup whipping cream
1 1/2 pounds unsalted butter,
  melted and cooled
Almonds and candied fruit for
  decoration

Line a colander with cheesecloth. Put in cottage cheese and drain in bowl in refrigerator with top weighted, for 4 days. After draining, force cottage cheese through a coarse sieve. Beat egg yolks until light and fluffy. Add vanilla and sugar; mix well. Stir in drained cottage cheese, whipping cream, and butter and blend well. Put into a flower pot lined with double thickness of damp cheesecloth. Put into bowl for draining (do not plug up hole). Weight top with plate and brick. Set in refrigerator and let drain for 2 or 3 days. Turn onto plate and decorate with almonds and fruit.
Yields: 30 servings

Food and Gladness
St. Francis Episcopal Church
Norris, Tennessee

CHOCOLATE CAKE

1/4 pound butter
3/4 cup sugar
2 tablespoons golden syrup
1 1/2 cups all-purpose flour
1 teaspoon baking powder
1 teaspoon baking soda
3 teaspoons cocoa
2 large eggs, beaten whole

Cream butter and sugar in a large bowl. Add golden syrup and stir well. Combine the flour, baking powder, baking soda, and cocoa in a bowl. Add eggs to the creamed mixture, alternating with the flour mixture. If a little too dry, add a little milk and mix in. Pour into a well-greased oblong pan, with buttered paper on the bottom. Bake at 350° for 25 to 30 minutes. Be careful not to overcook as this cake has a tendency to burn. Cool on rack and ice with chocolate icing.
Yields: 8 to 10 servings

A Book of Favorite Recipes
Grace Episcopal Church and
Grace Day School
Massapequa, New York

MOUTH-LICKING CHOCOLATE CAKE

1 (2-layer) devil's food
  cake mix
1/2 cup sugar
3/4 cup vegetable oil
4 large eggs
1/2 cup water
1 teaspoon vanilla
1 (8-ounce) carton sour cream
  or yogurt
Frosting

Combine all ingredients in a large mixer bowl. Blend just until moistened on low speed; beat until enough air has been incorporated to make the cake rise high and fluffy. Pour into greased 9 × 13-inch baking pan. Bake at 350° for 40 to 45 minutes, or until done when tested with toothpick. Cool, then cover with Frosting.
Yields: 12 to 15 servings

FROSTING
1 cup sugar
1/4 cup cornstarch
2 squares unsweetened
  chocolate
1 1/2 cups boiling water
2 tablespoons butter or
  margarine
1 teaspoon vanilla
1/4 teaspoon salt

In small pan mix sugar and cornstarch. Break chocolate into halves and add to sugar mixture. Stir water slowly into mixture; blend well. Cook on medium heat, stirring constantly. Stir in butter, vanilla, and salt. Cool to lukewarm before adding to cake.

...and Sew We Eat!
Diocese of Hawaii
Honolulu, Hawaii

CHOCOLATE COCA-COLA CAKE

2 cups all-purpose flour
2 cups sugar
1 cup butter or margarine
3 tablespoons dry cocoa
1 cup Coca-Cola
1/2 cup buttermilk
2 large eggs, beaten
1 teaspoon baking soda
1 teaspoon vanilla
2 cups miniature marshmallows
Icing

Combine flour and sugar in a large bowl. Heat butter, cocoa, and Coca-Cola in saucepan; bring to a boil. Pour over flour mixture; mix well. Add buttermilk, eggs, soda, vanilla, and marshmallows; mix well. Pour into a 9 × 13-inch baking pan. Bake at 350° for 35 minutes. Spread Icing on cake while still warm.

Yields: 10 to 12 servings

ICING
1/2 cup butter or margarine
3 tablespoons cocoa
6 tablespoons Coca-Cola
1 pound confectioners' sugar
1 cup chopped pecans
1 teaspoon vanilla

Combine butter and next 2 ingredients in a saucepan. Heat until boiling. Pour over sugar in a large bowl; beat well. Stir in nuts and vanilla.

Kitchen Confessions
St. Edward's Episcopal Church
Lawrenceville, Georgia

❖

JUST AFTER DAYBREAK, JESUS STOOD ON THE BEACH; BUT THE DISCIPLES DID NOT KNOW THAT IT WAS JESUS. JESUS SAID TO THEM, "CHILDREN, YOU HAVE NO FISH, HAVE YOU?" THEY ANSWERED HIM, "NO." HE SAID TO THEM, "CAST THE NET TO THE RIGHT SIDE OF THE BOAT, AND YOU WILL FIND SOME." SO THEY CAST IT, AND NOW THEY WERE NOT ABLE TO HAUL IT IN BECAUSE THERE WERE SO MANY FISH. THAT DISCIPLE WHOM JESUS LOVED SAID TO PETER, "IT IS THE LORD!" WHEN SIMON PETER HEARD THAT IT WAS THE LORD, HE PUT ON SOME CLOTHES, FOR HE WAS NAKED, AND JUMPED INTO THE SEA. BUT THE OTHER DISCIPLES CAME IN THE BOAT, DRAGGING THE NET FULL OF FISH, FOR THEY WERE NOT FAR FROM THE LAND, ONLY ABOUT A HUNDRED YARDS OFF.

WHEN THEY HAD GONE ASHORE, THEY SAW A CHARCOAL FIRE THERE, WITH FISH ON IT, AND BREAD. JESUS SAID TO THEM, "BRING SOME OF THE FISH THAT YOU HAVE JUST CAUGHT." SO SIMON PETER WENT ABOARD AND HAULED THE NET ASHORE, FULL OF LARGE FISH, A HUNDRED FIFTY-THREE OF THEM; AND THOUGH THERE WERE SO MANY, THE NET WAS NOT TORN. JESUS SAID TO THEM, "COME AND HAVE BREAKFAST." NOW NONE OF THE DISCIPLES DARED TO ASK HIM, "WHO ARE YOU?" BECAUSE THEY KNEW IT WAS THE LORD. JESUS CAME AND TOOK THE BREAD AND GAVE IT TO THEM, AND DID THE SAME WITH THE FISH.

JOHN 21:4–13
(JESUS APPEARS TO THE DISCIPLES WHILE THEY ARE FISHING)

PUMPKIN PIE CAKE

1 (2-layer) yellow cake mix
1/4 cup melted margarine
1 large egg
1 (29-ounce) can pumpkin
1 1/2 cups sugar
1 teaspoon cinnamon
2 large eggs
1 (5-ounce) can evaporated
  milk
1/2 teaspoon salt
1/2 teaspoon ginger
1/4 teaspoon cloves
1/4 cup all-purpose flour
1/4 cup firmly packed brown
  sugar
1/4 cup margarine, softened

Combine cake mix, 1/4 cup melted margarine, and egg in a bowl; mix well. Set aside 1 cup mixture for the topping. Press remaining mixture into a 9 × 13-inch baking pan. Combine the pumpkin and next 7 ingredients in a large bowl; mix well. Spread over cake crust. Combine the reserved cup cake mix batter and the remaining 3 ingredients; mix well. Drop in dollops here and there on top of the pumpkin mix. Bake at 350° for 40 to 50 minutes. Garnish with whipped cream, if desired.
Yields: about 12 servings

Parish Collection
Epiphany Episcopal Church
Cape Coral, Florida

CARROT CAKE

3 cups finely grated carrots
2 cups sugar
1 1/2 cups vegetable oil
2 cups sifted plain flour
2 teaspoons salt
2 teaspoons cinnamon
2 teaspoons baking soda
4 large eggs
Cream Cheese Frosting

Mix carrots, sugar, and oil in a large bowl; beat well. Combine dry ingredients in a bowl and sift; add to carrot mixture. Add eggs; beat well. Spoon batter into 3 round cake pans. Bake at 300° for 35 minutes. Cool, then frost with Cream Cheese Frosting.
Yields: 10 to 12 servings

CREAM CHEESE FROSTING
1 (16-ounce) box confectioners'
  sugar
2 teaspoons vanilla
1 (8-ounce) package cream
  cheese
1 stick margarine
1 cup chopped pecans

Combine the first 4 ingredients; beat well with a mixer. Stir in pecans.

Down Plantation Road
St. Philip Episcopal Church
Bartlett, Tennessee

CARROT BUNDT CAKE

1 cup sugar
2 1/4 cups all-purpose flour
1 cup firmly packed brown
   sugar
1 1/2 teaspoons baking soda
1 teaspoon salt
2 tablespoons cinnamon
3 (4-ounce) jars baby food
   strained carrots
1/4 cup raisins
3 large eggs
1/2 cup dates
3/4 cup vegetable oil
1/2 cup chopped nuts
1 teaspoon vanilla

Grease and flour a 12-cup fluted Bundt pan. In large bowl, combine all ingredients; blend until moistened. Beat 3 minutes at medium speed (portable mixer at high speed), scraping bowl occasionally. Pour batter into prepared pan. Bake at 350° for 60 to 65 minutes, or until toothpick inserted in center comes out clean. Cool upright in pan 45 minutes. Turn out; cool.
Yields: 10 to 12 servings

Christ Episcopal Church Cookbook
Christ Episcopal Church
Pearisburg, Virginia

FRESH APPLE CAKE

1 cup vegetable oil
2 cups sugar
3 large eggs
1 teaspoon vanilla
2 cups self-rising flour
3 cups chopped tart cooking
   apples
1 cup pecans or walnuts
1 teaspoon cinnamon
1 teaspoon nutmeg
Glaze

Combine oil, sugar, and eggs in a large bowl; add vanilla. Add flour; beat thoroughly. Add remaining ingredients and stir to blend well. Turn into a greased and floured 9 × 13-inch pan. Bake at 350° for 40 to 45 minutes. Spread Glaze on cake while it is still warm.
Yields: 10 to 12 servings

GLAZE
1/2 stick margarine
1/2 cup firmly packed light
   brown sugar
1/2 teaspoon vanilla
2 tablespoons milk

Combine all ingredients in a medium saucepan; boil for 1 minute.

Potluck Sunday
St. Mary's Episcopal Church
Madisonville, Kentucky

BLUEBERRY CAKE

2 large egg whites
1 cup sugar, divided
1/2 cup shortening
2 large egg yolks
1 teaspoon vanilla
1/2 teaspoon salt
1 1/2 cups all-purpose flour
1 teaspoon baking powder
1/2 cup milk
1 tablespoon all-purpose flour
1 1/2 cups blueberries
Sugar and cinnamon

Beat egg whites in a bowl; add about 1/4 cup sugar. Cream shortening in a separate large bowl; add remaining sugar and egg yolks, and beat until light and creamy. Add vanilla and salt. Sift together 1 1/2 cups flour and baking powder; add alternately with milk to creamed mixture. Sprinkle 1 tablespoon flour over berries. Fold berries and egg whites into batter. Sprinkle with sugar and cinnamon. Bake at 350° for 45 to 50 minutes.

Yields: 8 to 10 servings

Treasure of Personal Recipes
Church of Our Fathers
Hulls Cove, Maine

PINEAPPLE UPSIDE-DOWN CAKE

1 cup butter or margarine
1–2 cups firmly packed brown
   sugar
1 (16-ounce) can sliced
   pineapple
4 tablespoons chopped nuts or
   chopped maraschino cherries
6 large eggs, separated
2 cups sugar, divided
10 tablespoons pineapple juice
2 cups sifted cake flour
2 teaspoon baking powder
1/2 teaspoon salt

Melt butter in a 9 × 13-inch baking pan. Sprinkle brown sugar evenly in pan. Drain pineapple slices but reserve juice; arrange slices on top of brown sugar, filling spaces with nuts or maraschino cherries. Beat egg yolks until light, adding 1 1/2 cups sugar gradually. Add pineapple juice. Combine flour, baking powder, and salt; add to yolk mixture. Beat 6 egg whites with remaining 1/2 cup sugar until stiff; then fold into the flour batter. Pour over pineapple mixture in pan. Bake at 350° for about 45 minutes or until cake tests done with toothpick. Wait 10 minutes, then turn upside down on platter.

Yields: 8 servings

...and Sew We Eat!
Diocese of Hawaii
Honolulu, Hawaii

SIMNEL CAKE

(In olden days, this was a fine fruitcake made for Christmas, Easter, and other religious holidays. Such cakes were not ordinary fare for the common people in older times and represented a real treat. This version is supposed to be served on Mothering Sunday, the fourth Sunday in Lent, and perhaps it still is somewhere in England. Occasionally, this cake was baked in a circular form and charms were tucked into various spots before baking. The person who got the ring would be the next to marry; the thimble indicated luck.)

1 stick butter
1 cup sugar
4 large eggs
2 cups all-purpose flour
4 ounces candied chopped
  citron
3 cups currants
White Icing

Cream butter and sugar until fluffy, then add eggs one at a time, beating well after each one. Sift and measure flour, then use some of it to mix with citron and currants. This is necessary to keep fruit separated in fruitcake batter. Add coated fruit to batter and mix well, then add remaining flour. Blend all thoroughly, but not too long. Spoon batter into a greased and floured 9 × 13-inch cake pan. Bake cake at 275° to 300° until a tester comes out clean, about 1 hour. Spread top with thin White Icing when cake is cool.
Yields: 12 to 15 servings

WHITE ICING
Sifted confectioners' sugar
Butter
Hot milk

Combine the ingredients in a small bowl until you reach a spreadable consistency.

Grandma's Pantry Cookbook
St. Mark's Episcopal Church
Marco Island, Florida

ON THE THIRD DAY THERE WAS A WEDDING IN CANA OF GALILEE, AND THE MOTHER OF JESUS WAS THERE. JESUS AND HIS DISCIPLES HAD ALSO BEEN INVITED TO THE WEDDING. WHEN THE WINE GAVE OUT, THE MOTHER OF JESUS SAID TO HIM, "THEY HAVE NO WINE." AND JESUS SAID TO HER, "WOMAN, WHAT CONCERN IS THAT TO YOU AND TO ME? MY HOUR HAS NOT YET COME." HIS MOTHER SAID TO THE SERVANTS, "DO WHATEVER HE TELLS YOU."

NOW STANDING THERE WERE SIX STONE WATER JARS FOR THE JEWISH RITES OF PURIFICATION, EACH HOLDING TWENTY OR THIRTY GALLONS. JESUS SAID TO THEM, "FILL THE JARS WITH WATER." AND THEY FILLED THEM UP TO THE BRIM. HE SAID TO THEM, "NOW DRAW SOME OUT, AND TAKE IT TO THE CHIEF STEWARD." SO THEY TOOK IT. WHEN THE STEWARD TASTED THE WATER THAT HAD BECOME WINE, AND DID NOT KNOW WHERE IT CAME FROM (THOUGH THE SERVANTS WHO HAD DRAWN THE WATER KNEW), THE STEWARD CALLED THE BRIDEGROOM AND SAID TO HIM, "EVERYONE SERVES THE GOOD WINE FIRST, AND THEN THE INFERIOR WINE AFTER THE GUESTS HAVE BECOME DRUNK. BUT YOU HAVE KEPT THE GOOD WINE UNTIL NOW." JESUS DID THIS, THE FIRST OF HIS SIGNS, IN CANA OF GALILEE, AND REVEALED HIS GLORY; AND HIS DISCIPLES BELIEVED HIM.

JOHN 2:1–11
(JESUS TURNS WATER INTO WINE)

BURNT-SUGAR CAKE

3/4 cup shortening
1 1/2 cups sugar
2 large eggs
1 teaspoon vanilla
2 1/2 cups all-purpose flour
2 teaspoons baking powder
1/2 teaspoon baking soda
1/4 teaspoon salt
1 cup milk
2 teaspoons Burnt-Sugar Syrup

Cream shortening and sugar in a large bowl; add eggs and vanilla. Combine dry ingredients. Add alternately with milk. Add Burnt-Sugar Syrup. Bake at 375° for about 25 minutes.
Yields: 8 to 10 servings

BURNT-SUGAR SYRUP
1/2 cup sugar
3/4 cup water

Place sugar in a heavy pan or skillet and heat until melted and deep golden brown in color. Add water, and boil until mixture becomes a thin syrup. Use sufficient syrup to color the cake to your liking.

Cook Book
Church of the Transfiguration
Bennington, Kansas

HARVEY WALLBANGER CAKE

1 (2-layer) package yellow cake
    mix
1 (4-ounce) package instant
    vanilla pudding
1/2 cup vegetable oil
1/2 cup sugar
4 large eggs
1 1/4 cups vodka
1/4 cup Galliano
3/4 cup orange juice
Orange Glaze

Mix all ingredients together in a large bowl. Beat for 4 minutes. Pour batter into well-greased and lightly floured Bundt pan. Bake at 350° for 40 to 50 minutes. Remove from oven; let set for about 10 minutes. Turn cake out on cooling rack. When cold, frost with Orange Glaze.
Note: You may use all orange juice instead of vodka and Galliano.
Yields: 10 to 12 servings

ORANGE GLAZE
Sifted confectioners' sugar
Melted butter
Orange juice

Combine ingredients in bowl, using enough of each to make a thin liquid to drizzle over cake.

Recipes—and Remembrances
Zion Episcopal Church
Avon, New York

CHOCOLATE CHIP CHEESE CAKE

1 cup vanilla wafer crumbs
1/4 cup butter, melted
2 (8-ounce) packages cream
  cheese, softened
3/4 cup sugar
1/2 cup sour cream
4 large eggs
1 teaspoon vanilla extract
1 (6-ounce) package semisweet
  chocolate chips
Topping

TOPPING
1 cup sour cream
1 1/2 teaspoons lemon juice
1 1/2 teaspoons vanilla extract
1/2 cup sugar

Combine crumbs and butter in a small bowl until blended. Press into bottom and 1/2 inch up sides of pan. Beat cream cheese, sugar, sour cream, eggs, and vanilla in a large bowl; mix well. Stir in chocolate chips. Pour batter into crust. Bake 40 minutes at 325° or until a 3-inch circle in the center jiggles when pan is shaken. Cheese cake will become firm as it cools. Remove from oven and cool in pan 20 minutes. Prepare Topping. Gently spoon over cheese cake. Bake 5 minutes at 475°. Cool before serving.
Yields: 10 servings

Combine all ingredients in a bowl; mix well.

Hometown Recipes of Palmetto
St. Mary's Episcopal Church
Palmetto, Florida

ULTIMATE NO-BAKE CHOCOLATE CHEESECAKE

1 1/2 cups graham wafer
  crumbs
1/3 cup brown sugar
1/2 cup firmly packed
  melted butter
2 large eggs, separated
1/4 cup firmly packed
  brown sugar
1/2 pint whipping cream
8 ounces semisweet
  chocolate bits
1 (8-ounce) package cream
  cheese, softened
1/2 cup firmly packed
  brown sugar
1 teaspoon vanilla

Blend crumbs and 1/3 cup brown sugar together with a fork. Stir in melted butter. Press evenly in the bottom and sides of a buttered 8-inch springform pan or a deep 9-inch pie plate. Refrigerate. Beat egg whites until soft peak stage. Beat in 1/4 cup brown sugar until they hold stiff glossy peaks; refrigerate. Without washing beaters, whip cream in another bowl until it holds soft peaks; refrigerate. Melt chocolate. Combine cream cheese, 1/2 cup brown sugar, egg yolks, and vanilla in a large mixing bowl. Without washing beaters, beat until well mixed. Beat in warm chocolate. Cool to room temperature. Add whipped cream into chocolate mixture, then beaten egg whites. Gently pour into chilled crust and refrigerate overnight.
Yields: 12 servings

What's Cooking?
St. John's Episcopal Church
Huntington, L.I., New York

MOCHA SOUR CREAM TORTE

1 cup heavy cream
2 cups firmly packed light
  brown sugar
2 tablespoons cocoa
2 teaspoons instant coffee
1 cup sour cream
1 small angel food cake
Shredded coconut

Beat cream in medium bowl at medium speed of an electric mixer; then add sugar, cocoa, and coffee, whipping until soft peaks form. Fold in sour cream. Cut cake horizontally in thirds. Place 1 layer on plate and spread on it about 1/4 cream mixture. Repeat layering of cake and cream mixture, ending with a cake layer. Frost sides and top with remaining cream. Garnish with coconut and refrigerate.
Yields: 10 servings

Cooking with Grace
Grace Church
Bath, Maine

ORLEANS TORTE

7 squares (1-ounce each)
  semisweet chocolate
1/2 cup butter
1 cup sugar, divided
7 large egg yolks
7 large egg whites
Sweetened whipped cream
Chocolate shavings
1 cup finely chopped pecans

Melt chocolate and butter in a saucepan over low heat. In small mixing bowl, beat chocolate, butter, egg yolks, and 1/4 cup sugar for 3 minutes at high speed. In separate bowl, beat egg whites until soft peaks form. Add remaining 3/4 cup sugar gradually and beat until whites hold their peaks. Fold egg whites into chocolate batter. Pour three-fourths of batter into ungreased 9-inch springform pan. Bake at 325° for 35 minutes. Let torte cool and set. Run knife around edge to loosen and remove springform frame. Pour remaining uncooked batter over the top and chill. Garnish with whipped cream and chocolate shavings. Press finely chopped pecans onto sides of torte.
Yields: 8 to 10 servings

La Bonne Cuisine, Lagniappe
All Saints' Episcopal Church
River Ridge, Louisiana

CHOCOLATE DESSERT

1 stick margarine or butter
1 cup chopped pecans
1 cup sifted all-purpose flour
1 (8-ounce) package cream
   cheese
1 cup confectioners' sugar
1 cup frozen whipped topping,
   thawed
1 (4-ounce) package chocolate
   instant pudding
1 (4-ounce) package vanilla
   instant pudding
2 1/2 cups milk
Frozen whipped topping,
   thawed
Chocolate shavings or
   chopped nuts

Combine margarine, nuts and flour in a large bowl; mix well. Press into 9 × 13-inch baking dish. Bake at 350° for 20 minutes; cool. Combine cream cheese and next 2 ingredients. Spread on cooled crust. Beat puddings and milk in a large bowl for about 2 minutes. Spread over cream cheese layer. Top with whipped topping and shaved chocolate or chopped nuts. Cut into squares. Keep refrigerated.
Yields: 12 to 15 servings

Parish Collection
St. Mary's Episcopal Church
Mitchell, South Dakota

BAKED APPLES

5 cooking apples
1/2 cup cranberries
1/2 cup walnuts
1/2 cup firmly packed brown
   sugar
1/2 cup plain bread crumbs
1 teaspoon cinnamon
Zest of 1 lemon
5 tablespoons unsalted butter

Wash and core apples; place in an oblong baking pan. Combine cranberries, nuts, sugar, bread crumbs, cinnamon, zest, and butter in a bowl; mix well. Stuff apples with filling and mound on top. Bake at 275° for about 25 minutes or until filling is bubbly. Serve hot or cold.
Yields: 5 servings

Parish Collection
St. John's Episcopal Church
Homestead, Florida

APPLE CRISP

1 quart apples, peeled, cored,
  and sliced
1 tablespoon lemon juice
1/2 tablespoon grated lemon
  rind
1/4 cup water
1/2 cup sugar
2 tablespoons quick tapioca
1 teaspoon ground cinnamon
1/2 teaspoon ground nutmeg
1/4 teaspoon salt
1 cup raisins
1/3 cup all-purpose flour
1/3 cup nonfat dry milk
  powder
2/3 cup sugar
1/2 teaspoon salt
1/3 cup butter or margarine

Toss apples with lemon juice, rind, and water in a large bowl. Add 1/2 cup sugar, tapioca, cinnamon, nutmeg, 1/4 teaspoon salt, and raisins; mix well. Spoon into an 11 × 7-inch baking dish. Combine flour and remaining ingredients; mix until crumbly. Sprinkle over apple mixture. Bake at 375° for 35 to 40 minutes or until apples are tender and crust is brown.
Yields: 6 to 8 servings

A Book of Favorite Recipes
St. Elizabeth's Episcopal Church
Elizabeth, New Jersey

EASY PEACH COBBLER

6 cups sliced fresh peaches
2 teaspoons lemon juice
1 teaspoon nutmeg
1 teaspoon cinnamon
2 cups self-rising flour
2 large eggs, slightly beaten
2 cups sugar
2 sticks butter or margarine,
  melted

Place peaches in a greased 9 × 13-inch baking dish. Sprinkle with lemon juice, nutmeg, and cinnamon. Combine flour, egg, and sugar in a large bowl until crumbly. Spread over peaches. Pour butter evenly over flour mixture. Bake, uncovered, at 350° for 30 to 35 minutes.
Yields: 8 to 10 servings

Saints Preserve Us Cookbook
St. Edward's Episcopal Church
Lawrenceville, Georgia

BLUEBERRY COBBLER

1 stick butter
1 cup self-rising flour
1 cup sugar
1 cup milk
1 1/2–2 cups blueberries

Place butter in 9 × 13-inch baking dish; melt butter in 375° oven. Combine flour, sugar, and milk in a bowl; stir until mixed. Some lumps will remain. Pour flour mixture on top of melted butter, then spoon in prepared blueberries. Bake for 45 minutes.
Note: Peaches can be added to blueberries.
Yields: 8 servings

Parish Collection
Church of the Cross
Bluffton, South Carolina

MRS. DESHA'S PLUM PUDDINGS

(This recipe has been used since 1925 to make the plum puddings that have helped provide funding for ECW projects. In the beginning, two to four were made annually, but in 1998, 430 puddings sold within eight weeks.)

1 (24-ounce) loaf white bread, left open to stale for at least four days
1 pound raisins
1 pound currants
1/4 pound cherries, chopped
1/4 pound chopped candied lemons
1/4 pound chopped candied orange
1/4 pound chopped candied citron
1/2 cup pecan pieces (or other nuts, as desired)
1/2 pound beef suet, ground finely
2 1/2 cups scalded milk (or more if needed)
4 large eggs
1 1/2 teaspoons vanilla
2 cups sugar
2 teaspoons nutmeg
1 teaspoon cinnamon
1/2 teaspoon salt

Tear stale bread into small fingernail-size pieces; set aside. Weigh and measure fruit and nuts; set aside. Mix bread and suet in very large bowl; pour in warm milk to melt suet and dampen bread. If bread has not become stale enough, more milk may be needed. Beat eggs and vanilla thoroughly, add sugar and dry spices, then pour this mix into the bread/suet bowl. Stir until combined. Add fruits and nuts and stir longer. Put this combination into 4 cans, if you are going to steam commercially. Use pudding molds for steaming at home. To steam, cover bowl with cloth tied on very securely. Place in boiling water. Steam for at least 1 1/2 hours.

To process commercially, get cans from cannery that are about the size of a large tomato can. Fill 3/4 full or better to weigh carefully, with allowance for the weight of the can. This size can provides 2 pounds of pudding. Take filled cans to cannery, where they can be steamed about an hour. Cap cans. Place in pressure cooker for about another hour. Plunge cans into cold water, then wipe off and set aside to cool.
Yields: four (2-pound) puddings

Parish Collection
R. E. Lee Memorial Episcopal Church
Lexington, Virginia

PERSIMMON PUDDING

2 cups self-rising flour
2 cups sugar
1 teaspoon cinnamon
2 large eggs, beaten
2 cups milk
2 cups persimmon pulp
1 cup shredded raw sweet
   potato
2 tablespoons melted butter

Combine flour, sugar, and cinnamon; mix well. Stir in eggs and milk. Add remaining ingredients and mix well. Pour in greased 13 × 9-inch pan. Bake at 350° for 45 minutes or until set. Serve warm with whipped topping or ice cream.
Yields: 6 to 8 servings

Parish Collection
St. Peter's Episcopal Church
Altavista, Virginia

SWEET POTATO PUDDING

3 cups mashed sweet potatoes
1 cup sugar
1/4 cup milk
2 large eggs
1/2 cup butter
1 cup firmly packed brown
   sugar
1 cup all-purpose flour
3/4 cup butter
1 cup pecans, chopped

Combine first 6 ingredients in a 2-quart baking dish; mix well. Combine remaining ingredients in a bowl; mix until crumbly. Sprinkle over top of sweet potato mixture. Bake at 350° for 30 minutes.
Yields: 4 to 6 servings

Treasured Recipes
St. Mark's Episcopal Church
Prattville, Alabama

WOJAPI
(Indian Pudding)

2 cups dried or canned fruit
4 cups water
Sugar to taste
Cornstarch and water

Place fruit, water, and sugar in a large saucepan. Cook until fruit is tender, then bring to a boil. Slowly pour a thin mixture of cornstarch and water into the fruit; stir well until mixture is like gravy. Serve warm.
Note: Wild fruit, such as chokecherries, grapes, buffalo berries, plums, were sundried and stored until needed. They were soaked in water before cooking.
Yields: 4 to 6 servings

Santee Dakota Sioux Recipe
St. John's Cathedral
Denver, Colorado

BREAD PUDDING WITH WHISKEY SAUCE

6 cups day-old French bread,
  cubed
1 apple, peeled and finely diced
1 cup raisins
1 cup broken pecans or
  black walnuts
3 large eggs
1 cup sugar
2 cups milk
1 teaspoon vanilla
1/2 teaspoon nutmeg
1/2 teaspoon salt

Combine bread, apple, raisins, and nuts; set aside. Beat eggs until frothy in a large bowl, then beat in sugar. Add milk, vanilla, nutmeg, and salt. Combine bread mixture with egg mixture. Let stand for 15 minutes. Pour mixture into a buttered 1 1/2-quart baking dish. Place this pan in a larger pan. Pour boiling water into outer pan to a depth of 1 inch. Bake at 375° for 40 to 45 minutes. Serve with warm Whiskey Sauce and vanilla ice cream, if desired.
Yields: 8 servings

WHISKEY SAUCE
1 1/3 cups water
1/2 cup firmly packed
  brown sugar
1/4 teaspoon nutmeg
1/4 cup whiskey
1 1/2 tablespoons cornstarch
2 tablespoons butter

Combine water, sugar, and nutmeg in a small saucepan and bring to a boil. In a separate cup, combine whiskey with cornstarch; blend well, then add to water mixture. Cook until thickened. Add butter; stir until melted. Serve immediately.

Angel Food
St. Timothy's Episcopal Church
Signal Mountain, Tennessee

CREAMY RICE PUDDING

1 quart milk
1/2 cup long grain rice
2 large eggs
1/4–1/2 cup sugar
  (according to taste)
1 teaspoon vanilla
1 (5-ounce) can undiluted
  evaporated milk
Nutmeg or cinnamon

Heat milk to simmer in a saucepan. Stir in rice and simmer 20 minutes or until rice is tender, stirring occasionally. Beat eggs with sugar, vanilla, and evaporated milk in a bowl. Add rice, one spoonful at a time, to egg mixture. Then return combination to saucepan and cook slowly until slightly more thickened. Pour into a bowl, stirring often, until cooled. Sprinkle with nutmeg or cinnamon, according to taste.
Yields: 4 to 6 servings

St. Raphael's Cookbook
St. Raphael's Episcopal Church
Brick, New Jersey

ARROZ CON LECHE
(Rice with Milk)

1 1/2 cups rice
10 cups water
1/2 teaspoon salt
4 pieces cinnamon
2 cups evaporated milk
2 (14-ounce) cans condensed milk
1/4 pound raisins

Mix the rice, water, salt, and cinnamon in a large saucepan. Cook at a low temperature for approximately 40 minutes. Once the rice is soft, add the milks and raisins and continue to cook for another 30 minutes. Let cool, place in plastic or glass containers, sprinkle with cinnamon, and serve cold.
Yields: 8 to 10 servings

Representative of National Board of ECW
San Pedro Sula, Honduras, C.A.

CARAMEL CUSTARD

1/2 cup sugar
5 large eggs
1 (14-ounce) can sweetened condensed milk
1 (12-ounce) can evaporated milk
3/4 cup water
Pinch of nutmeg
1/2 teaspoon almond extract

Heat sugar in top of double boiler until it becomes liquid. Spoon into baking dish and let crystallize. Combine eggs and remaining ingredients in a large bowl; mix well and strain. Pour over sugar. Bake at 350° for 1 hour or until knife inserted in center comes out clean.
Yields: 4 to 6 servings

St. Simons ECW Cookbook
St. Simons Episcopal Church
Miami, Florida

LEMON LUSH

1/4 pound butter
1 cup all-purpose flour
1/2 cup chopped nuts
1 (8-ounce) package cream cheese
1 cup confectioners' sugar
1/2 cup whipping cream, whipped
3 cups milk
2 (4-ounce) packages instant lemon pudding
Additional whipped cream for garnish (optional)

Combine butter, flour, and nuts in a bowl; mix until crumbly. Pat into a 9 × 13-inch baking pan. Bake at 350° for 15 minutes; cool. Cream together softened cream cheese and confectioners' sugar. Fold in whipped cream; spread over the baked crust. Mix the milk into the 2 pudding packages. Pour over the above mixture. Let stand overnight. To serve, top with more whipped cream, if desired.
Yields: 8 servings

Parish Collection
St. Luke's Episcopal Church
Delta, Colorado

PECAN TARTLETS

1 (3-ounce) package cream
  cheese, softened
1/2 cup butter or margarine,
  softened
1 cup all-purpose flour, sifted
3/4 cup firmly packed brown
  sugar
1 tablespoon margarine,
  softened
1 large egg
1 teaspoon vanilla
Dash of salt
2/3 cup pecans, coarsely
  chopped

Blend cream cheese and 1/2 cup butter in a large bowl. Stir in flour; mix well. Shape into 2 dozen (1-inch) balls. Place in small ungreased 1 3/4-inch muffin cups. Press dough on bottom and sides of cups to form pastry shells. Chill in refrigerator at least 1 hour or overnight. Mix brown sugar and 1 tablespoon margarine in bowl; then add egg, vanilla, and salt, mixing just until smooth. Divide half the pecans among pastry-lined cups. Add filling mixture, and top with remaining pecans. Bake at 325° for 35 to 40 minutes or until filling is set; cool. Remove from pans by inserting sharp knife around edge of cups.

Yields: 2 dozen servings

St. Anne's Guild Cookbook
St. James the Less Church
Scarsdale, New York

NUT CUPS

1 cup all-purpose flour
1 stick butter or margarine
1 (3-ounce) package cream
  cheese
Dash of salt
3/4 cup chopped nuts
3/4 cup firmly packed
  brown sugar
1 teaspoon vanilla
2 tablespoons butter or
  margarine, softened
1 large egg
Dash of salt
Confectioners' sugar

Cream together flour, 1 stick butter, cream cheese, and a dash of salt in a large bowl. Roll into 24 small even balls. Press into small muffin tins, spreading dough up sides of tin to form a crust. Add 1/2 teaspoon nuts to each cup. Combine brown sugar and next 4 ingredients in a bowl. Add filling to each cup. Sprinkle top with nuts. Bake at 350° for 20 to 30 minutes or until crust is golden brown. Carefully remove from pan. Cool, then sprinkle with confectioners' sugar.

Yields: 24 servings

Blest Be These Feasts
St. Francis of Assisi
Levittown, New York

EPISCOPALIAN BARS

3/4 cup butter or margarine
1 cup firmly packed brown
  sugar
1 large egg yolk
1 teaspoon vanilla
1 cup all-purpose flour
1 cup chocolate bits
1 (1-ounce) square baking
  chocolate

Cream together butter and sugar in a large bowl until light and fluffy. Add yolk and vanilla and blend. Add flour and mix well. Spread evenly in a 10 × 15-inch greased cookie pan. Bake at 350° for 12 to 15 minutes. Cool. Melt chocolates over boiling water, stirring until smooth. Spread over cookies. Let stand a few minutes to partially set. Cut into bars or squares. Cool until chocolate is firm.
Yields: 12 servings

Loaves and Fishes
St. Mark's Episcopal Church
Chenango Bridge, New York

SPICY OLD-FASHIONED RAISIN BARS

1 cup seedless raisins
1 cup water
1 cup sugar
1 large egg, lightly beaten
1/2 cup vegetable oil
1 3/4 cups all-purpose flour
1 teaspoon baking soda
1 teaspoon cinnamon
1 teaspoon nutmeg
1 teaspoon allspice
1/2 teaspoon cloves
1/4 teaspoon salt or to taste
1/2 cup chopped walnuts
Confectioners' sugar (optional)

Combine raisins and water in a saucepan; bring to a boil. Set aside to cool. Stir in sugar, egg, and oil. Sift together dry ingredients; stir into sugar mixture; mix well. Add nuts. Pour into 15 1/2 × 10 1/2-inch greased pan. Bake at 350° for 12 minutes or until done. Cut bars while warm. Dust with confectioners' sugar if desired.
Yields: 15 to 18 servings

Seasoned with Love
St. Andrew's Episcopal Church
Taft, California

PRALINE BARS

6–8 graham crackers
1/2 cup butter
1/2 cup firmly packed
  brown sugar
1/2 cup chopped pecans,
  walnuts, or almonds

Break graham crackers into quarters and arrange side by side in a 9 × 13-inch baking pan. Combine remaining ingredients in a small saucepan. Bring to a boil and spread onto graham crackers. Bake at 350° for 10 minutes. Remove from pan and transfer immediately to a cold cookie sheet; separate while still very hot so they won't stick.
Yields: 24 to 32 servings

St. John the Baptist Centennial Cookbook
St. John the Baptist Episcopal Church
Seattle, Washington

CREAM CHEESE BARS

2 (8-count) packages
  refrigerator crescent rolls
2 (8-ounce) packages
  cream cheese
1 cup sugar
1 teaspoon vanilla
1 large egg yolk
1 large egg white, beaten
Topping

TOPPING
1/2 cup sugar
1/2 cup chopped nuts
1 1/2 teaspoons cinnamon

Spread 1 package rolls in a 9 × 13-inch baking pan. Combine the cream cheese, sugar, vanilla, and egg yolk and spread over the rolls. Cover with remaining package of rolls. Brush top crust with egg white. Sprinkle Topping over egg white. Bake at 375° for 25 to 30 minutes.
Yields: about 15 bars

Combine all ingredients in a small bowl.

Parish Collection
Holy Trinity Episcopal Church
Iron Mountain, Michigan

THEREFORE, MY DEAR FRIENDS, FLEE FROM THE WORSHIP OF IDOLS. I SPEAK AS TO SENSIBLE PEOPLE; JUDGE FOR YOURSELVES WHAT I SAY. THE CUP OF BLESSING THAT WE BLESS, IS IT NOT A SHARING IN THE BLOOD OF CHRIST? THE BREAD THAT WE BREAK, IS IT NOT A SHARING IN THE BODY OF CHRIST? BECAUSE THERE IS ONE BREAD, WE WHO ARE MANY ARE ONE BODY, FOR WE ALL PARTAKE OF ONE BREAD.
1 CORINTHIANS 10:14–17
(JESUS SPEAKS OF THE LORD'S SUPPER)

18TH-CENTURY GINGER CAKES

(These were served with spiced tea at Pohick during Virginia Garden Week.)

3/4 cup soft butter
3/4 cup solid shortening
2 cups sugar
2 large eggs
1/2 cup dark molasses
4 cups sifted all-purpose flour
2 teaspoons baking soda
2 teaspoons cinnamon
2 teaspoons ginger
2 teaspoons ground cloves
3/4 cup sugar

Cream butter, shortening, and 2 cups sugar in a large bowl until soft and light. Beat in eggs and molasses. Sift in flour, baking soda, cinnamon, ginger, and cloves until well mixed. Dough will be soft. Chill at least 1 hour. Roll pieces of dough into 1-inch balls. Roll each ball in remaining 3/4 cup sugar. Place on well-greased baking sheet about 3 inches apart. Bake at 375° for 12 to 15 minutes. Cool slightly; remove to wire rack to cool completely.

Yields: 90 to 100 cookies

Pohickory Cookbook
Pohick Church
Lorton, Virginia

OLD-FASHIONED SUGAR COOKIES

3 cups all-purpose flour
1 teaspoon baking powder
1 teaspoon baking soda
1/8 teaspoon salt
1 cup butter or margarine
2 large eggs
1 1/2 cups sugar
1 teaspoon vanilla

Lightly spoon flour into measuring cup; level off. In large bowl, combine flour, baking powder, baking soda, and salt; mix well. Using fork or pastry blender, cut in 1 cup butter until mixture is crumbly. In small bowl, beat eggs. Gradually add sugar, vanilla, and lemon extract, beating until light. Add to flour mixture. Stir by hand until dough forms. (If necessary, knead dough with hands to mix in dry ingredients.) Cover with plastic wrap and refrigerate 1 hour for easier handling. On lightly floured surface, roll out dough, one-third at a time, to 1/8-inch thickness. Cut with 2 1/2- to 3-inch floured cookie cutters. Place 1 inch apart on ungreased cookie sheets. Bake at 375° for 6 to 11 minutes or until edges are light golden brown. Immediately remove from cookie sheets and cool completely. Decorate with colored sugar (before baking) or decorating gels.

Yields: 4 to 5 dozen

Our Favorite Recipes
St. Thomas' Episcopal Church
Pittstown, New Jersey

SOFT MOLASSES COOKIES

1 cup shortening
1 cup firmly packed
  dark brown sugar
1 cup hot coffee mixed with
  1 teaspoon baking soda
2 large eggs, well beaten
2 teaspoons baking powder
1 teaspoon ginger
1/2 teaspoon cloves
1 teaspoon salt
1 cup dark molasses
1 teaspoon vinegar
3 cups all-purpose flour
1 teaspoon cinnamon

Combine all ingredients in a large bowl; mix well. Dough should be very stiff. Add more flour if necessary. Drop by spoonfuls onto an ungreased cookie sheet. Bake at 350° for 10 to 12 minutes. Cool on a wire rack.

Yields: 2 to 3 dozen

Cook Book
St. Anne's Episcopal School
Denver, Colorado

DOUBLE CHOCOLATE CHIP COOKIES

8 (1-ounce) squares semisweet
  chocolate
3 (1-ounce) squares
  unsweetened chocolate
6 tablespoons butter
1/2 cup all-purpose flour
1/4 teaspoon baking powder
1/4 teaspoon salt
3 large eggs
1 cup sugar
2 teaspoons vanilla
1 1/2 cups semisweet
  chocolate chips
1 cup chopped pecans
1 cup chopped walnuts

Melt squares of chocolate with butter in a heavy saucepan over low heat, stirring until smooth; cool. Sift together flour, baking powder, and salt in a large bowl; set aside. Beat eggs, sugar, and vanilla until slightly thickened. Stir into dry ingredients. Add melted chocolate, mixing well. Stir in chocolate chips and nuts. Drop by heaping tablespoons onto lightly greased cookie sheets, spacing cookies 3 inches apart. Bake at 350° for 8 to 10 minutes. Cool on a wire rack.

Yields: 3 dozen

Food for the Flock
St. Catherine's Episcopal Church
Jacksonville, Florida

CHOCOLATE-NUT TASSIES

1/2 cup butter, softened
1 (3-ounce) package cream
  cheese, softened
3 tablespoons sugar
1/2 teaspoon vanilla
1 cup sifted all-purpose flour
1/4 cup finely ground blanched
  almonds
1/4 cup raspberry, strawberry,
  or apricot jam
2 squares semisweet chocolate
1 tablespoon butter

Beat butter, cream cheese, sugar, and vanilla in a large bowl until light and fluffy. Stir in flour until smooth. Stir in nuts. Wrap dough in plastic wrap and refrigerate several hours or overnight. Divide dough into 24 pieces. Gently press each piece into and up sides of two ungreased muffin tins to form shells. Bake at 350° for 13 minutes. Cool slightly on wire rack. Loosen cookies gently and remove to cool completely. When cool, spoon about 1/2 teaspoon jam into each. Melt chocolate and butter over hot water. Cool slightly. Spoon over jam layer. Refrigerate until chocolate sets. Keep refrigerated.
Yields: 2 dozen

St. Uriel's Guild Cookbook
Church of St. Uriel the Archangel
Sea Girt, New Jersey

STAINED GLASS COOKIES

1 (12-ounce) package
  semisweet chocolate chips
1 cup crunchy peanut butter
1 (12-ounce) package colored
  miniature marshmallows

In a double boiler, melt but don't cook chocolate and peanut butter. Cool for 10 minutes. Then add marshmallows; mix well. Cut 3 pieces of paper, about 12 × 18 inches, one of foil on bottom, then two of waxed paper on top. Dump about half of mixture on top paper and form a 12-inch-long log. Wrap in other piece of wax paper and then foil to give it body. Repeat procedure with other half. Refrigerate for 4 to 6 hours; unwrap and slice.
Yields: 48 servings

Heavenly Tastes, Earthly Recipes
St. Andrew's Episcopal Church
Lake Worth, Florida

CREBS
(A German cookie)

1 1/2 pounds butter
9 cups sifted all-purpose flour
3/4 cups chopped walnuts
2 teaspoon vanilla
9 tablespoons superfine sugar
Additional superfine sugar

Combine ingredients in a large bowl in order given. Form mixture into small balls and place on ungreased cookie sheet an inch apart. Bake at 350° for about 15 minutes. Roll cookies in more superfine sugar as soon as they are cool enough to handle. Store in airtight tins.
Yields: differs according to size of balls

Grandma's Pantry Cookbook
St. Mark's Episcopal Church
Marco Island, Florida

EASY TIME SQUARES

1 1/2 cups sugar
1 cup butter
4 large eggs
2 cups all-purpose flour
1 tablespoon lemon extract
   or juice
1 can cherry pie filling
Confectioners' sugar

Gradually add sugar to butter in a large bowl; add eggs, one at a time, beating after each addition. Add flour and lemon extract. Pour into well-greased 15 × 10-inch jelly roll pan. Mark off into 20 squares. Place 1 heaping table-spoon of pie filling in center of each square. Bake 45 to 50 minutes at 350°. While warm, sift confectioners' sugar over cake. Cool and cut into squares.
Yields: 20 servings

Trinity Episcopal Church Cookbook
Trinity Episcopal Church
Gladstone, Michigan

KENTUCKY COLONEL BOURBON BALLS

1 stick margarine
1 (16-ounce) package
   confectioners' sugar
1/4 cup bourbon
Pecans
1 (8-ounce) square
   unsweetened chocolate
1 square paraffin

Cream margarine, sugar, and bourbon in a large bowl. Refrigerate until firm. Form into balls and top with a pecan. Refrigerate again. Melt chocolate and paraffin in top of a double boiler. Dip balls quickly in chocolate mix-ture, using a fork or toothpick. Drop onto a baking sheet lined with waxed paper; refrigerate until firm. Wrap indi-vidually in waxed paper.
Yields: 2 dozen

Christ Church Classics
Christ Church
Lexington, Kentucky

NO-BAKE CHOCOLATE CREAMS
(A Napoleonic confection with the American touch of ease)

CRUST
1 cup butter, melted
10 tablespoons cocoa
2 large eggs, beaten
4 cups graham cracker crumbs
1 cup nuts, chopped

Melt butter in a saucepan; add cocoa and mix well. Remove from heat and cool about 10 minutes. Stir in beaten eggs, graham cracker crumbs, and nuts. Press mixture into bottom of buttered 16 × 12-inch baking pan. Chill.

FILLING
1 (16-ounce) box confectioners' sugar
1/4 cup butter, softened
2 1/2 tablespoons vanilla instant pudding
1/2 teaspoon vanilla
6 tablespoons evaporated milk

Combine confectioner's sugar, 1/4 cup softened butter, vanilla pudding, vanilla, and evaporated milk; mix to a smooth spreading consistency. Spread over crust and chill.

GLAZE
1 (12-ounce) package semisweet chocolate chips
7 tablespoons hot water

Melt chocolate chips in the top of a double boiler, adding enough hot water to enable chocolate to be poured. Pour evenly over filling; chill well.

Before serving, cut into diamond shapes. Store covered in the refrigerator.
Yields: 5 dozen

Cooking with Love
St. Timothy's Episcopal Church
Fairfield, Connecticut

ALMOND ROCA

1 pound butter
2 cups sugar
3 tablespoons water
8 ounces blanched almonds
1 tablespoon vanilla

Melt butter in heavy saucepan. Add sugar, water, and almonds and bring to boil. Cook, stirring constantly until candy caramelizes, or almonds are golden brown. Remove from heat and add vanilla. Pour in greased flat pan and let cool. Break into pieces.
Yields: 16 to 20 servings

Parish Collection
St. Mary's Episcopal Church
Mitchell, South Dakota

CREAMY CREOLE PRALINES

1 cup sugar
1 cup firmly packed
  dark brown sugar
2 tablespoons light corn syrup
1/2 cup whipping cream
2 tablespoons butter
1 teaspoon vanilla
1 cup pecan halves or pieces

In a saucepan dissolve the sugars and corn syrup in the cream over medium heat. Bring the mixture to a boil and continue cooking until a candy thermometer registers 228°, stirring occasionally. Add the butter, vanilla, and pecans; cook to 236° and remove from the heat. Cool the candy to 225° and beat just until thickened. Drop the candy by tablespoonfuls on wax paper, working rapidly. The candy will flatten out. When cool, wrap each in waxed paper, and store in a covered container.
Yields: 10 to 15 pralines

La Bonne Cuisine
All Saints' Episcopal Church
River Ridge, Louisiana

MICROWAVE PEANUT BRITTLE

1 1/2 cup shelled raw peanuts
  (about 1/2 pound)
1 cup sugar
1/2 cup light corn syrup
Light dash of salt
1 tablespoon lightly salted
  butter or margarine
1 teaspoon vanilla extract
1 teaspoon baking soda

Mix peanuts, sugar, corn syrup, and salt in a glass mixing bowl. Cook 7 to 9 minutes on high in microwave; mixture should be bubbling and peanuts browned. Quickly stir in butter and vanilla; cook 2 to 3 minutes longer. Add baking soda and stir quickly, just until mixture is foamy. Pour immediately onto a greased baking sheet. Let cool 15 minutes or longer. Break up peanut brittle and store in an airtight container.
Yields: about 1 pound, 3 ounces

Holy Tidbits
St. Christopher's Episcopal Church
Fairborn, Ohio

BUCKEYES

(These delicious and easy candies are supposed to have originated in Ohio. Wherever they started, here they are for you to try out. Don't expect to keep them very long.)

1 stick butter, melted
2 3/4 cups sifted confectioners' sugar
1 cup peanut butter
6 ounces semisweet chocolate chips
1 ounce paraffin

Combine melted butter, sugar, and peanut butter in a large bowl. Roll into balls about the size of a pecan and refrigerate 2 hours or more. Melt chocolate chips with paraffin in top of double boiler over boiling water. Insert a toothpick into top of each peanut butter ball and immerse in chocolate 3/4 of the way up, leaving a small circle of peanut butter mixture to show on top. Place dipped candies on cookie sheet covered with waxed paper until chocolate hardens.
Yields: about 50 candies

Grandma's Pantry Cookbook
St. Mark's Episcopal Church
Marco Island, Florida

SOUR CREAM FUDGE

2 cups sugar
1/2 teaspoon salt
1 cup sour cream
2 tablespoons butter or margarine
1 teaspoon vanilla
1 cup black walnuts, chopped

Combine sugar, salt, and sour cream in a saucepan. Stir over low heat until sugar is dissolved. Continue cooking until mixture reaches the soft ball stage (about 234° on the candy thermometer), stirring frequently. Remove mixture from the heat, add butter, and let cool. Stir in vanilla. Beat until thickened. Add nuts and pour into greased container. Let set for a few hours or overnight.
Yields: 4 to 6 servings

Parish Recipes
Emmanuel Episcopal Church
Staunton, Virginia

FROZEN PUMPKIN DESSERT

1 1/2 cups graham crackers,
  crushed
1/4 cup sugar
1/2 cup melted margarine
  (1 stick)
1 cup canned pumpkin
1/2 cup firmly packed
  brown sugar
1/2 teaspoon salt
1/2 teaspoon cinnamon
1/2 teaspoon ground ginger
1/4 teaspoon nutmeg
1 quart softened vanilla
  ice cream
Whipped cream
Walnut or pecan halves

Combine the graham crackers and next 2 ingredients in a bowl; mix well. Press firmly into a 9 × 13-inch freezer-proof pan. Combine the pumpkin and next 5 ingredients in a bowl. Stir in the ice cream, making sure no lumps remain. Spread the filling over the crust and freeze. Then score top and place a dollop of whipped cream and a walnut half on each square. Refreeze until 20 minutes before serving.
Yields: 12 servings

Love, Loaves, and Fishes
St. John's Episcopal Church
Lafayette, Indiana

APRICOT FREEZE

1 cup (22) crushed vanilla
  wafers
3 tablespoons melted
  margarine
1/3 cup sliced almonds
1 teaspoon almond extract
1 quart softened vanilla
  ice cream
12 ounces apricot preserves

Combine crushed cookies, margarine, almonds, and extract in a bowl. Reserve 1/4 cup for topping. Press remaining mixture into a square freezer-proof dish. Blend ice cream and preserves with electric mixer quickly so as not to melt the ice cream. Spread over crumbs. Top with 1/4 cup reserved crumbs. Cover and freeze for at least 6 hours.
Yields: 6 to 8 servings

The Book of Common Fare
Grace-St. Luke's Church
Memphis, Tennessee

CRANBERRY ICE

(A refreshing dessert or a delightful first course for a holiday meal)

4 cups cranberries
2 cups water
1 (3-ounce) package
  unflavored gelatin
1 1/2 cups orange juice,
  divided
1 1/2 cups sugar
6 tablespoons lemon juice

Simmer cranberries in water in a saucepan until soft; then mash through a colander. Soften gelatin in half cup of orange juice in a saucepan and add sugar. Stir over low heat until dissolved. Cool thoroughly, then add the remaining 1 cup orange juice and lemon juice. Mix with mashed cranberries. Freeze until mushy; stir and return to freezer. When almost hard, beat with a rotary mixer until very light pink and fluffy. Return to freezer.
Yields: 1 1/2 quarts

Angels in the Kitchen
Holy Trinity Episcopal Church
Gainesville, Florida

FRUIT SHERBET

1 banana, mashed
1 cup orange juice
Juice of 1 1/2 lemons
1 (8-ounce) jar cherries, cut up
1 cup sugar, divided
2 large eggs, divided

Combine banana in a bowl with orange and lemon juices. Drain cherries and add to banana; add enough water to cherry juice to make 1 cup. Add cherry juice to banana mixture. Add all the sugar except 2 tablespoons. Beat egg yolks in a small bowl; stir into banana mixture. Spoon into a freezer-proof container. Freeze to mush. Beat egg whites with 2 tablespoons sugar. Fold into banana slush mixture. Freeze, stirring frequently.
Yields: 2 to 3 cups

Saint Peter's Recipes
St. Peter's Episcopal Church
Rockland, Maine

CHOCOLATE ICE CREAM

1 (14-ounce) can sweetened
  condensed milk
1 (12-ounce) container frozen
  whipped topping, thawed
1/2 gallon chocolate milk

Mix condensed milk and whipped topping together in a large bowl. Add chocolate milk; mix well. Place in electric ice cream freezer/maker and blend until hardened.
Yields: 6 to 8 servings

St. Martin's Spoon-Lickers
St. Martin's Episcopal Church
Chattanooga, Tennessee

CARAMEL ICE CREAM

2 large eggs
2 tablespoons all-purpose flour
1 cup sugar
Pinch of salt
1 pint milk
1 cup sugar
1 quart cream
1 teaspoon vanilla

Beat together the first 4 ingredients in a large saucepan until smooth and lemon-colored. Add milk. Cook until smooth and thick. Burn sugar in a small skillet to make caramel. Stir into custard; cool. Add cream and vanilla. Freeze in old-fashioned crank ice cream machine.
Yields: 6 to 8 cups

The Parish Pantry
St. John's Episcopal Church
Thomaston, Maine

FRESH PEACH ICE CREAM

4–5 ripe peaches, chopped and
  mashed until almost pureed
  (canned peaches may be
  substituted when fresh are
  not in season)
2 (12-ounce) cans condensed
  evaporated milk
3 cups sugar
1 (12-ounce) can apricot nectar
Whole milk

Mix all ingredients and pour into ice-cream freezer container. Fill to fill-line with whole milk. Turn freezer packed with ice and salt until ice cream is done.
Yields: 8 to 10 servings

Wholly Cookery
Trinity Episcopal Church
Tulsa, Oklahoma

Menus

PROGRESSIVE DINNER

Being neighborly doesn't get much better than this. Welcome new church members or new neighbors by preparing a progressive dinner. Meet at the first home to partake of good fellowship and appetizers ranging from tender Bleu Cheese Cake to Roasted Red Pepper Dip. After appetizers, progress to the next home for the salad course, then on to the entrée. If you have any room left, end the evening at the fourth home with desserts including Cranberry Ice and Mocha Sour Cream Torte.

APPETIZER COURSE
Bleu Cheese Cake
Roasted Red Pepper Dip
Crumb-Coated Zucchini Diagonals
Salmon Cheese Paté
Fresh Fruit
Wine

SALAD COURSE
Greek Green Beans and Feta Salad
Spinach-Strawberry Salad
Frozen Fruit Salad
No-Knead Rolls
Angel Biscuits

MAIN COURSE
Beef Tenderloin with Roasted Shallots, Bacon, and Port
Mashed Potato Casserole
Tomato Pie
Baked Carrots

DESSERT COURSE
Mocha Sour Cream Torte
Cranberry Ice
Old-Fashioned Sugar Cookies
Coffee
Tea
Mint Iced Tea

PANCAKE SUPPER

Once a year, cajole the men of the church into sharing their good will and cooking talents at a Pancake Supper. Have them plan the menu, prepare the food, and clean up. A suggested menu might consist of hot pancakes lathered with butter and syrup and Irish baked ham slices. And, of course, no pancake supper would be complete without scrambled eggs.

Pancakes
Irish Baked Ham slices
Scrambled Eggs
Pineapple Casserole
Butter
Syrup
Orange Juice
Coffee
Tea

FISH FRY FOR A CROWD

Invite ECW members for a fun-filled Friday-evening get-together. One inspiration might be an old-fashioned fish fry. Gather a few large grills in your backyard, get out your apron and chef's hat, and throw on the fresh fillets. Serve with tasty tarragon butter. If you are supplying the fish and the beverages, guests might volunteer to bring some of the side dishes, such as Baked Macaroni and Cheese and Sweet Hush Puppies that melt in your mouth.

Fish Fillets with Tarragon Butter
Baked Macaroni and Cheese
Roasted Summer Vegetables
St. Christopher's Cranberry Salad
Sweet Hush Puppies
Blueberry Cake

CAROLING PARTY

One of the festive events of the Christmas season is when the youth group gathers to sing carols to the elderly and to the ill. With adults driving them from location to location, the young people have a pleasant time with their peers and, in turn, help brighten the day for those who hear their chorus of voices. After the caroling, return to the church to find an enticing aroma of French chocolate waiting to warm them and snacks to tempt their sweet cravings.

Pumpkin Pie Cake
Nut Cups
Spicy Old-Fashioned Raisin Bars
Double Chocolate Chip Cookies
Sour Cream Fudge
French Chocolate
Pink Lassies

BASKET OF HAPPINESS

A neighbor has just had a baby. Packing a meal for the family is your way of saying, "I am so happy for all of you. Perhaps this food will help feed the family while everyone is adoring the new arrival." Casserole items usually are the best to give, since the neighbors can eat what they want and reheat or freeze the leftovers. And, chicken is the safest bet for a food most people enjoy. Don't forget the dessert. A Millionaire Pie or Carrot Cake will satisfy even the pickiest of eaters.

Orange Chicken
Potato Croquettes
Corn Pudding
Carrot Cake or Millionaire Pie

SUNDAY BRUNCH

Family and friends gather at your house for a celebration, such as a christening. Make-ahead items work best for this after-church occasion. A German coffee cake only needs warming, as does the main casserole. So mix up the Banana Punch, start the coffee, and decorate your table. When guests arrive, you should have plenty of time to enjoy them.

Festival Brunch Dish
Fresh Fruit
German Coffee Cake
Cinnamon Rolls
Banana Punch
Coffee
Tea

CHURCH SUPPER ON THE LAWN

On a lovely spring day, after an afternoon of socializing and games, offer a simple supper for everyone to enjoy. Finger-licking Tortilla Rollups, followed by pies filled with turkey or oysters, some refreshing salads, and something special for those with a sweet tooth. This meal could follow a Sunday School picnic or an ECW spring bazaar.

Tortilla Rollups
Oyster Quiche
Picante Turkey Pie
Pasta Salad with Pesto Mayonnaise
Garlicky Tossed Salad
Pickled Okra
French Apple Pie
Burnt Sugar Cake
Banana Punch

ANNIVERSARY DINNER

The joining of two lives in holy matrimony is a special sacred moment, and the celebration of that anniversary should be special—whether it is one year or fifty. Preparing a dinner for two at home should be a joint venture. The enjoyment of cooking together can be just as delightful as dining together on this happy occasion. And, don't rush the meal. Enjoy Shrimp Louis on the deck as the sun slowly sets over the horizon. Savor the salad while the veal is slowly cooking, and pair the bread pudding with an after-dinner drink while you reminisce about the good things you've shared.

Shrimp Louis
Bean Sprout Salad
Veal Supreme
Gingered Spinach in Tomato Cups
Bread Pudding with Whiskey Sauce

GRADUATION SUPPER

High school or college graduation requires proper celebration. Invite the special graduates and their friends for a simple meal of lasagna, vegetable, and bread. It gives them one more chance to socialize and dream before their lives take on different directions.

Mexican Lasagna
Sweet and Sour Green Beans
Ice Box Rolls
Chocolate Cake
Honey Limeade

POTLUCK DINNER

Once a month, before Wednesday night services, families can each contribute a dish to the Potluck Dinner. Chicken or pork will please most hungry attendees. Round out the meal with a few vegetable dishes, some type of bread, and a choice of desserts. With full stomachs, church members can then attend the service and feed their souls.

Pork Chops, Family Style
Chicken Enchilada Casserole
Ranch House Beans
Corn Fritters
Spoon Bread
Blueberry Cobbler
Episcopalian Bars
Spring Punch

FOURTH OF JULY PICNIC

Wave the flag and pass the chicken wings during this festive outdoor celebration. No hamburgers and hot dogs this year. A lobster and clam bake will help you and your friends enjoy the Fourth of July in style. While the lobster, clams, and corn cook over your outdoor fireplace, your guests can enjoy badminton, croquet, and Frisbee. After this delicious meal, allow the appetites to rebuild before serving the luscious desserts. Roll them out about the time the fireworks begin to light up the night sky.

Chicken Wings
Down East Lobster and Clam Bake
Creamy Potato Salad
Fresh Apple Cake
Grandma's Banana Bread
Mint Iced Tea
Old-Fashioned Lemonade

ICE CREAM SOCIAL

Have a summer yard sale and ice cream party. Offer sherbets and ice creams, with a variety of toppings for all to enjoy. No Ice Cream Social would be complete without some sweet cookies or cakes and a fruity punch to wash it all down.

Fruit Sherbet
Chocolate Ice Cream
Fresh Peach Ice Cream
Chocolate Sauce
Butterscotch Sauce
Praline Bars
Chocolate-Nut Tassies
St. Francis Punch

Graces

As we say this grace, we give you thanks, O God, for this good earth, and for every kitchen and communion table where life is nourished and hunger is fed.

We give you thanks for women and men through the generations who kneaded the dough, kindled the fires, poured the wine, and opened the door to share their sustenance with those in need.

We remember Jesus, the joyful host, who welcomed the least and the last and gave them the seats of honor. We extend the same hospitality as we work and pray for the day when all people will gather together around the table to share good food, to enjoy good company, and to live in peace for the good of the earth.

By your Spirit of Hope, bless this bread and bless this wine, bless the earth and bless your people, that in the fullness of time, every cup will be filled to overflowing and every life will be filled with abundant love. Amen.

Prepared for "Visions and Voices"
the Third National Women's
Gathering of the United Church of
Christ (June, 1996)

Give us grateful hearts, our Father, for all thy mercies, bless them to our use. We thank thee for our home, our neighbors and loved ones far and near. Guide us by thy Spirit and feed us evermore with the Bread of Life. Amen.

Christ Episcopal Church
Bradenton, Florida

Our Father, we humbly pray thy blessing upon our food. Enable us to rejoice in the presence of the unseen Guest who came that we might have life and have it more abundantly. Amen.

Christ Episcopal Church
Bradenton, Florida

Be present at our table Lord. Be here and everywhere adored. These creatures bless and grant that we may feast in Paradise with thee. Amen.

From Cornwall, England
St. Andrew's Episcopal Church
Gill, Massachusetts

Lord, grant that the true spirit of the Christmas season, its joy, its beauty, its hope, and above all its abiding faith, may live among us. Let the blessings of peace be ours, peace to build and grow and to live in harmony and sympathy with others. Amen.

St. Mark's Episcopal Church
Marco Island, Florida

Blessed are you, Lord God the Father and the Son and the Holy Spirit. Help us to be ever grateful for thy bounty, and teach us never to forget the needs of others. Amen.

St. Francis of Assisi
Levittown, New York

Merciful Lord, we thank you for your great goodness and mercy, which has caused the earth to bring forth this food for our use. We pray that you bless the loving hands that have prepared it. As we receive it, make us ever mindful of the needs of those less fortunate than we and keep them in your care. Now bless this food to the nourishment of our bodies and bless us to thy service. In Jesus' name we pray. Amen.

St. Edward's Episcopal Church
Lawrenceville, Georgia

D ear God, who has blessed us with so many gifts, we thank you for bringing us together to share this food, which we receive as a gift of your love. Keep us always together in our family and in our faith, for we pray this in Jesus' name. Amen.

The Reverend Christopher T. Connell
St. Raphael's Episcopal Church
Brick, New Jersey

T hank God for dirty dishes,
  They have a tale to tell.
While other folks go hungry,
We're eating very well.
With home and health and happiness,
We shouldn't want to fuss.
For by this stack of evidence,
God's very good to us. Amen.

Diocese of Southwest Florida

A lmighty Giver of Good, we thank thee for thy loving kindness to us. Thou openest thy hand, and we are fed. Be at this table, we pray thee, and bless our gathering together. Amen.

Diocese of El Camino Real

F or the food that we eat, and the hands that prepare it,
  For health to enjoy it, and good friends to share it,
We thank you, Lord. Amen.

St. Stephen's Episcopal Church
Spokane, Washington

Accept our thanks, Heavenly Father, for the food provided for our use. Grant that it may nourish and strengthen our bodies as we partake thereof. Amen.

Grace Episcopal Church
Martinez, California

Every place is a place of devotion. Anytime is the time, and the prayer offered with hands in the dishpan is given the same loving attention as the one offered with hands folded over the rail. Amen.

Margaret Benson and Helen Smith
St. Luke's Episcopal Church
Farmington, Maine

Bless O Lord, this food to our use
And us to thy service.
Give us grateful hearts
And supply the needs of others,
For Christ's sake. Amen.

Wendy Waer's English Grandfather
ECW Diocese of New Jersey

Bless this food upon our dishes
As you did the loaves and fishes.
And, as the sugar in our tea,
May our lives be stirred by thee. Amen.

An Irish Blessing
ECW Diocese of New Jersey

Our Father in Heaven, we thank you for the magic of this life, for this healthy family, for the warm sun and rains that make our crops grow. Amen.

> *Adapted by Elyse Eckler*
> *St. Uriel's Episcopal Church*
> *Manasquan Park, New Jersey*

Most Gracious God, by whose hand we receive all the blessings of this life, bless the hands that have prepared this meal and the hands that serve it. Bless us as we join hands around this table that we might find nourishment for our bodies and nurture for our souls. Grant us grace that we might use our hands to bring your blessing to others. All this we pray in Christ's name. Amen.

> *The Reverend Gayle Hansen Browne*
> *St. Stephen's Episcopal Church*
> *Oak Ridge, Tennessee*

Bless us, Lord, and bless this food, and help us this day to be good. In Jesus' name we pray. Amen.

> *Boys' Home, Inc.*
> *Covington, Virginia*

Dear God, as we come to this table we ask your blessings. Bless this food, our families, our hearts and souls.
Bless our friends, neighbors, and those who wish us ill.
All of this we ask through your son Jesus Christ.
In his name we pray. Amen.

> *Senior High Church School Class*
> *St. Paul's Episcopal Church*
> *Salem, Virginia*

As our bodies are sustained with this food, may our hearts be nourished with true friendship and our souls fed with truth. Amen.

From A Grateful Heart
Submitted by Grace Episcopal Church
Chattanooga, Tennessee

Lord, we give thanks to thee for this food and for all thy blessings. We ask thy blessings to continue upon us and our home. Amen.

Betty Crichton
St. Christopher's Episcopal Church
Fairborn, Ohio

Heavenly and loving Father, I give you thanks for the food that you give us. Bless the hands that have prepared it and be propitious to the needs of those who call upon you. In your name, we pray. Amen.

Betty Torres
ECW Board Representative
Province IX
San Pedro Sula, Honduras

Divine Creator, Giver of all gifts, we thank you for the food we are about to share and for the fellowship of our table. May this food strengthen us and keep us well until we gather again in your name. Amen.

Isabel Polk
St. Peter's Episcopal Church
Rockland, Maine

B lessed Lord,
Thank you for all that you are.
Thank you for all that you do.
Thank you for all that you share.
Help us, Lord, to be more like you in all that we say and do.
Help us to make our lives more holy in your sight.
Bless these gifts, which you have given us, and bless us to your service.
In the name of your Son, Jesus Christ, we pray. Amen.

Evelyn Huyck
St. Hilary's Episcopal Church
Fort Myers, Florida

T each me, Father, when I pray, not to ask for more,
But let me give my thanks for what is at my door.
For food and drink and gentle rain, for sunny skies above,
For home and friends, peace and joy, but most of all for love! Amen.

Lolly Burbank
St. Francis of Assisi
Ooltewah, Tennessee

C ome Lord Jesus, our guest to be.
Bless these gifts bestowed by thee.
Bless our loved ones everywhere;
And, keep them in your loving care.

Submitted by Church of Our Father
Hulls Cove, Maine
and
Christ Episcopal Church
Charlotte, North Carolina

Blessed are you, Lord God, for you bring forth food from the earth and wine to gladden our hearts, oil to make a cheerful face, and bread to strengthen the heart. Bless everyone who bakes and cooks, and pour out your spiritual blessing on the food they prepare that it may bless us with health of body and mind and the joy of a grateful heart. Amen.

The Reverend Bob King (retired)
St. Mary's Episcopal Church
Madisonville, Kentucky

Lord of the Harvest, move us this day to a deeper commitment to share your harvest with others as you have wonderfully shared it with us. While we experience the pleasure of plenty, many experience the pain of want. Increase our awareness, our prayer, and our action so that this gap may disappear, and finally, all who pray "give us this day our daily bread" will be answered, and your will be done on earth as it is in Heaven. In the name of Christ. Amen.

Portion of prayer from For Starters
by the Right Reverend
Michael W. Creighton
Bishop of Central Pennsylvania

May the Lord God take our hands in his,
May he lead us to the land of green pastures and sparkling waters.
May his countenance shine upon us.
And when our days are accomplished,
May he take us to his house—
There to live with him evermore. Amen.

David Rudd
Christ Church
Norway, Maine

L ord our God, you invite us to the banquet of your wisdom, giving us for nourishment both the bread of the earth and your living words. Bless this meal and grant us entry to your banquets, in the name of the Father, and of the Son, and of the Holy Spirit. Amen.

From Table Prayer
by M.O. Bouyer
St. Andrew's Episcopal Church
Periodical Club
Taft, California

G racious God, we give you thanks for the wonder of your creation, and the gift of another day of life in your world. We give you thanks for this gathering of your people, and your presence in our midst. And we give you thanks for this food: Bless those who produced it, those who prepared it, and we who are about to eat it, through Jesus Christ our Lord. Amen.

The Reverend Charles F. Brumbaugh
Church of Ascension and Holy Trinity
Diocese of Southern Ohio

D ear God, we thank you for our food.
We know that it is very good.
Help us dear Lord to think of others—
Our hungry sisters and our brothers. Amen.

Catherine Asker
Grace Episcopal Church
Bath, Maine

Contributors

All Angels by the Sea Episcopal Church
All Angels Fare
Longboat Key, Florida

All Saints' Episcopal Church
All Saints' Cookbook
Morristown, Tennessee

All Saints' Episcopal Church
All Saints' Cooks
Kapaa, Kauai, Hawaii

All Saints' Episcopal Church
Cooking New Orleans Style, La Bonne Cuisine, and *Lagniappe*
River Ridge, Louisiana

All Saints' Episcopal Church
Suppers in Season
Wolfeboro, New Hampshire

All Saints' Episcopal Church
The Way to a Man's Heart
Norton, Virginia

Boys' Home Inc.
Recipes from "the Hill"
Covington, Virginia

Calvary Episcopal Church
Shrimp Mousse and Other Waffle Shop Recipes
Memphis, Tennessee

Canterbury School of Florida
Canterbury Feasts
St. Petersburg, Florida

Christ Church
Christ Church Classics
Lexington, Kentucky

Christ Church
Norway, Maine

Christ Church, the Episcopal Parish
Not by Bread Alone
Shrewsbury, New Jersey

Christ Episcopal Church
Charlotte, North Carolina

Christ Episcopal Church
Gracing Your Table
Hudson, Ohio

Christ Episcopal Church
Parish Collection
Bradenton, Florida

Christ Episcopal Church
Christ Episcopal Church Cookbook
Pearisburg, Virginia

Christ Episcopal Church
Heavenly Scents
Toms River, New Jersey

Christ Episcopal Church
Our Favorite Recipes II
Greensburg, Pennsylvania

Church of Ascension and Holy Trinity
Holy Chow
Wyoming, Ohio

Church of Our Fathers
Treasure of Personal Recipes
Hulls Cove, Maine

Church of St. Uriel the Archangel
St. Uriel's Guild Cookbook
Sea Girt, New Jersey

Church of the Advent
Gifts from the Kitchen
Cynthiana, Kentucky

Church of the Ascension
Keep the Feast
Middletown, Ohio

Church of the Cross
Parish Collection
Bluffton, South Carolina

Church of the Epiphany
What's Cookin' at Epiphany?
Richmond, Virginia

Church of the Holy Comforter
Holy Cow, Chicago's Cooking!
Kenilworth, Illinois

Church of the Incarnation
Our Daily Bread
Mineral, Virginia

Church of the Redeemer
A Book of Favorite Recipes
Ruston, Louisiana

Church of the Transfiguration
Episcopal Churchwomen Cookbook
Ironwood, Michigan

Church of the Transfiguration
Cook Book
Bennington, Kansas

Diocese of Central Pennsylvania
Diocese Board Collection

Diocese of El Camino Real
What's Cooking Along the King's Highway
Monterey, California

Diocese of Hawaii
Diocesan Altar Guild
…and Sew We Eat!
Honolulu, Hawaii

Diocese of Louisiana Southwest Deanery
A Cook's Tour of the Bayou Country

Diocese of Southwest Florida
The Garden of Eatin' Cook Book

Diocese of West Missouri
Served with Love
Kansas City, Missouri

ECW Diocese of New Jersey
Diocese Board Collection

Emmanuel Episcopal Church
Parish Recipes
Staunton, Virginia

Emmanuel Episcopal Church
Angels in the Kitchen, II
Bristol, Virginia

Epiphany Episcopal Church
Parish Collection
Cape Coral, Florida

Episcopal Church of the Resurrection
The Vicar's Guild Cookbook
Loudon, Tennessee

Good Shepherd Church
Navajo Indian Recipes
Fort Defiance, Arizona

Good Shepherd Church
Parish Collection
Fort Defiance, Arizona

Grace Church
Cooking with Grace
Bath, Maine

Grace Episcopal Church and Grace
    Day School
A Book of Favorite Recipes
Massapequa, New York

Grace Episcopal Church
Burnt Offerings
Vernon, Texas

Grace Episcopal Church
Entertaining Grace-fully
Hutchinson, Kansas

Grace Episcopal Church
Grace Cooks
Chattanooga, Tennessee

Grace Episcopal Church
Prize Recipes of Martinez
Martinez, California

Grace Memorial Episcopal Church
Give Us This Day
Lynchburg, Virginia

Grace-St. Luke's Church
The Book of Common Fare
Memphis, Tennessee

Holy Trinity Episcopal Church
Angels in the Kitchen
Gainesville, Florida

Holy Trinity Episcopal Church
Parish Collection
Iron Mountain, Michigan

Holy Trinity Episcopal Church
Second Helpings
Ukiah, California

Iglesia Episcopal Costarricense
Diocese Collection
Costa Rica

Pohick Church
Pohickory Cookbook
Lorton, Virginia

R. E. Lee Memorial Episcopal Church
Parish Collection
Lexington, Virginia

Representative of National Board of ECW
San Pedro Sula, Honduras, C.A.

Sabor a Mas
Guatemala, Guatemala

St. Albans Episcopal Church
Savoring Grace
Hixson, Tennessee

St. Andrew's Episcopal Church
Cooking with Love
Downers Grove, Illinois

St. Andrew's Episcopal Church
Favorite Recipes Home-Style
Readfield, Maine

St. Andrew's Episcopal Church
Feeding Our Flock
Longmeadow, Massachusetts

St. Andrew's Episcopal Church
Gill, Massachusetts

St. Andrew's Episcopal Church
Heavenly Tastes, Earthly Recipes
Lake Worth, Florida

St. Andrew's Episcopal Church
Loaves & Fishes and Other Dishes
Turners Falls, Massachusetts

St. Andrew's Episcopal Church
Seasoned with Love
Taft, California

St. Andrew's Episcopal Church
St. Andrew's 75th Celebration
Maryville, Tennessee

St. Anne's Episcopal School
Cook Book
Denver, Colorado

St. Augustine's Church
Potluck Favorites
Kingston, Rhode Island

St. Barnabas Episcopal Church
Cooks of St. Barnabas
Augusta, Maine

St. Basil's Episcopal Church
Another Touch of Basil
Tahlequah, Oklahoma

St. Catherine's Episcopal Church
Food for the Flock
Jacksonville, Florida

St. Christopher's Episcopal Church
St. Christopher's Cookbook
El Paso, Texas

St. Christopher's Episcopal Church
Holy Tidbits
Fairborn, Ohio

St. Christopher's Episcopal Church
Our Daily Bread and More
Kingsport, Tennessee

St. David's Episcopal Church
St. David's Cookbook
Nashville, Tennessee

St. Edward's Episcopal Church
Parish Collection, *Kitchen Confessions I
and II,* and *Saints Preserve Us Cookbook*
Lawrenceville, Georgia

St. Elizabeth's Episcopal Church
A Book of Favorite Recipes
Elizabeth, New Jersey

St. Francis by the Sea Episcopal Church
Cooking with St. Francis by the Sea II
Blue Hill, Maine

St. Francis of Assisi
Blest Be These Feasts
Levittown, New York

St. Francis Episcopal Church
Food and Gladness
Norris, Tennessee

St. Francis in-the-Fields
A Taste of Heaven
Somerset, Pennsylvania

St. George's-by-the-River
Canterbury Fare
Rumson, New Jersey

St. Hilary's Church
Parish Collection
Fort Myers, Florida

St. James Episcopal Church
Shared Treasures and *Blessed Are the Cooks*
Wichita, Kansas

St. James the Less Church
St. Anne's Guild Cookbook
Scarsdale, New York

St. John the Baptist Episcopal Church
St. John the Baptist Centennial Cookbook
Seattle, Washington

St. John's Cathedral
Parish Collection/Santee Dakota Sioux Recipe
Denver, Colorado

St. John's Episcopal Church
Heavenly Hosts
Naples, Florida

St. John's Episcopal Church
Love, Loaves, and Fishes
Lafayette, Indiana

St. John's Episcopal Church
The Parish Pantry
Thomaston, Maine

St. John's Episcopal Church
Parish Collection
Homestead, Florida

St. John's Episcopal Church
What's Cooking?
Huntington, L.I., New York

St. Luke the Evangelist
Parish Collection
Roselle, New Jersey

St. Luke Episcopal Church
125 Years of Cooking
Niles, Ohio

St. Luke's Episcopal Church
Cooking with Grace
Lanesboro, Massachusetts

St. Luke's Episcopal Church
Miracles in the Kitchen
Farmington, Maine

St. Luke's Episcopal Church
Parish Collection
Delta, Colorado

St. Luke's on the Lake
More Manna… and a Little Quail
Austin, Texas

St. Mark's Episcopal Church
Grandma's Pantry Cookbook
Marco Island, Florida

St. Mark's Episcopal Church
Loaves and Fishes
Chenango Bridge, New York

St. Mark's Episcopal Church
Lunches & Brunches
Plainview, Texas

St. Mark's Episcopal Church
Treasured Recipes
Prattville, Alabama

St. Martin's Episcopal Church
St. Martin's Spoon-Lickers
Chattanooga, Tennessee

St. Mary's Episcopal Church
Angels' Food
Napa, California

St. Mary's Episcopal Church
Hometown Recipes of Palmetto
Palmetto, Florida

St. Mary's Episcopal Church
Potluck Sunday
Madisonville, Kentucky

St. Mary's Episcopal Church
Parish Collection
Mitchell, South Dakota

St. Mary's Episcopal Church
St. Mary's Favorite Recipes
Reedville, Virginia

St. Matthew's Episcopal Church
Butter 'n Love Recipes
Unadilla, New York

St. Matthew's Episcopal Church
Family Collections
Snellville, Georgia

St. Matthias Episcopal Church
Home Cookin'
Monument, Colorado

St. Nicholas Episcopal Church
Breaking Bread with St. Nicholas
Midland, Texas

St. Paul's Episcopal Church
Goodness Graces
Albany, Georgia

St. Paul's Episcopal Church
Heavenly Delights
Waterloo, New York

St. Paul's Episcopal Church
Memories from the Kitchen
Mount Lebanon, Pennsylvania

St. Paul's Episcopal Church
One Hundred Years of Heavenly Cooking
Lynchburg, Virginia

St. Paul's Episcopal Church
Recipes from St. Paul's 1981
Naples, Florida

St. Paul's Episcopal Church
Salem, Virginia

St. Peter's Episcopal Church
Feed My Sheep
Lebanon, Indiana

St. Peter's Episcopal Church
Parish Collection
Altavista, Virginia

St. Peter's Episcopal Church
Saint Peter's Recipes
Rockland, Maine

St. Peter's Episcopal Church
Taste & See
Louisville, Kentucky

St. Peter's Episcopal Church
The Culinary Key
Cheshire, Connecticut

St. Philip Episcopal Church
Down Plantation Road
Bartlett, Tennessee

St. Philip's Episcopal Church
St. Philip's Cooks
Brevard, North Carolina

St. Raphael's Episcopal Church
St. Raphael's Cookbook and *Vol. II*
Brick, New Jersey

St. Simons Episcopal Church
St. Simons ECW Cookbook
Miami, Florida

St. Stephen's Episcopal Church
Best of Bayou Cuisine
Indianola, Mississippi

St. Stephen's Episcopal Church
Favorite Recipes of St. Stephen's
Spokane, Washington

St. Stephen's Episcopal Church
St. Stephen's Parish Cookbook
Schuylerville, New York

St. Stephen's Episcopal Church
The Loaves and Fishes, Act III
Oak Ridge, Tennessee

St. Thomas Episcopal Church
Keeping the Feast
Abingdon, Virginia

St. Thomas' Episcopal Church
Celebrating Our Roots
Knoxville, Tennessee

St. Thomas' Episcopal Church
Our Favorite Recipes
Pittstown, New Jersey

St. Timothy's Episcopal Church
Angel Food
Signal Mountain, Tennessee

St. Timothy's Episcopal Church
Cooking with Love
Fairfield, Connecticut

St. Timothy's Episcopal Church
Recipes & Remembrances
Cincinnati, Ohio

Stras Memorial Episcopal Church
Parish Collection
Tazewell, Virginia

Trinity Episcopal Church
Not by Bread Alone
Oak Ridge, Virginia

Trinity Episcopal Church
Parish Collection
Richlands, Virginia

Trinity Episcopal Church
Potluck
Ware, Massachusetts

Trinity Episcopal Church
Sharing Our Best
Houghton, Michigan

Trinity Episcopal Church
Taste & See
Red Bank, New Jersey

Trinity Episcopal Church
The Galveston Island Cookbook
Galveston, Texas

Trinity Episcopal Church
Trinity Episcopal Church Cookbook
Gladstone, Michigan

Trinity Episcopal Church
Wholly Cookery
Tulsa, Oklahoma

Wives of Bishops, Episcopal Church
We Gather Together

Zion Episcopal Church
Recipes—and Remembrances
Avon, New York

Index

Notes

Notes

Notes

Notes

Notes